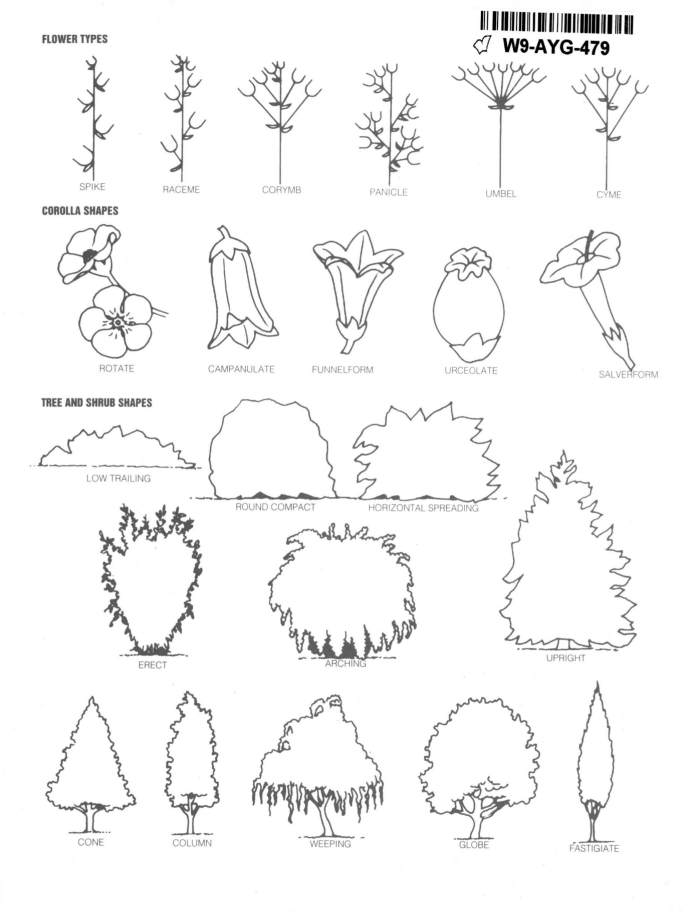

FLOWER TYPES

SPIKE RACEME CORYMB PANICLE UMBEL CYME

COROLLA SHAPES

ROTATE CAMPANULATE FUNNELFORM URCEOLATE SALVERFORM

TREE AND SHRUB SHAPES

LOW TRAILING ROUND COMPACT HORIZONTAL SPREADING

ERECT ARCHING UPRIGHT

CONE COLUMN WEEPING GLOBE FASTIGIATE

THE AMERICAN GARDEN GUIDES

trees

General Consultants:
Robert Bowden, Harry P. Leu Gardens, Orlando
Dorthe Hviid, Berkshire Botanical Gardens
Mary Irish, Desert Botanical Garden, Phoenix
Rick Lewandowski, Morris Arboretum of the University of Pennsylvania
Julie Morris, Blithewold Mansion & Gardens, Bristol, Rhode Island
Michael Ruggiero, The New York Botanical Garden
Dr. Gerald Straley, University of British Columbia Botanical Garden
Susan Thomas, Hoyt Arboretum, Portland, Oregon

Botany Consultant: Dr. Lucile H. McCook

trees

Chicago Botanic Garden

The Holden Arboretum

Galen Gates
CHICAGO BOTANIC GARDEN

Ethan Johnson
THE HOLDEN ARBORETUM

With Ruth Rogers Clausen
Preface by Kris Jarantoski
Series Editor: Elvin McDonald
Principal Photography by Galen Gates

Pantheon Books,
Knopf Publishing Group
New York
1996

Acknowledgments
This book was created with the help, expertise, and encouragement of a
great many people. We would like to thank all the consultants who con-
tributed so much to it and Ruth Clausen who helped us write it. We also
appreciate the efforts of C. W. Eliot Paine, Peter Bristol, Charles
Tubesing, Denise Salinger, Gary Weinheimer, and Paula Barnes of The
Holden Arboretum, Celeste VanderMey, Sarah Gates, Kris Jarantoski,
Kathy Grasso, Susan Ralston, Amanda Gordon, Ian Adams, Allan
Kellock, Albert Squillace, Joey Tomocik, Shlomo and Tamar Stein,
David Pryor, Michelle Stein, and Deena Stein. Special thanks to the
Morton Arboretum in Lisle, Illinois for permission to reproduce material
on planting trees from their recent publication.

We would like to thank Henry Holt and Company for permission to
publish an excerpt from "Birches" by Robert Frost, from *The Poetry of
Robert Frost,* edited by Edward Connery Lathem, © 1969.

Project Director: Lori Stein
Book Design Consultant: Albert Squillace
Editorial Director: Jay Hyams
Associate Art Director: Chani Yammer

Library of Congress Cataloging-in-Publication Data
Gates, Galen.
Trees / by Galen Gates, Ethan Johnson, with Ruth Rogers Clausen.
"The Holden Arboretum [and] Chicago Botanic Garden."
Includes index.
ISBN: 0-679-75862-3
1. Ornamental trees--United States. 2. Ornamental trees--Canada.
3. Ornamental trees--Pictorial works.   1. Johnson, Ethan.
II. Clausen, Ruth Rogers, 1938-   III. Holden Arboretum.
IV. Chicago Botanic Garden. V. Title. VI. Series.
SB435.5.G38 1996   95-23963
635.9'77'097--dc20   CIP

Manufactured in Singapore

First edition

Opposite: Sassafras albidum at The Holden Arboretum.

contents

Wooded area near Holden Arboretum.

the american garden guides

The network of botanical gardens and arboreta in the United States and Canada constitutes a great treasure chest of knowledge about plants and what they need. Some of the most talented, experienced, and dedicated plantspeople in the world work full-time at these institutions; they are the people who actually grow plants, make gardens, and teach others about the process. They are the gardeners who are responsible for the gardens in which millions of visitors exclaim, "Why won't that plant grow that way for me?"

Over thirty of the most respected and beautiful gardens on the continent are participating in the creation of *The American Garden Guides*. The books in the series originate with manuscripts generated by gardeners in one or several of the gardens. Drawing on their decades of experience, these originating gardeners write down the techniques they use in their own gardens, recommend and describe the plants that grow best for them, and discuss their successes and failures. The manuscripts are then passed to several other participating gardens; in each, the specialist in that area adds recommended plants and other suggestions based on regional differences and different opinions.

The series has three major philosophical points carried throughout:

1) Successful gardens are by nature user-friendly toward the gardener and the environment. We advocate water conservation through the precepts of Xeriscaping and garden health care through Integrated Pest Management (IPM). Simply put, one does not set into motion any garden that is going to require undue irrigation during normal levels of rainfall, nor apply any pesticide or other treatment without first assessing its impact on all other life—plant, animal, and soil.

2) Gardening is an inexact science, learned by observation and by doing. Even the most experienced gardeners often develop markedly dissimilar ways of doing the same thing, or have completely divergent views of what any plant requires in order to thrive. Gardeners are an opinionated lot, and we have encouraged all participants to air and share their differences–and so, to make it clear that everyone who gardens will find his or her own way of dealing with plants. Although it is important to know the rules and the most accepted practices, it is also important to recognize that whatever works in the long run for you is the right way.

3) Part of the fun of gardening lies in finding new plants, not necessarily using over and over the same ones in the same old color schemes. In this book and others in the series, we have purposely included some lesser-known or underused plants, some of them native to our vast and wonderful continent. Wherever we can, we call attention to endangered species and suggest ways to nurture them back to their natural state of plenty.

Elvin McDonald
Houston, Texas

director's preface

This book is a celebration of trees–the most important aspect of a landscape. No other type of plant–shrub, annual, or herbaceous perennial–matches the beauty, strength, function, and scale of a tree. Trees establish the tone and character of a landscape. Few other plants are as permanent or as prominent. Selecting the right tree is very important. It will impact the landscape more than any other plant. If cared for properly, it will live for generations of human owners.

People are learning to appreciate the various attributes of trees more than ever. Trees have year-round interest. Evergreen trees provide stability to the landscape and warmth in winter. Deciduous trees can provide a variety of foliage colors, patterns, and textures during the growing season, fantastic autumn color, and fascinating branching patterns during the winter. The added attractions of fragrant colorful flowers, longlasting fruit, and textured colorful bark has a year-round impact on the landscape. Trees can greatly affect our environment and are planted for cool summer shade and for screening out noise and winter winds.

There are many possible choices and selections of trees to uses in the landscape, from the hot climate of Harry P. Leu Gardens in Orlando to the cooler, mild climate of the University of British Columbia Botanical Garden in Vancouver. The Chicago Botanic Garden alone has almost 900 kinds of trees on display in its landscaped collections. Why do we then see the same trees used over and over again in various regions of North America?

This book presents a large diversity of trees for many different situations and many users, whether in the home landscape or commercial landscape, whether professional or amateur. This book will explain the use of trees in the landscape and provide the guidance needed to choose the right tree for the right environment for the proper use intended. The proper design will ensure increased enjoyment of the tree over time. Is there a need for a tree with flowers? A tree for small property? A tree sheared into a screen? A tree with winter fruit or interesting bark? This book will help you select the appropriate tree for the appropriate site.

There is a tree for almost any situation. The Chicago Botanic Garden's trees have been planted on poorly drained, disturbed soil, similar to many housing and commercial developments. Galen Gates has been working with our collections over many years and has an in-depth understanding of trees in our climate and their proper care. Ethan Johnson's experience with the Holden Arboretum's extensive collections has given him an appreciation of the personalities and possibilities of trees. Our consultants round out the wealth of knowledge from Rhode Island to Phoenix.

It's time to increase the diversity of trees used in our landscape and care for them properly. This book is a great resource toward a greener, more beautiful, future.

Kris S. Jarantoski
Director, Chicago Botanic Garden

INTRODUCTION 1

In nature and in our gardens, trees contribute to the landscape and the environment visibly and in many hidden ways. *Above: Cornus florida* lines a driveway; it is attractive in summer, covered in dark green glossy leaves, and in autumn when those leaves turn dark red; in spring, drenched in flowers, it is a vision.
Right: Trees in natural settings often grow differently than in our gardens.
Opposite top: Cornus alternifolia in a home setting.
Opposite bottom: A weeping willow blends beautifully with surrounding trees, yet stands out as a superb specimen, indicating the variety possible in form, textures, and shade of green; a lakeside setting is perfect for this tree.

Preceding pages: This view at Chicago Botanic Garden includes *Fraxinus americana* 'Autumn Purple', *Robinia pseudoacacia* 'Frisia', *Acer saccharum* ssp. *nigrum,* and the shrub *Cornus sericea* 'Cardinal'.

A cherry tree in full bloom, a sugar maple dressed in autumn colors, a grove of towering hemlocks: the beauty of trees is everywhere apparent, but the importance of trees to humanity and the environment in which we live is not so immediately visible. The world would be irreparably damaged by the loss of trees. They are a major factor in why our ecosystem works, providing, through photosynthesis, the oxygen we breath. Trees, particularly the vast rain forests, produce far more of the elements necessary to our environment than any other type of plant. Trees also have immense economic value, not just for their fruits and nuts, but also for their wood, our first fuel, which we use to build homes and furniture, and which provided the shipbuilding materials that brought us to this side of the world. The leaves, branches, and bark of trees provide fibers, including those used to make paper and rayon; innumerable drugs are made from every part. The bark of trees is a major source of tannins; other chemicals from trees make rubber and various resins, which can be refined to make such products as turpentine. Trees control erosion, hold up riverbanks, create shade with their leafy branches, and provide shelter for wildlife. Around a home they add privacy, enhance a scene or screen objectionable views, purify the atmosphere, and control the climate. That they are beautiful to behold is only an added bonus.

DEFINITION A tree is a perennial with woody stems that can be single-trunked or multistemmed. Trees are a minimum of 15 feet tall. Easily confused with shrubs, they differ in having elevated crowns of foliage you can sit and walk under (shrubs are branched from or near the base). In many cases, the differences between large shrubs and small trees blur, and both shrub and tree forms exist in most genera; some species can be grown as either shrubs or trees depending on the climate and the way they are pruned. The importance to the gardener is how they are used, and any plant a gardener grows as a tree can certainly be called one.

USING TREES Planting a tree in your yard is probably the most important horticultural decision you can make. Annuals, perennials, even shrubs can be relocated or even discarded if they don't thrive, but a tree is an investment of money, time, and space. Few of us have space for more than a few trees. If well chosen, these trees become monuments, permanent structures of beauty and sources of enjoyment for us and for generations to come; they improve the appearance of the entire garden, and, not inconsequentially, increase the value of the real estate. In addition to shade, wind protection, and reduced air pollution, trees enhance architecture, provide perspective and a sense of permanence. On the other hand, a poorly chosen tree can become a nuisance,

HISTORICAL NOTES

Rocks in Australia bear fossils of the first terrestrial plants, including the oldest known tree, *Baragwanathia longifolia,* which had a single stem about 1 inch in diameter covered with pointy leaves. Such first trees appeared early in the Devonian period, more than 400 million years ago, when the most notable animals were fish. By the Cretaceous period, 136 million years ago, many of the tree genera that exist today had appeared, including the magnolia, eucalyptus, willow, and larch. These were followed by the palms, fig, birch, oak, and chestnut. By the Paleocene period, roughly 65 million years ago, trees were practically identical to those of today.

And they were widespread, covering parts of the land in vast forests as dense as grass on a lawn. Early humans were daunted by these immense forests, which seemed impassable and divided early peoples as effectively as oceans. Classical writers refer to forests in Europe that no longer exist; the first men to penetrate them were hailed as heroes. Questioning Germans on the far borders of the Roman Empire, Julius Caesar heard of forests in which one could travel for more than two months without reaching an end.

Trees fed the growth of European civilization, cut down to provide housing, tools and furnishings, medicines, fuel for warmth, and ships. The discovery of the Americas came when the slopes of Europe were growing bare; it also coincided with and partially caused the scientific revolution. The new lands were covered with forests, and the earliest colonists quickly discovered trees unknown to Europeans; among the first of these was the bald cypress (*Taxodium distichum*), first described by colonists at Roanoke Island. The Europeans were enormously interested in these new trees and the possibilities of new products from them, in particular remedies to diseases. Many new uses were discovered for American trees. Some did indeed offer chemicals for medicine. Some had sap for turpentine and tar, some were good for making sugar. There were also new kinds of trees with beautiful blooms, enormous trees, and trees with exotic wood. Ships traveling between the American colonies and Europe brought new plants and maintained ongoing communication between American and European botanists.

Countless American trees had to come down to make room for people; once again civilization advanced to the ringing of axes. Early Americans had neither the time nor the inclination for pleasure gardens, but planted gardens of medicinal plants or potherbs; they also had orchards, particularly of apples, for cider was an early national drink. The Indians had planted trees to shade their gardens, and New Englanders applied this in the planting along streets of what they called common trees, usually elms. Before their use in parks, trees were planted in cemeteries, usually laurels and weeping varieties, such as willows. The colonists were proud of their trees: the first coins made in North America (1652-82) were silver shillings bearing a picture of a pine tree and thus known as pine tree shillings.

Washington and Jefferson studied gardening books and planted trees on their properties; William Penn planned tree-lined parks; and Benjamin Franklin promoted the planting of trees along streets as beneficial to public health. The pioneer American botanist John Bartram corresponded with nearly all the great European botanists of the day and made journeys in the Alleghenies and Catskills, the Carolinas and Florida, in search of new trees. Humphry Marshall, a relative of Bartram, wrote the first book on American trees, published in 1785, *Arbustum Americanum, The American Grove,* an alphabetical catalog of trees that was a landmark in American botany and contains several of the earliest descriptions of trees and shrubs now used in ornamental plantings. In the early 1800s Dr. David Hosack, a New York physician, botanist, and college professor, founded the first American botanical garden, the Elgin Botanic Garden (near where Rockefeller Center now stands) and surrounded it with a "belt of forest trees."

In 1823 Hosack was among the many American botanists to welcome the Scotsman David Douglas to New York. Douglas was one of the great nineteenth-century "plant hunters," those far-ranging botanical and horticultural collectors who sought out new species. During this first trip to the Northeast he sent back to England various new species of fruit trees. He was next off to the Pacific Northwest, Alaska, and Hawaii, where he discovered and introduced many trees, including the fir that bears his name, Douglas fir (*Pseudotsuga menziesii*), the sugar pine (*Pinus lambertiana*), the noble fir (*Abies procera*), silver fir (*A. amabilis*), and giant fir (*A. grandis*), as well as the sitka spruce (*Picea sitchensis*), destined for large-scale use in reforestation projects in Europe. Other plant hunters followed (see page 85 for more tales of adventure and discovery).

The North American landscape has changed dramatically since the European discovery of the New World, but efforts to preserve America's trees began even as the trees were being discovered. Many of our ancestors knew that the emotions they experienced when standing amid an "American grove" would be essential for the physical and spiritual well-being of coming generations.

blocking views and shedding litter throughout the garden, a huge, unhappy, and shabby reminder of a bad decision. Because of their permanence, trees become part of our lives, essential elements not only in the appearance of a home but the memories attached to it. When we plant a tree we are doing so for posterity; many of the trees we enjoy today are gifts from gardeners of the past; those we plant will be treasured by future generations.

REQUIREMENTS Trees are available for just about any site, but a tree's requirements should be thoroughly investigated before planting. When planting herbaceous plants, you can adjust the site, providing shade with a small shrub, improving poor soil, watering, and fertilizing regularly. This is not necessarily true when planting a tree that may be in the same spot for 200 years. The single most important point that the authors of this book would like to make is that it is best to choose a tree that fits your site rather than attempt to adjust the site to fit a tree you like. In some cases, different types of the same tree will thrive under markedly different conditions; live oaks (*Quercus virginiana*) will not survive northern winters, but many other oak species are perfect for cold climates. Even within a single species, different cultivars (cultivated varieties) have been selected for use in different areas: *Acer rubrum* (red maple) 'October Brilliance' is an excellent choice for Georgia, while 'Northwood' was selected for the region around Minnesota; *Magnolia grandiflora* 'Victoria' is a very hardy cultivar, but the compact 'Little Gem' is better for smaller sites; *Albizia* 'E. H. Wilson', *Cercis canadensis* 'Columbus Strain', and *Liquidambar styraciflua* 'Moraine' were all selected for cold hardiness. Consider planting a tree native to or well-adapted to your area; it may not be exotic, but it will stay healthy. Talk to horticulturists at local botanic gardens and arboreta as well as reputable nurserypeople and your neighbors to find out the best choices for your specific circumstances.

Soil Most trees flourish in any well-drained soil, but not every tree needs the

Trees can turn barren highways into gardens; they affect both air quality and quality of life. *Above:* A treeless stretch of city in a midwestern city. *Below:* A similar scene, transformed by trees, in Boston.

A BRIEF LESSON IN BOTANY

Plants are living things and share many traits with animals. Plants are composed of millions of individual cells that are organized into complex organ systems. Plants breathe (take in and expel gases) and extract energy from food; to do this they require water, nutrients, and atmospheric gases. Like animals, plants reproduce sexually, and their offspring inherit characteristics through a genetic code passed along as DNA.

Plants, however, can do one thing that no animal can do. Through a process called photosynthesis, plants can capture energy from the sun and convert that energy into compounds such as proteins, fats, and carbohydrates. These energy-rich compounds are the source of energy for all animal life, including humans.

THE IMPORTANCE OF PLANTS

Because no living animals can produce the energy they need to live, all their energy comes from plants. Like other animals, we eat green plants directly, in the form of fruits, vegetables, and grains (breads and cereals), or we eat animals and animal products that were fed green plants.

The oxygen we need to live on Earth is constantly pumped out of green plants as a byproduct of photosynthesis. Plants prevent the erosion of our precious soils and hinder water loss to the atmosphere.

Plants are also an important source of drugs. Fully one-quarter of all prescriptions contain at least one plant-derived product. Aspirin, one of the most commonly used drugs, was originally isolated from the bark of the willow tree.

THE WHOLE PLANT

Basically, a plant is made up of leaves, stems, and roots; all these parts are connected by a vascular system, much like our circulatory system. The vascular system can be seen in the veins of a leaf, or in the rings in a tree.

LEAVES

Leaves are generally flattened and expanded tissues that are green due to the presence of chlorophyll, the pigment that is necessary for photosynthesis. Most leaves are connected to the stem by a stalk, or petiole, which allows the leaves to alter their position in relation to the sun and capture as much energy as possible.

Leaves come in an astounding variety of shapes, textures, and sizes. Some leaves are composed of a single structure, or blade, and are termed simple. Other leaves are made up of many units, or leaflets, and are called compound (see endpapers).

STEMS

Technically, a stem is the tissue that supports leaves and that connects the leaves with the roots via a vascular system. Stems also bear the flowers on a plant. Therefore, a stem can be identified by the presence of buds, which are the unexpanded leaves, stems, or flowers that will develop later.

A single plant can produce more than one kind of stem; the upright, above-ground stem produces leaves and flowers, while a horizontal, below-ground stem can swell and store food products from photosynthesis. Underground stems can overwinter and produce new plants when conditions are favorable.

The stem of a plant often changes as the plant matures. When a tree is young, its stems are green and soft; as the tree grows and ages, however, the stem develops woody tissues. Wood is composed of hardened cells that provide strength to the stem and that allow water, gases, and nutrients to move both vertically and horizontally through the stem. Concentric circles inside a woody stem are called annual rings. The oldest wood is in the center of the rings, and the youngest wood is in the outer ring. Light-colored rings, or early wood, are composed of cells that were added early in the growing season of each year; these cells are larger and are less densely packed together. Late wood is darker in color because the cells are smaller and packed more closely. Each set of a light and dark ring represents one year in the life of the growing plant stem. When a plant grows under constant environmental conditions, with no changes in tem-

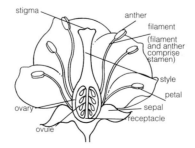

perature or moisture during the year (like in some tropical rain forests), the wood is uniform in color and lacks annual rings.

Bark forms on the outside of woody stems and is made up mostly of dead cells. This corky tissue is very valuable to the stem because it protects the new wood, allows gas exchange into the stem, and lets the stem grow in diameter. All of the bark is not dead tissue, however; the innermost layer is living vascular tissue. If a stem is girdled or the bark is damaged, this vascular tissue, which moves the food products of photosynthesis around in the plant, will be destroyed, and the plant will die.

ROOTS

Although out of sight, roots are extremely important to the life of the plant. Roots anchor a plant in the soil, absorb water and nutrients, and store excess food, such as starches, for the plants' future use. Basically, there are two types of roots: taproots and fibrous roots. Taproots, such as the edible part of a carrot, are thick unbranched roots that grow straight down. A taproot takes advantage of moisture and nutrients far below the soil surface and is a storehouse for carbohydrates. Fibrous roots are fine, branching roots that often form dense mats, making them excellent agents of soil stabilization. Fibrous roots absorb moisture and nutrients from a shallow zone of soil and may be more susceptible to drought. Roots obviously need to come into contact with water, but they also need air in order to work properly. Except for those adapted to aquatic environments, plants require well-drained soils.

VASCULAR SYSTEMS

Plants have a well-developed vascular system that extends throughout the plant body and that allows movement of water and compounds from one part of a plant to another. Roots absorb water and minerals, and the vascular system funnels them to the leaves for use in photosynthesis. Likewise, energy-rich compounds that are produced in the leaves must travel to the stems and roots to provide nutrition for further growth. The vascular system also strengthens plant tissues.

PHOTOSYNTHESIS

A green plant is like a factory that takes raw

materials from the environment and converts them into other forms of energy. In a complex series of energy transfer and chemical conversion events called photosynthesis, plants take energy from the sun, minerals and water from the soil, and gases from the atmosphere; these raw materials are converted into chemical forms of energy that are used for plant growth. These same energy-rich compounds (proteins, sugars and starches, fats and oils) can be utilized by animals as a source of food and nutrition. All this is possible because of a green pigment, chlorophyll.

Photosynthesis is an extremely complex series of reactions that takes place in the cells of leaves, the byproducts of which are connected to other reactions throughout the cell. The most basic reactions of photosynthesis occurs like this: Energy from the sun strikes the leaf surface, and electrons in the chlorophyll molecule become "excited" and are boosted to a higher energy level. Excited electrons are routed through a chain of reactions that extracts and stores energy in the form of sugars. As a byproduct of electron loss, water molecules are split; hydrogen moves in to replenish the electrons lost from chlorophyll, and oxygen is released, finding its way into our atmosphere. In another photosynthetic reaction, carbon dioxide from the atmosphere is "fixed," or converted into organic compounds within the plant cell. These first chemical compounds are the building blocks for more complex reactions and are the precursors for the formation of many elaborate chemical compounds.

PLANT NUTRITION

Plants require mineral nutrients from the soil, water, and the atmosphere in order to maintain healthy growth and reproduction. Macronutrients, those nutrients needed in large amounts, include hydrogen, oxygen, and carbon–all of which are abundant in our atmosphere. Other macronutrients are nitrogen, phosphorus, potassium, sulfur, and calcium. If macronutrients are in limited supply, growth and development in the plant will be strongly curtailed. Nitrogen is an important component of chlorophyll, DNA, and proteins and is therefore an essential element for leaf growth and photosynthesis. Adding nitrogen to garden soil will generally result in greener, more lush plant growth. But beware of too much of a good thing; too

much nitrogen can burn tender plants. Or, you may have large and lovely azalea leaves, but with no flowers! Phosphorus is also used in building DNA and is important in cell development. Phosphorus is necessary for flowering and fruiting and is often added to garden soil. Potassium is important in the development of tubers, roots, and other storage organs.

LIFE CYCLE

Higher plants (except for ferns) begin life as a seed. Given the right set of conditions (temperature, moisture, light), a seed will germinate and develop its first roots and leaves using food stored in the seed (humans and other animals take advantage of the high-quality food in seeds when they eat wheat and corn, just to name a few). Because of the presence of chlorophyll in the leaves, the small plant is soon able to produce its own food, which is used immediately for further growth and development. As the seedling grows, it also grows in complexity. The first, simple root gives way to a complex root system that may include underground storage organs. The stem is transformed into an intricate system of vascular tissue that moves water from the ground up into the leafy part of the plant, while other tissues transport energy-rich compounds made in the leaves downward to be stored in stem and root systems.

Once the plant reaches maturity, flower initiation begins. Flowers hold the sexual apparatus for the plant; their brilliant colors and glorious odors are advertisements to attract pollinators such as insects or birds. In a basic, complete flower, there are four different parts, given below. However, many plants have incomplete flowers with one or more of these parts missing, or the parts may be highly modified.

1. Sepals. The outermost part of the flower, sepals cover the young floral buds. Although they are often green, they may be variously colored.

2. Petals. The next layer of parts in the flower, petals, are often colorful and play an important role in attracting pollinators.

3. Stamens. Stamens are located next to the petals, or may even be basally fused to the petals. The stamens are the male reproductive parts of the flower; they produce the pollen. Pollen grains are fine, dust-like particles that will divide to form sperm cells. The tissue at the end of the stamen that holds

pollen is called the anther.

4. Pistil. The innermost part of the flower holds the plant's female reproductive apparatus. The stigma, located at the tip of the pistil, is often covered with a sticky substance and is the site where pollen is deposited. The stigma is held by a floral tube, call the style. At the base of the style, the ovary holds one to many ovules, which contain eggs that represent undeveloped seeds.

Pollination is the transfer of pollen from an anther to a stigma and is the first step in the production of seeds. Pollen can be transferred by an insect visiting the flower, by the wind, or even by the splashing of raindrops. After being deposited on a compatible stigma, the pollen grains grow into tubes that travel from the stigma, down the floral tube into the ovary, depositing sperm cells to the ovules. If all goes well, sperm cells unite with the eggs inside the ovules, and fertilization takes place.

After fertilization, the entire floral structure is transformed into a fruit. Fruit can be fleshy, like an apple, or dry like a pea pod. Within each fruit, fertilized eggs develop into seeds, complete with a cache of storage tissue and a seed coat.

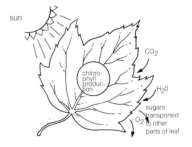

sun

CO_2

H_2O

chlorophyll production

sugars transported to other parts of leaf

O_2

The beauty of flowering trees, like *Magnolia* x *soulangiana,* above, is undeniable. But don't forget that trees like oaks (top) produce lovely blooms as well—or that flowers are not the only ornamental feature of a tree. *Right: Fagus sylvatica* 'Pendula' shows its shape in winter. In summer the hot-pink-edged leaves of *Fagus sylvatica* 'Roseomarginata' (opposite bottom right), the bright pink flowers (followed by ornamental cones) of *Picea orientalis* (opposite top right) and the glistening dark red bark of *Prunus serrulata* (opposite left) provide vivid color.

same type of soil. Most need a fairly fertile, somewhat acidic soil, but some, like *Tilia americana,* Chinese toon tree, and honey locust actually do better in alkaline soil; live oak thrives in both the limestone soils of central Texas and the acidic soils of the Gulf Coast.

Light In nature, trees live in a wide variety of environments, from forest floor to open plain: pioneers like junipers, for example, thrive in full sun, while understory plants, such as hornbeam, fringe tree, dogwood, and witch hazel require only dappled sunlight. A certain amount of shade is crucial for broad-leaved evergreen trees (like rhododendron), which can be damaged even by winter sunlight.

Water Established trees, planted in a suitable environment, require very little water other than that provided by nature, except in the case of severe drought. Some trees, like ironwood and paloverde, are adapted to dry climates and can live for years without water. Others, like the *Acer rubrum* or bald cypress, can grow in marshy areas along the banks of rivers.

Space One of the most common mistakes made when planting a tree is not leaving enough room for it to grow to maturity. In an effort to achieve immediate results, small young trees are crowded into too little space. Make sure you know how big your tree will be ten, twenty, and fifty years down the line as well as at maturity.

CHOOSING TREES If there is a tree for every landscape, there is also one for every use—but it takes some thought to understand all the ways we can use trees. Another critical factor in gardening with trees is the need to consider not only the overstory of the garden but also the numerous opportunities for shade-tolerant, ornamental understory trees—like amelanchier, cercis, and

hamamelis—that can accent the space closest to our everyday lives.

People—like pollinating birds and bees—are often attracted to flowers. But flowers are not the most important aspect to take into consideration. Most trees flower for only a few weeks; some, like goldenchain tree, silverbell, and albizia, are only attractive during that time. If you prefer a tree that is useful all year, take all its elements into consideration:

Foliage The large, attractive leaves of trees such as aralia, katsura, and catalpa are fresh and green all summer; they provide shade as well as color. Some trees, like copper or purple beeches and Japanese maples, have colored leaves from spring through fall.

Fall color Autumn is the best season for many trees, and in some cases, particular species or cultivars provide better color than others. The tupelo, red oak, and parrotia trees are attractive in summer, but become magnificent in fall. Some apple trees lose their leaves before they color; others become purple or red, adding another season to their usefulness.

Fruit Some trees, such as the pawpaw and persimmon, provide edible fruit as well as ornament. On others, such as hollies and crabapples, fruit and berries are only ornamental—but they add significantly to the autumn garden.

Shade The enjoyment of our gardens on hot summer days is much enhanced by the possibility of watching them from under the shade of a tree; trees also cool our home, reducing the need for air conditioning. Pay particular attention to size when choosing a tree for shade; a very tall tree may provide shade for upper stories. Try to site trees so that they shade the house from the hottest, early afternoon sun. If you choose deciduous trees, the sun will still be able to warm the house in winter.

Architecture The shape of a tree can be beautiful in itself, whether covered by

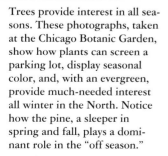

Trees provide interest in all seasons. These photographs, taken at the Chicago Botanic Garden, show how plants can screen a parking lot, display seasonal color, and, with an evergreen, provide much-needed interest all winter in the North. Notice how the pine, a sleeper in spring and fall, plays a dominant role in the "off season."

leaves or bare. Weeping forms, arching branches, and pyramidal shapes are all available. In its bare state, the tree's structure or architecture can present a dramatic vision against a windswept landscape; glistening with ice or covered with snow, a bare tree is as lovely as one in fullest leaf and flower.

Bark Some trees, like cherries, have smooth, glistening barks; others (like *Acer griseum*, the paperbark maple) have interesting peeling barks that reveal a panoply of colors beneath them. The bark is an important ornamental feature of your tree, particularly in the winter garden.

Evergreens Evergreen trees retain foliage all year; they lose their leaves, but not all at the same time. Most evergreens are conifers (cone-bearers), with narrow, needle-like leaves. An evergreen tree provides green color and screening all year long.

Flowers And finally, flowers should not be forgotten. Perhaps cherry and magnolia trees only flower for a few weeks; but for those weeks, they are magnificent. Many flowering trees have other values, but their flowers cannot be denied their beauty.

ABOUT THE GARDENERS Ethan Johnson began his horticultural career at Harvard's Arnold Arboretum and has served since 1989 as plant recorder for the Holden Arboretum near Cleveland, keeping track of all that grows among the garden's 3,100 acres. He is an enthusiast of Integrated Pest Management–the idea that by carefully monitoring the life cycle, food preferences, and habits of the pest, you can create the conditions that will best allow the hoist to protect itself. "Know your enemy" is Johnson's succinct horticultural motto.

Galen Gates is Manager, Horticultural Collections, at the Chicago Botanic Garden where he oversees a diverse collection of over one million plants. He has 25 years experience in horticulture ranging from hands-on maintenance work to involvement in the design and development of several million-dollar public display gardens. His lifelong interest in plants has led him to search out plants in the United States, Canada, Europe, and Siberia (where he collected a number of plants new to the field of horticulture). His background in plant evaluation, teaching, construction, and maintenance has made him a respected consultant to the horticulture industry. Galen is a frequent lecturer on a variety of horticultural topics and to date has contributed to 30 gardening books. His mission as a horticulturist is to encourage gardeners to try new approaches to gardening and investigate the use of a broader range of plants. Galen feels the garden is a place of learning, "a resource from which everyone who visits–children, the gardener, his friends and family–should come away with new insights and new ideas the year round. Above all, he stresses the notion of a garden as ever-changing, a living tapestry where color and texture are continually altered through experimentation, the seasons, new plant choices, and the efforts of the gardener.

Of all plants, trees are the most prominent, the most permanent, and a major component in our environmental picture. "Trees are telling and decisive," says Gates. "In a city, they dictate its atmosphere, character, and image. On a more personal scale, trees provide shade, noise abatement, privacy, and comfortable living space. They also create a sense of scale, articulate space, and add significantly to the value of our home landscapes. Trees should always be the first consideration in planning, evaluating, or planting any property."

SCIENTIFIC NOMENCLATURE

Botanists and horticulturists use a binomial, or two-name, system to label the over 250,000 species of living plants. Because the names are in Latin, this system crosses both time and language barriers and allows people all over the world to communicate about plants. Occasionally, a scientific name will be changed to reflect additions to our knowledge about plants. A scientific name consists of the genus (singular; genera is plural) and the species–as in the scientific name for sugar maple, *Acer saccharum*. The genus name is always first and always capitalized; the species name follows and is generally not capitalized.

Cultivated plants are often selected for a particular attribute, such as leaf or flower color or fruit size. These selections are given a cultivar, or cultivated variety, name in addition to the species and genus. Cultivar names are capitalized and surrounded by single quotes, such as *Acer saccharum* 'Green Mountain' or *Populus nigra* 'Italica'. A particular plant may have many common names–cottonwood, American planetree, and sycamore are all used for *Platanus occidentalis,* for example–but it has only one correct scientific name.

Varieties are arranged alphabeti-
cally, according to their Latin
names. See the index or contents
page for translations of Latin
names.
Some common trees and their
genus names:
Alder: *Alnus*
Arborvitae: *Thuja*
Ash: *Fraxinus*
Beech: *Fagus*
Birch: *Betula*
Cedar: *Cedrus*
Cherry: *Prunus*
Crabapple: *Malus*
Cypress: *Cupressus*
Dogwood: *Cornus*
Elm: *Ulmus*
False cypress: *Chamaecyparis*
Fir: *Abies*
Hemlock: *Tsuga*
Holly: *Ilex*
Hornbeam: *Carpinus*
Horse chestnut: *Aesculus*
Linden: *Tilia*
Maple: *Acer*
Mimosa: *Acacia, Albizia*
Oak: *Quercus*
Pear: *Pyrus*
Pine: *Pinus*
Plum: *Prunus*
Poplar: *Populus*
Redbud: *Cercis*
Sour gum: *Nyssa*
Sourwood: *Oxydendrum*
Spruce: *Picea*
Sycamore: *Platanus*
Willow: *Salix*
Yew: *Taxus*

Though gardening is essentially a hands-on endeavor, some of its greatest pleasures are vicarious: for most gardeners, nothing surpasses the joy of discovering a new plant. Since thousands of different trees are currently under cultivation—and nurseries, botanists, and private gardeners the world over are dedicated to finding and introducing more—there will never be a shortage of horticultural treasures from which to choose.

This chapter is designed to help you sift through those treasures and make a choice. Our authors have selected more than 150 trees that work well for them, mixing common, easy-to-find varieties with others you might not know about, but should; experts from other botanic gardens around the country then added plants that thrive in their own regions. Because most of the gardeners couldn't bear to leave out their favorites, we've included additional recommended plants at the end of many of the entries; and a brief description of many other shrubs at the end of the chapter.

The first part of the Plant Selector lists varieties according to size, growth habit, ornamental features, and requirements for sun and water. Following that is the main portion of the chapter—detailed "plant portraits" describing the plants' qualities, the best conditions for the plants' health, routine care, propagation, pest and disease tolerance, and uses in the landscape. Two hundred of the recommended plants are illustrated, with captions noting their mature size and hardiness zone.

There are only a few keys to successful gardening; choosing the right plant is among them and that goes double for trees. If a well-tended plant refuses to thrive or succumbs to disease, it probably doesn't belong in its present site. Before deciding on a plant, you need to understand the special conditions of your own garden. Is it sunny, shady, or a combination of both? Is rainfall abundant, or nearly nonexistent? Is the soil sandy, loamy, heavy? How much organic matter does it contain? Does it drain well? What is your soil's natural pH? Information on how to answer these questions is located in Chapter 4; your local nursery, botanical garden, or agricultural extension service can also help. But don't forget that your site is unique, with a microclimate of its own created by the contours of the landscape, shade, and natural barriers; it may be different from those next door, let alone at a nursery ten miles down the road.

To help match plant and gardener, each plant portrait includes information on the following:

Sun Because trees will stay in the same place for many years, you'll need to consider the future as well as current exposure. A tree growing nearby might provide more shade than the plant needs in just a few years.

Soil It isn't practical to adjust soil for trees extensively. You make minor adjustments so that the tree can establish itself or survive an unusual drought. But don't try to grow a plant that thrives on nutrients in poor, dry soil; you'll spend the rest of your life pampering it and it will never do as well as a more practical choice.

Water There are plenty of plants that thrive in dry climates—and not all of them are cacti. Notations throughout this chapter point out plants that are adapted to dry climates; see page 214 for information on gardening in dry climates. Because water supplies everywhere are becoming more scarce, all gardeners would do well to heed the basic principles of xeriscaping: proper garden design, maintenance, and especially plant selection.

Hardiness Consider your area's general climate, but keep in mind too that planting in a protected area might allow you to gain one warmer zone–if you don't mind the risk of perhaps, in some years, experiencing winter damage. See page 212 for information on gardening in cold climates. In the West, climate zones are not as important as summer highs and rainfall.

Pests and diseases We've noted problems that are common to particular plants; if these pests or diseases are rampant in your area, avoid the plants in question. See pages 203-5 for more information on pests and diseases.

Mature size So many factors affect the growth rates of trees that information about mature size is often useless. A tree that grows to 150 feet in its native habitat might reach only 40 feet in your backyard, particularly if your climate is colder or your soil less fertile than the plant prefers. We've given *average* sizes for trees in temperate zones at ten, twenty, and fifty years and at maturity.

The map below was created by the United States Department of Agriculture. It divides the United States and Canada into climate zones. Most nurseries (and this book) use these classifications to advise where plants will be hardy. Although this is a useful system, it is not foolproof; it is based on average minimum temperature, and a particularly cold winter might destroy some plants that are listed as hardy in your climate zone. More often, you will be able to grow plants that are not listed as hardy in your zone, particularly if they are in a sheltered area.

There are other climate-zone classifications; the Arnold Arboretum's is also used quite often. The climate zones referred to in this volume are those of the USDA.

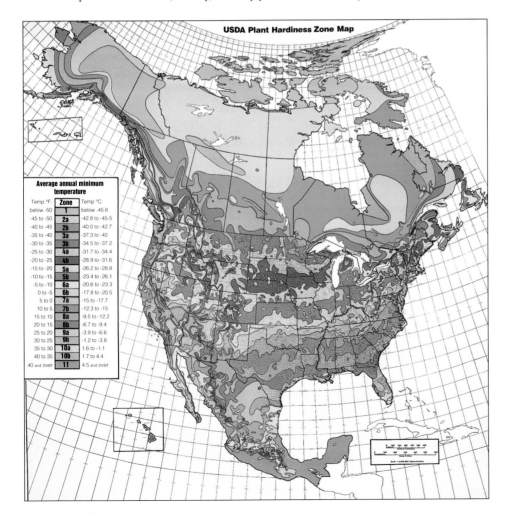

USDA Plant Hardiness Zone Map

Average annual minimum temperature		
Temp °F.	Zone	Temp °C.
below -50	1	below -45.6
-45 to -50	2a	-42.8 to -45-5
-40 to -45	2b	-40.0 to -42.7
-35 to -40	3a	-37.3 to -40
-30 to -35	3b	-34.5 to -37.2
-25 to -30	4a	-31.7 to -34.4
-20 to -25	4b	-28.9 to -31.6
-15 to -20	5a	-26.2 to -28.8
-10 to -15	5b	-23.4 to -26.1
-5 to -10	6a	-20.6 to -23.3
0 to -5	6b	-17.8 to -20.5
5 to 0	7a	-15 to -17.7
10 to 5	7b	-12.3 to -15
15 to 10	8a	-9.5 to -12.2
20 to 15	8b	-6.7 to -9.4
25 to 20	9a	-3.9 to -6.6
30 to 25	9b	-1.2 to -3.8
35 to 30	10a	1.6 to -1.1
40 to 35	10b	1.7 to 4.4
40 and over	11	4.5 and over

TREES WITH PYRAMIDAL HABITS

Abies, 30
Acer, 35
Arbutus, 45
Asimina, 45
Carpinus, 55'
Cedrus, 61
Chamaecyparis, 66
Cornus, 70
Corylus, 75
Cryptomeria, 78
Cunninghamia, 78
Cupressus, 81
Cupressocyparis, 81
Fagus, 87
Firmiana, 90
Fraxinus, 92
Ilex, 98
Juniperus, 102
Koelreuteria, 104
Larix, 107
Magnolia, 111
Nyssa, 122
Ostrya, 123
Oxydendrum, 124
Picea, 128
Pinus, 129
Pseudolarix, 145
Pseudotsuga, 145
Quercus, 148
Rhododendron, 152
Sciadopitys, 158
Sequoiadendron, 159
Stewartia, 161
Syringa, 163
Taxus, 164
Tilia, 167
Umbellularia, 174

TREES WITH ROUNDED HABITS

Acer, 33
Aesculus, 39
Carpinus, 55
Celtis, 62
Cornus, 71
Cotinus, 75
Crataegus, 76
Euonymus, 85
Fraxinus, 92
Juglans, 101
Kalopanax, 102
Magnolia, 111
Malus, 115
Morus, 120
Poncirus, 137
Prunus, 139
Pyrus, 146
Quercus, 148
Robinia, 154
Sorbus, 159
Tsuga, 169
Ulmus, 170

TREES WITH COLUMNAR HABITS

Acer, 33
Betula, 46
Carpinus, 55
Chamaecyparis, 66
Crataegus, 76
Cupressus, 81
Fagus, 87
Ginkgo, 92
Gleditsia, 93
Juniperus, 102
Laburnum, 105
Liriodendron, 108
Magnolia, 111
Malus, 115
Picea, 128
Pinus, 129
Populus, 139
Quercus, 148
Sophora, 159

Taxodium, 163
Thuja, 167
Tilia, 167
Tsuga, 169

FRAGRANT TREES

Abies, 30
Acacia, 32
Cedrus, 61
Cercidiphyllum, 64
Chionanthus, 67
Cladrastis, 69
Davidia, 82
Eleaegnus, 83
Franklinia, 90
Fraxinus, 92
Hamamelis, 97
Koelreuteria, 104
Maackia, 110
Magnolia, 111
Oxydendrum, 124
Pauwlonia, 127
Pinus, 129
Poncirus, 137
Prunus, 139
Pterostyrax, 146
Robinia, 153
Sassafras, 156
Syringa, 163
Umbellularia, 174
Viburnum, 174

EVERGREEN TREES, NEEDLE

Abies, 30
Araucaria, 44
Cedrus, 61
Chamaecyparis, 66
Cryptomeria, 78

Cunninghamia, 78
Cupressus, 81
Juniperus, 102
Picea, 128
Pinus, 129
Platycladus, 136
Pseudolarix, 145
Pseudotsuga, 145
Sciadopitys, 158
Sequoia, 158
Taxodium, 163
Taxus, 164
Thuja, 167
Tsuga, 169

EVERGREEN TREES, BROAD-LEAF

Arbutus, 45
Camellia, 52
Ficus, 88
Ilex, 98
Magnolia, 111
Maytenus, 118
Quercus, 148
Rhododendron, 152
Umbellularia, 172

TREES WITH ORNAMENTAL OR EDIBLE FRUIT

Asimina, 45
Carya, 56
Celtis, 62
Chionanthus, 67
Corylus, 75
Cratageus, 76
Cydonia, 81
Diospyros, 82
Evodia, 87
Ficus, 88
Hippophae, 98
Ilex, 98
Juglans, 101
Juniperus, 102
Malus, 115
Morus, 120
Phellodendron, 127
Poncirus, 137
Prunus, 139
Viburnum, 174

Left: The general appearance or shape of a tree is called its habit. *Far left: Acer saccharum* 'Fastigiata'; fastigiate trees have branches that are pressed upwards. *Center: Fraxinus excelsior* 'Nana', with a rounded crown. *Left: Acer saccharum* 'Endowment Column, with a columnar habit.

Acer saccharum

Acer griseum

(above list courtesy of Nan Sinton, Director, horticultural programs, *Horticulture* magazine)

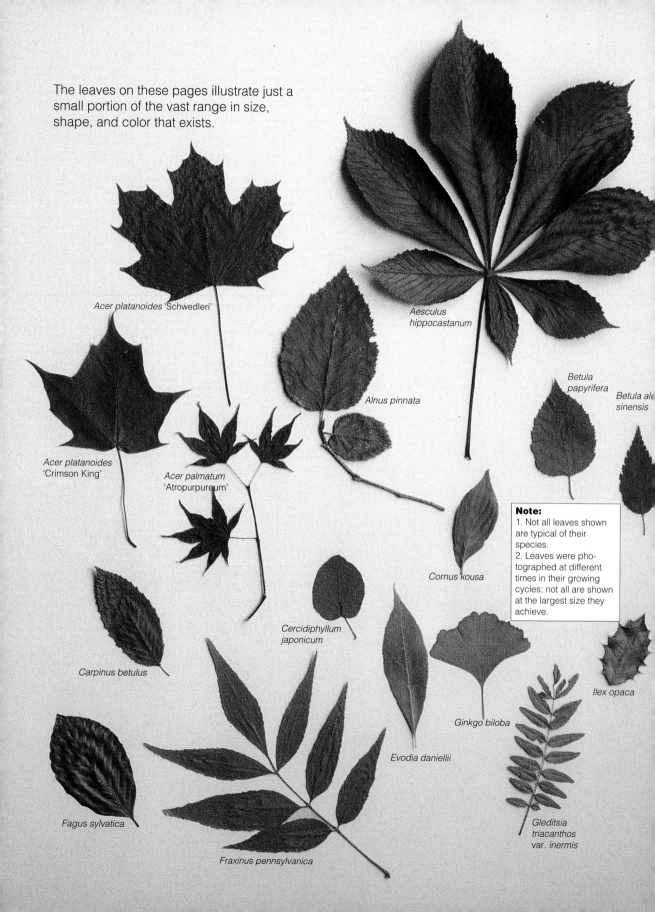

The leaves on these pages illustrate just a small portion of the vast range in size, shape, and color that exists.

Acer platanoides 'Schwedleri'

Acer platanoides 'Crimson King'

Acer palmatum 'Atropurpureum'

Alnus pinnata

Aesculus hippocastanum

Betula papyrifera

Betula alu sinensis

Cornus kousa

Carpinus betulus

Cercidiphyllum japonicum

Note:
1. Not all leaves shown are typical of their species.
2. Leaves were photographed at different times in their growing cycles; not all are shown at the largest size they achieve.

Ginkgo biloba

Ilex opaca

Evodia daniellii

Fagus sylvatica

Fraxinus pennsylvanica

Gleditsia triacanthos var. *inermis*

Magnolia
soulangiana

Parrotia
persica

Prunus serrulata

Platanus
occidentalis

Quercus
palustris

Quercus robur

Sassafras
albidum

Salix
babylonica

Sophora japonica

Sorbus 'Gypsii'

Ulmus
americana

Tilia heterophylla

Tilia cordata

Conifers are trees that produce cones containing seeds that produce future generations. *Above: Abies delavayi* cones; other firs with ornamental cones include *Abies koreana* and *Abies procera.*

ABIES FIR *Pinaceae (Pine family)*

The word *abies* is derived from the Latin *abeo*, meaning upreaching or ascendant. These popular evergreen conifers, native mostly to mountainous regions in the northern hemisphere, grow to 60 feet or more and develop into dense, conical trees. Their horizontal branches are covered with deep green or blue-green needles and are highlighted by upright cones. Firs are prized for their woodsy scent and make excellent Christmas trees. Most species live up to 100 years.

BEST CONDITIONS Firs thrive in full sun, but will also tolerate partial shade, particularly when young. The ideal soil is moist, well drained, and fertile, with somewhat acidic pH. They tend to wilt in long, hot, dry summers.

PLANTING Look for balled-and-burlapped trees with a single leader. Plant in spring or fall. Fir trees have shallow root systems and transplant easily. They grow very slowly from seed; a tree planted from seeds in Maine grew to only 3 feet after eight years.

ROUTINE CARE Provide water during dry spells. A 2-inch layer of mulch is beneficial.

PRUNING Branch tips may be cut during the summer to achieve fuller, more symmetrical growth as Christmas trees. Branches that are cut back hard do not resprout.

PESTS, DISEASES, OTHER PROBLEMS Usually pest and disease free, but young trees with thin bark are susceptible to damage from aphids..

PROPAGATION Propagate by seeds sown in fall or stratified cold and moist for one month or more. Cuttings do not root easily, but cultivars can be grafted and rarely prove incompatible.

USE Firs are choice specimens and can be used as screens, backdrops, and accents. They are best for larger properties, particularly near a deck or patio from which their handsome cones can be viewed. They are not suited to street tree conditions.

SELECTIONS *A. balsamea,* balsam fir, rarely lives longer than 40 years, but is the best Christmas tree fir because of its strong fragrance and superior needle retention. In cultivation, it grows to 50 feet tall and 20 feet wide and bears 3-inch-long purple-tinged cones on its upper branches. Its needles are soft and deep green. This tree needs high humidity and cool temperatures. ***A. b. var. phanaerolepis*** (Canaan fir) is native to wet soils in West Virginia and has recently been distributed to Christmas tree growers.

A. fraseri, fraser fir, southern balsam) from the Smokey Mountains is another popular Christmas tree with a broader spread than balsam fir. Its cones are bedecked with bracts. This species is now endangered. Zones 4-7.

A. concolor, white fir, grows to 80 by 25 feet at an average rate of 1 foot per year at The Holden Arboretum. Growth is sparse and slow in deep shade or compacted clay soil; at Holden, specimens in clay grow at ⅔ the rate of those in loamy soil, and a tree in deep shade grew to only 6 feet tall in 60 years. Its needles are up to 2½ inches long (long for a fir) and bluish or whitish green. Purplish cones appear after 40 years. White fir adapts to hot summers better than most other species, but is the worst choice for compacted, clay soils and can be severely damaged by wind. It needs water only during establishment. White fir contrasts beautifully with other evergreens. The cultivar **'Candicans'** has striking blue spring foliage that turns whitish or powder blue by fall. Zone 4-7.

ABIES CONCOLOR (WHITE FIR) Evergreen. 10 years: 6 feet; 20 years: 20 feet, 50 years: 50-55 feet; maturity: to 100 feet. Narrow pyramidal form with horizontal branching. Blue-green needles to 2 inches long. Full sun or light shade, cool moist climate, slightly acidic well-drained soil. Zones 4-7.

ABIES KOREANA (KOREAN FIR) Evergreen. 10 years: 6 feet; 20 years: 15 feet; 50 years: 35-40 feet; maturity: to 70 feet. Dark green, shiny needles to1 inch long, pyramidal form with horizontal branching. Full sun or light shade, cool moist climate, slightly acidic well-drained soil. Tolerates heat better than most firs. Zones 4-7.

ABIES NORDMANNIANA (NORDMAN FIR) Evergreen. 10 years: 6 feet; 20 years: 20 feet; 50 years: 50-55 feet; maturity: to 100 feet. Dark green, shiny needles to 1 inch long. Full sun or light shade, cool moist climate, slightly acidic well-drained soil. Tolerates heat better than most firs. Zones 4-7.

ACACIA FARNESIANA (SWEET ACACIA) Evergreen. 10 years: 4 feet; 20 years: 8 feet; 50 years: 20 feet; maturity: to 25 feet. Finely divided blue-green foliage, abundant clusters of yellow flowers in early spring. Full sun, tolerates heat and poor, dry soil. Zones 9-10.

Above: Conifer needles, from top to bottom: *Picea abies, Chamaecyparis obtusa, Cedrus atlantica* 'Glauca', *Taxus baccata, Pinus koraiensis.*

A. koreana, Korean fir, has glossy, deep green leaves with contrasting white lines on the undersides and bears attractive purple cones after 10 years. It was introduced to the U.S. by Ernest Wilson at The Arnold Arboretum in 1918, where one tree is now 60 feet tall and 25 feet wide. It does best in areas where summers are cool, from the coast of Maine to the Pacific Northwest. The young foliage of the cultivar **'Horstmann's Silberlocke'** is particularly attractive: recurved and displaying white undersides as if decorated with tinsel.

A. nordmanniana, Nordman fir, Caucasian fir, is a tall, dense, narrow dark green conifer with a deeper root system than most firs. It is a fine specimen for a meadow border and contrasts well with the blossoms of early spring bloomers like magnolias and with striking fall foliage of deciduous trees.

A. cilicica, Cilician fir, is a lighter green than *A. nordmanniana.*

A. pinsapo, Spanish fir, has stiffer needles than most firs and grows to 50 feet tall. It is more heat tolerant than most species, thriving up to Zones 7 or 8. The cultivar **'Glauca'** has blue-green needles. **A. numidica,** Algerian fir, is a closely related species that also has a stiff, angular appearance. Its 5- to 7-inch cones are light green, tinged with purple.

A. procera, noble fir, is native to the Pacific Northwest and is a magnificent tree in that region, growing to 250 feet tall with 8- to 11-inch cones on even young trees; it is a choice Christmas tree in the Pacific Northwest. It is not recommended for the Midwest or East, as it requires high moisture and perishes in heat.

A. homolepis, Nikko fir, is a beautiful 60-foot-tall tree with strong horizontal branches and 4-inch-long purple cones. This and white fir were Charles Sprague Sargent's choices for the Boston area.

A. lasiocarpa, subalpine fir, performed well in clay soil at The Holden Arboretum for 40 years, but has not proven reliable at The Arnold Arboretum. It does well in sandy or clay soil, and is probably best in the West. It has soft green to blue-green foliage and grows 50 feet tall and 25 feet wide. Zones 2-5. **A. l. var. arizonica,** corkbark fir, is a native of the southern Rockies and has blue foliage. Zones 4-7.

ACACIA WATTLE, MIMOSA *Fabaceae (Pea family)*

Hardy only in Zone 9 and warmer, wattles are extremely valuable in the Southeast and Southwest. Many are tolerant of drought and humidity and produce abundant fragrant flowers in late winter or early spring.

BEST CONDITIONS Wattles need full sun and warm temperatures; some types will not even survive in coastal southern California. They thrive in almost any soil, including poor, dry soil.

PLANTING Acacias need some extra care in planting. Plant young trees from pots in spring; harden off before placing in ground and water after planting..

ROUTINE CARE The long roots of established acacias will find water and nutrients; it is better not to provide surface moisture or fertilizer, for this discourages the establishment of a good root system. When watering is necessary–during establishment (three years) and in severe drought–water deeply and infrequently.

PRUNING Prune to desired shape. To encourage branching, cut a few inches off the main branch on top. To induce a tree shape, keep the main branch and prune lower branches. Some forms, such as *A. farnesiana,* can be sheared as a hedge. Remove suckers regularly.

PESTS, DISEASES, OTHER PROBLEMS Because their wood is very brittle, acacias are usually short-lived. They are susceptible to mimosa wilt, a fungus disease, and webworms, which can skeletonize the tree. Affected trees should be treated aggressively.

PROPAGATION Propagate by seeds or cuttings.

USE Acacias are popular shade trees in the southern part of the United States. Their fragrant flowers and silvery foliage are often used in arrangements.

SELECTIONS *A. baileyana,* Cootamundra wattle, grows very quickly to about 30 feet tall and produces 3-inch-long racemes of feathery pale yellow flowers. Zone 10.

A. dealbata, silver wattle, grows to 60 feet and is extremely drought tolerant. Its foliage is silver-gray, and its flowers appear as soft yellow balls. This species needs more fertile soil than most.

A. erioloba, camelthorn, is a tall, gray-green acacia useful in the Arizona desert.

A. farnesiana, sweet acacia, is a fine shade tree in both Arizona and Florida; it produces fragrant yellow flowers through much of the year and tolerates heat and drought very well. .

ACER MAPLE *Aceraceae (Maple family)*

Maples are among the most loved, beautiful, and practical trees available to the homeowner. The maples include about 200 species, most of which are native to northern temperate regions. They are valued for their early spring flowers, fall color, and ornamental bark. There is an enormous variety within the genus in appearance and cultural requirements. Maples range from shrubby Japanese maples with finely dissected burgundy foliage to towering Norway maples that line city boulevards; many species provide excellent shade and extraordinary fall color.

As seen in this grouping, maples are a variable group, with a great range in leaf color, size, shape, and height.

ACER X FREEMANII 'MARMO' (MARMO FREEMAN MAPLE) Deciduous. 10 years: 20 feet; 20 years: 40-45 feet; 50 years: 75-85 feet; maturity: to 110 feet. Upright, columnar habit, outstanding red and green fall color. Full sun, any fertile soil, tolerates cold, drought, and excess moisture well. Zones 4-8.

ACER GRISEUM (PAPERBARK MAPLE) Deciduous. 10 years: 8 feet; 20 years: 18 feet; 50 years: 25-30 feet; maturity: to 45 feet. Open rounded form. Compound green leaves turn rich red in fall. Exquisite exfoliating cinnamon brown bark. Full sun, any soil, slightly alkaline acceptable, not drought tolerant. Zones 6-9, 5 with protection.

ACER TRIFLORUM (THREE-FLOWERED MAPLE) Deciduous. 10 years: 6 feet; 20 years: 15-20 feet; 50 years: 20-25 feet; maturity: to 40 feet. Rounded crown. Very attractive flaking bark. Trifoliate green leaves turn red to orange in fall. Full sun, any fertile soil, not drought tolerant. Zone 5-8.

ACER PALMATUM (JAPANESE MAPLE) Deciduous. 10 years: 6 feet; 20 years: 15 feet; 50 years: 30 feet; maturity: to 40 feet. Shrubby, mounded habit. Dense, deeply lobed green or red foliage, turns bright red in fall. Full sun (some tolerate partial shade), any fertile soil, not drought tolerant. Zone 5-8.

ACER X FREEMANII FREEMAN MAPLE *Aceraceae (Maple family)*

A hybrid between the red maple (*A. rubrum*) and silver maple (*A. saccharinum*), this extremely adaptable tree is found where the two species overlap, in much of the eastern half of the U.S. It is a relatively new plant on the market and may be difficult to find, but it shows much promise and is worth the effort to track down.

BEST CONDITIONS Site in full sun if possible. Freeman maple adapts to both cold and warm temperatures, and is unfazed by the rigorous winters of the Midwest. It tolerates excess moisture and drought well and thrives in a wide range of soils.

PLANTING Plant in spring so that it is established before the stress of summer heat. Plant at the same level as the rootball and keep well watered to encourage a deep root system. Site where there is plenty of space for future growth.

ROUTINE CARE Keep well watered until established and during severe drought. Mulch for first few years. Plant a groundcover for shade and reduce moisture loss at the roots. Turf fertility should be sufficient, without additional feeding.

PRUNING Prune to maintain central leader, and routinely remove dead or crossing branches. Do not cut branches severely; insect and disease problems may result.

PEST, DISEASES, OTHER PROBLEMS None serious.

PROPAGATION From cuttings, or buy stock grown on their own roots.

USE This excellent shade tree displays good fall color. Although it grows fast, it is not as weak wooded as some maples. Its extensive root system limits what can be grown beneath it; in later years, consider leaving the lower branches.

SELECTIONS Autumn Blaze ['Jeffersred'] rapidly forms a broad tree to 50 feet tall and 45 feet wide. It combines the vigor and pH tolerance of silver maple with the stronger wood, red-orange fall color, and central leader of red maple. Zone 4. **'Marmo'** has an upright columnar habit. Its outstanding red and green fall color lasts for several weeks. A Chicagoland Grows® program introduction, Zone 4.

ACER RUBRUM RED MAPLE, SWAMP MAPLE *Aceraceae (Maple family)*

This flood plain tree, a staple of the tree industry and perhaps the most common tree in some parts of the country, is noted for its early red flowers and fall color. It has a pyramidal shape and gray bark; 40-50 feet tall.

BEST CONDITIONS Site in full sun if possible, where the soil is moist and acidic to neutral. It does not tolerate high pH soils or heavily polluted conditions well.

PLANTING, ROUTINE CARE, PRUNING, PROPAGATION As above.

PEST, DISEASES, OTHER PROBLEMS Verticillium wilt, anthracnose, weak wood.

USE This workhorse is used as a shade or specimen tree.

SELECTIONS Although hardy in Zones 3-9, look for the many cultivars adapted to particular areas. Consider **Red Sunset** ['Franksred'] for Zones 4-8; **'October Glory'** in Zones 5-8. As a street tree in Zones 4-8, **'Bowhall'** has the desired upright habit, and adapts to neutral to acid soil.

ACER GRISEUM PAPERBARK MAPLE *Aceraceae (Maple family)*

This slow-growing Chinese native is considered to be among the finest of the small trees available for American gardens. It is ornamental during all seasons, with splendid fall color of reds and oranges, and its cinnamon-colored, exfoliating bark enlivens the winter months. Autumn coloration is best when trees are grown in a sunny location, although they tolerate partially shaded positions well.

BEST CONDITIONS Paperbark maple grows best in well-drained, acid to slightly

Above: Acer palmatum 'Bloodgood'. Top: Acer palmatum 'Tsukubane'. Acer palmatum cultivars are among the most sought-after of trees, particularly useful in small gardens. Their leaf color and textures are unbeatable.

Above: Acer ginnala, Chrysanthemum
'Wolverine'.

alkaline soils, but is quite adaptable, and clay soils are also successful. Sun or light shade.

PLANTING Select healthy plants with dark green, unblemished leaves and good bark color. The latter varies considerably and is a major attribute of the plant. Plant in spring so that it is established before the stress of summer heat. Plant at the same level as the rootball and keep well watered to encourage a deep root system. Site where there is plenty of space for future growth.

ROUTINE CARE Keep well watered until established and during severe drought. Mulch for the first few years. Plant a groundcover to afford shade and reduce moisture loss at the roots. Fertilizer is seldom necessary; turf fertility should be sufficient, without additional feeding.

PRUNING Prune to maintain a central leader, and routinely remove dead or crossing branches. Do not cut branches back severely; insect and disease problems may result.

PESTS, DISEASES, OTHER PROBLEMS No serious pests or diseases.

PROPAGATION Not easy to propagate; paperbark maples are difficult both from seed and cuttings.

USE Since their native habitat is at elevations of 4,000-6,000 feet, the heat of southern climates is not to their liking. This tree is reliably hardy in Zones 6-7, but will survive with protection in Zone 5 and in Zone 8 in the Pacific Northwest. Good specimens are quite costly, due to their difficulty in propagation by seed or cuttings and their slow growth rate.

SELECTIONS *A. triflorum* is a northern counterpart of *A. griseum*. It reaches 15-25 feet and although its bark is not quite as outstanding, it displays good red to orange fall color. It tolerates a wide range of pH. Anthracnose may be a problem.

A. pensylvanicum 'Erythrocladum', 12-15 feet, has exquisite watermelon pink stems

ACER PLATANOIDES (NORWAY MAPLE) Deciduous. 10 years: 10 feet; 20 years: 20-25 feet; 50 years: 50-60 feet; maturity: to 100 feet. Dense, bright green lobed leaves, sometimes turn clear yellow in fall. Small yellow flowers in spring. Full sun, any fertile soil, not drought tolerant. Seedlings can be invasive. Zones 3-8.

ACER PLATANOIDES 'CRIMSON KING' (CRIMSON KING NORWAY MAPLE) Deciduous. 10 years: 10 feet; 20 years: 20-25 feet; 50 years: 50-60 feet; maturity: to 100 feet. Deeply lobed dark red leaves, broadly rounded crown. Full sun, any fertile soil, not drought tolerant. Seedlings can be invasive. Zones 3-8.

ACER SACCHARUM 'GREEN MOUNTAIN' (SUGAR MAPLE) Deciduous. 10 years: 10 feet; 20 years: 20-25 feet; 50 years: 50-60 feet; maturity: to 100 feet. Wide, rounded crown. Dense foliage, bright green in summer turns orange and gold in autumn. Moderately fertile, well-drained, loamy soil on the acidic side; full sun to half shade in the North and ¾-¼ sun in the South. Zones 3-8.

ACER CIRCINATUM (VINE MAPLE) Deciduous. 10 years: 6 feet; 20 years: 15 feet; 50 years: 25-30 feet; maturity: to 35 feet. Dense green lobed leaves turning red or orange in fall, ornamental purplish and white flowers, widespreading habit. Full sun or up to half shade, any fertile soil. Zones 5-8.

with white striations, exposed to view as the leaves fall.

A. palmatum, Japanese maple, is often grown as a shrub though many cultivars grow to 20-30 feet tall. Some varieties, such as **'Atropurpureum',** have dark red or bright red leaves; some like 'Butterfly' have variegated leaves.. Others, including **'Dissectum'** (cutleaf Japanese maple), have graceful lacy leaves, often startling red, that add incomparable interest wherever they are planted.

ACER SACCHARUM SUGAR MAPLE *Aceraceae (Maple family)*

This beautiful native tree, with its upright to rounded habit to 75 feet tall, is found in the wild from eastern Canada to Georgia, Wisconsin, Texas, and Mississippi. As an ornamental it is valued for its clean foliage which turns brilliant reds, oranges, and yellows in fall. Sugar maple is the primary source of maple syrup. The sap is tapped and boiled down; it takes 40 gallons of sap to produce 1 gallon of syrup.

BEST CONDITIONS Fall coloration is best in full sun; susceptible to salt and air pollution. It does best in the North and East in sunny areas where the soil is rich and well drained. It does tolerate extended hot dry conditions well, but is unsuitable as a street tree, especially where salt is used on the roads. Where it is planted in hot, dry places, try to site on the north side of buildings to afford some shade, and use a groundcover to provide shade and conserve moisture at the roots.

PLANTING Spring planting is best for balled-and-burlapped stock. Plant so that the top of the rootball is level with the soil surface, avoiding deep planting. Keep well watered. Bear in mind the eventual size of the tree so that it will not become crowded.

ROUTINE CARE Keep well watered until established and during severe drought. Mulch for the first few years. Plant a groundcover to afford shade and reduce moisture loss at the roots. Turf fertility should be sufficient, without additional feeding.

PRUNING Prune to maintain a central leader, and routinely remove dead or crossing branches. Do not cut branches back severely or limb up low branches; insect and disease problems may result.

PESTS, DISEASES, OTHER PROBLEMS Verticillium wilt can be a problem, but can usu-

A. palmatum.

ally be alleviated with good care. Water well during times of stress and fertilize if necessary. Leaf scorch is also a result of insufficient water. This species is not salt tolerant.

PROPAGATION It is best to buy cultivars. Can be grown from seed.

USE This tree shows off best in large landscapes. Site it so that it can be appreciated from the living space, especially when it displays its brilliant fall spectacle, ideally lighted from behind by the setting sun in autumn. Because the tree has shallow roots and a heavy canopy, it is difficult to plant shrubs or grass beneath it.

SELECTIONS At the Chicago Botanic Garden **'Green Mountain'** has shown exceptional tolerance to drought and leaf scorch. In very poor soil and under high-temperature stress in parking lots it has remained healthy for 23 years with no more attention than routine mulching. This excellent, vigorous selection has an upright oval crown and in the Midwest colors orange and scarlet in fall. Ethan Johnson suspects this cultivar is a natural hybrid of *A. saccharum* and *A. nigrum,* due to its vigor, adaptability to high pH, and partial resemblance to the latter. Zones 3-8.

A. platanoides, Norway maple, is popular and there are many cultivars available. For the upper parts of the country, where hardiness may be a problem, two of the best are **'Pond'** ['Emerald Lustre'] and **'Columnare'.** 'Pond', Zones 4-8, has an excellent branching habit and yellow fall color; 'Columnare', Zones 3-9, is an upright grower, ideal for narrow planting areas. It also tolerates stress well and makes a good street tree. Of the red-leaved selections, **'Crimson King'**, Zones 3-8, is among the best. It reaches 35 feet tall and 25 feet across, with purple-green foliage even in the summer. Its parent **'Schwendleri'** is somewhat hardier, but its red-purple spring foliage becomes bronze-green later on. It has a narrower growth habit making it useful as a street tree.

A. nigrum, black maple, is more adaptable to alkalinity than sugar maple, but has markedly duller fall foliage. Common in the Midwest, it is hardy in Zones 4-7.

A. barbatum, southern sugar maple or Florida maple, has smaller leaves (to 4 inches across) and is recommended for Zones 8-9.

A. circinatum (vine maple) is native to the West Coast and is one of the better maples for warm areas. Its twisting branches start from the base of the tree, leading to its name, and its clusters of small red-purple and white flowers are particularly ornamental.

Aesculus hippocastanum.

AESCULUS HORSE CHESTNUT, BUCKEYE *Hippocastanaceae (Horse Chestnut family)*

The horse chestnut does not bear edible fruit; it is, however, prized for its neatly rounded shape and shiny, dark green foliage. It grows 40-80 feet tall, with a crown nearly as wide, and bears clusters of large red, pink, or white flowers in late spring. Leaves drop before autumn, so it does not produce an autumn display.

BEST CONDITIONS The horse chestnut is hardy to Zone 3 and tolerates the heat of Zone 8 as well, though in very warm or dry seasons the leaves may turn brown; brown leaves are more often the cause of vascular problems. It needs full sun, but will thrive in almost any well-drained soil.

PLANTING Plant in spring or fall; balled-and-burlapped transplants work best. Fertilize and water generously until established.

ROUTINE CARE Once established, additional water is not necessary except in

AESCULUS GLABRA (OHIO BUCKEYE) Deciduous. 10 years: 9 feet; 20 years: 20 feet; 50 years: 35-40 feet; maturity: to 70 feet. Rounded crown. Large green compound leaves turn bright orange in fall; yellow flowers, not very showy. Ordinary, well-drained soil, full sun. Zones 3-8.

ALBIZIA JULIBRISSIN (SILK TREE, MIMOSA TREE) Deciduous. 10 years: 8 feet; 20 years: 15-20 feet; 50 years: 20-30 feet; maturity: to 35 feet. Broad flat crown, dainty leaves, flowers with long silky pink stamens. Full sun, tolerates poor dry soil. Zones 6-9.

ALNUS RUBRA (RED ALDER) Deciduous. 10 years: 20 feet; 20 years: 40 feet; 50 years: 60-80 feet; maturity: to 100 feet. Dense dark green foliage, gray to white mottled bark. Tolerates pollution and marshy areas. Zones 7-9.

ALNUS SINUATA (SITKA ALDER) Deciduous. 10 years: 5 feet; 20 years: 10 feet; 50 years: 25 feet; maturity: to 30 feet. Bright green rounded leaves. Tolerates pollution and marshy areas. Zones 7-9.

extremely dry seasons. Water if leaves turn brown or look scorched, but only if soil is dry. Additional fertilizer is not necessary. Remove dead leaves from underneath tree to avoid disease; take care when removing fruit as it can be spiny.

PRUNING This tree naturally forms a pleasing shape; prune only to remove dead wood.

PESTS, DISEASES, OTHER PROBLEMS Fungal infections and rust sometimes strike; keeping the area around the tree free of dead leaves and debris helps avoid this problem. Horse chestnuts drop fruits, leaves, twigs, and flowers; many gardeners consider it a messy tree.

PROPAGATION Cuttings can be taken in winter; grafting is also often successful. Seeds should be sown as soon as they ripen in the fall.

USE The wide spread of the horse chestnut makes it an excellent shade tree; its naturally symmetrical shape and showy flowers make it useful as a specimen. It does not serve well as a background to a flower border since its spiny fruits and twigs are difficult to remove.

SELECTIONS *A. x carnea* produces the typical red flowers and grows to 75 feet tall. The cultivar **'Plantieriensis'** does not produce fruit, making it more desirable. Native *A. glabra,* Ohio buckeye, also grows to 40 feet and has smaller yellow flowers; it is useful in autumn, when its leaves turn bright orange.

A. hippocastanum, which was brought to America by early colonists, produces pyramids of white flowers and grows to 80 feet. *A. h.* **'Baumannii',** a double-flowered form, bears the showiest flowers in spikes often reaching 12 inches long.

Alnus glutinosa has pendulous flowers and miniature cones called strobiles.

ALBIZIA SILK TREE, MIMOSA TREE *Mimosaceae*

Because of its delicate, showy pink blossoms and dainty foliage, many people think the silk tree is fragile or even tropical. Actually, it is tolerant of fairly severe weather–up to Zone 6–and harsh pollution. It is often used as a city street tree, where its fluffy blooms appear in midsummer when many other trees are looking tired and dry. The tree grows to 40 feet tall in the South, but usually does not exceed 30 feet in cooler climates.

BEST CONDITIONS Although it is usually hardy to Zone 6, the silk tree prefers a sheltered location and performs better in warm climates; it is not always hardy in lower New York but does well in sandy soil on Long Island. It needs full sun, but thrives in poor, dry soil of virtually any pH value as long as it is well drained.

PLANTING Plant in spring or winter; water generously after planting and through the first season.

ROUTINE CARE After establishment, water and fertilizer are not needed. Monitor for insect pests.

PRUNING Prune lightly to shape or to rejuvenate scraggly specimens.

PESTS, DISEASES, OTHER PROBLEMS Although it blooms better in warm climates, the silk tree often develops mimosa wilt if the weather is warm and the soil is wet. Do not plant in poorly drained areas. Webworms often colonize the trees; remove and destroy affected branches.

PROPAGATION Cuttings may be taken in the winter. Seed may be sown in spring, but it should be scarified first.

USE Often used as a street tree, silk tree is a nice specimen for small gardens where it flowers toward the middle of the summer.

ARBOR DAY

Almost forgotten today, Arbor Day was a source of great excitement among American schoolchildren from the 1880s until World War II. Set aside as a day "to teach the importance of forestry," it was usually observed by parading the students to a local park to plant trees. The idea and name were creations of Julius Sterling Morton (1832-1902), a Nebraska agriculturalist and politician. Nebraska celebrated the first Arbor Day on April 10, 1872; when it was made a legal holiday in Nebraska in 1885, the day was moved to April 22, Morton's birthday. Within a decade the holiday was being celebrated in 40 states, although the exact date varied in accordance with local planting seasons: it fell in January in Florida, on various days in April or May in the more northerly states, and was so popular in Pennsylvania that it was celebrated twice a year, in spring and fall. Morton, who went on to serve as Secretary of Agriculture under Grover Cleveland, was a descendent of Richard Morton, an Englishman who came to America on the *Little Ann,* the ship otherwise known as "the second Mayflower." Julius Morton's son, Joy, made the family name a household word in 1911 with his salt company's slogan, "When it rains, it pours."

SELECTIONS *A. julibrissin* is the only species commonly available. The cultivar **'Charlotte'** is wilt-resistant and suitable for warm areas. *A. j.* **'Ernest Wilson'** is hardier than most, surviving in Zone 5.

ALNUS ALDER *Betulaceae (Birch family)*

Alders are good trees for difficult spots. Because they release nitrogen rather than using it up, they do well in infertile soil; they also thrive in city pollution and in marshy areas. The showiest element of these trees is their catkins, which appear in early spring and often become woody.

BEST CONDITIONS Alders are not fussy about soil and will thrive in almost any type; they can be used in poorly drained areas where many other trees will rot. They are hardy in Zones 4-7.

PLANTING In spring or fall.

ROUTINE CARE None necessary. These trees thrive on neglect.

PRUNING Prune to keep in bounds.

PESTS, DISEASES, OTHER PROBLEMS Tent caterpillars and aphids often need control.

PROPAGATION Propagate by cuttings, seeds, or grafts.

USE Alders are usually used in wet or marshy areas.

SELECTIONS *A. cordata,* Italian alder, has glossy green foliage.

A. glutinosa, common alder, grows 50 feet tall and spreads 30 feet. *A. g.* **'Laciniata'** has deeply lobed leaves.

A. incana has yellow catkins and blue-gray foliage and is hardier than other alders, surviving in Zone 2.

A. rubra, red alder, is suitable for the West Coast; 60 feet tall, often weedy.

A. sinuata is native to the West Coast from California to Alaska; it grows 50-60 feet tall and is usually multitrunked, forming a bowl-shaped crown.

AMELANCHIER X GRANDIFLORA APPLE SERVICEBERRY *Rosaceae (Rose family)*

This easy to grow hybrid of *A. arborea* and *A. laevis* makes a fine small scale tree for home landscapes. In spring it has white flowers, which are followed by edible purplish blue fruit, a favorite of songbirds. Plum-colored foliage emerges during the flowering stage and contrasts beautifully; it turns green as it matures. Even in shade it has excellent fall color; in the winter its silvery bark is attractive. Apple serviceberry has been grown in the U.S. for over 100 years.

BEST CONDITIONS It thrives in full sun, but colors well in fall even if sited in partial shade. Well-drained, acid to neutral soils are best with good moisture retention. In highly alkaline soils (7.5 and over), the leaves are susceptible to chlorosis (yellowing). Tolerant of dry conditions once established. In Chicago the amelanchiers continued to grow when other plants had quit during a dry spring. Not affected by humidity.

PLANTING Balled-and-burlapped stock should be set out in spring; container plants may be planted later. Water weekly until established.

ROUTINE CARE Keep well watered until established and during severe drought. Mulch for the first few years. Plant a groundcover to afford shade and reduce moisture loss at the roots. Fertilizer is seldom necessary; turf fertility should be sufficient, without additional feeding.

PRUNING Pruning is rarely necessary.

AMELANCHIER CANADENSIS (EASTERN SERVICEBERRY) Deciduous. 10 years: 5 feet; 20 years: 10 feet; 50 years: 20 feet; maturity: to 20 feet. 10-15 feet wide. Small, pointed oval leaves turn yellow to gold in fall; white flowers in spring, bluish fruit, attractive silvery bark. Full sun or partial shade, moist well-drained soil, acid to neutral. Zones 4-9.

ARALIA ELATA (ANGELICA TREE) Deciduous. 10 years: 8 feet; 20 years: 15 feet; 50 years: 25-30 feet; maturity: to 40 feet. Dull green leaves, spikes of small white flowers, very thorny branches, small black berries in fall. Moist fertile soil, full sun. Zones 3-8.

ARAUCARIA ARAUCANA (MONKEY-PUZZLE TREE) Evergreen. 10 years: 10 feet; 20 years: 20 feet; 50 years: 45-55 feet; maturity: to 90 feet. Ropelike, twisted branches with dark green needles. Prefers rich soil, tolerates dry, poor soil. Full sun. Zones 7-10.

ARBUTUS MENZIESII (PACIFIC MADRONE) Evergreen. 10 years: 10 feet; 20 years: 20 feet; 50 years: 45-55 feet; maturity: to 80 feet. Pyramidal shape. Glossy green oblong leaves, red bark, clusters of white flowers, showy red berries in fall. Full sun, any soil (dry or poor soil is fine). Zones 7-9.

The Great Khan has had made an earthwork, that is to say a mound, fully 100 paces in height and over a mile in circumference. This mound is covered with a dense growth of trees, all evergreens that never shed their leaves. And I assure you that whenever the Great Khan hears tell of a particularly fine tree he has it pulled up, roots and all and with a quantity of earth, and transported to this mound by elephants. No matter how big the tree may be, he is not deterred from transplanting it. In this way he has assembled here the finest trees in the world. In addition, he has had the mound covered with lapis lazuli, which is intensely green, so that trees and rock alike are as green as green can be and there is no other color to be seen. For this reason it is called the Green Mound.

MARCO POLO, *THE TRAVELS*

PESTS, DISEASES, OTHER PROBLEMS Seldom a problem.

PROPAGATION It is best to buy vegetatively propagated named selections. Many are propagated by tissue culture.

USE Its upright, vase shape makes apple serviceberry a perfect subject for planting near a patio, terrace, or path, where it can be appreciated at close quarters. To get the full impact of its seasonal glory, plant it in front of an evergreen background. The multistemmed form is also attractive.

SELECTIONS 'Autumn Brilliance' is a fast-growing, leaf-spot-resistant selection. It has superior red fall color. **'Forest Prince'**, a robust selection by Roy Klehm, has leathery emerald green foliage which turns orange-red in fall. **'Robin Hill'** is a more upright grower with pink flower buds which open to pale pink in cool weather. Its fall color is red. **'Strata'**, named by Dr. Ed Hasselkus (University of Wisconsin) for its strong horizontal branching habit, grows as wide as tall; bright red fall color. Princeton Nursery introduced the upright growing **'Cumulus'**. Its fall foliage is orange to red.

A. canadensis (shadblow, Eastern serviceberry) has small white flowers that appear on erect racemes in early spring, along with gray-green foliage. Its purplish berries and red or yellow color are effective in June.

A. laevis has foliage that emerges red and turns gray-green. It grows to 40 feet.

ARALIA ANGELICA TREE *Araliaceae (Ginseng family)*

This is an unusual tree that can provide a dramatic effect if used properly. They grow 10-30 feet tall and produce large dull green leaves and very large panicles of small white flowers on thorny branches in August. Birds appreciate its small black berries in early fall.

BEST CONDITIONS Angelica tree needs fertile, moist soil and full sun; it will grow, but less quickly, in part shade. It is hardy to Zone 3.

PLANTING Plant in spring or fall. Provide water and fertilizer generously during establishment.

ROUTINE CARE Once established, it requires little care; water only during drought.

PRUNING Pruning is usually unnecessary and can only harm the naturally graceful shape of this plant.

PESTS, DISEASES, OTHER PROBLEMS None serious.

PROPAGATION Propagate by division, budding, or grafting; seeds will need to be stratified before they are sown.

USE Use angelica where a dramatic specimen is desired. If you're looking for bold foliage with a tropical effect, angelica tree will provide it.

SELECTIONS *A. elata,* Japanese angelica tree, is described above. *A. e.* **'Variegata'** has boldly marked leaves.

A. spinosa, devil's walking stick, is sometimes weedy and is hardy to Zone 4.

A. cordata bears an edible fruit, called udo, that is used in Japanese cooking.

ARAUCARIA NORFOLK ISLAND PINE, MONKEY-PUZZLE TREE
Araucariaceae (Araucaria family)

Unlike some conifers, araucarias rarely blend into the background. Their ropelike, twisted branches and dark green needlelike to wedge-shaped leaves combine to form a striking, if sometimes ungainly, specimen tree.

BEST CONDITIONS This conifer needs warm temperatures; *A. araucana* is hardy to

Zone 7, most other species only to Zone 10. It prefers deep, rich, moist soil, but will tolerate dryness well.

PLANTING Sow seed directly into sandy, peaty soil; protect from wind for the first few seasons.

ROUTINE CARE Enrich soil with peat. This plant will adapt to dry conditions, so water only if drought is unusually severe once established.

PRUNING Improper pruning results in asymmetrical trees. Take care to prune evenly on all sides of the tree.

PESTS, DISEASES, OTHER PROBLEMS None serious.

PROPAGATION Propagate from seeds or from cuttings taken from the top of a tree.

USE Use as a specimen tree or foundation planting in warm climates.

SELECTIONS *A. araucana,* the monkey-puzzle tree, grows to 90 feet; it is recommended for the Pacific Northwest.

A. heterophylla, the Norfolk Island pine, grows to 100 feet. It can also be used as an indoor pot plant. Zones 9-10.

Asimina triloba flower.

ARBUTUS PACIFIC MADRONE *Ericaceae (Heath family)*

Pacific madrone, a broad-leaved evergreen native to the west coast from southwest British Columbia to northwest Mexico, is a valuable tree with a graceful, pyramidal shape and red bark. It is interesting in all seasons, for its clusters of flowers in spring, showy orange berries in fall, and glossy dark green leaves and cinnamon red bark in summer and winter.

BEST CONDITIONS The Pacific madrone is hardy to Zone 7. It needs full sun, but will grow in dry, poor soil.

PLANTING Pacific madrone is difficult to transplant. Plant seedlings 18 inches tall or smaller and place where they are to grow.

ROUTINE CARE Provide additional water and fertilizer only during the first two seasons. Cleanup is sometimes difficult because the tree drops leaves, branches, fruits, and bark.

PRUNING Rarely necessary; this tree has a naturally graceful shape.

PESTS, DISEASES, OTHER PROBLEMS No serious pest or disease problems; leaf drop sometimes causes problems.

PROPAGATION By cuttings or seeds.

USE The rich green leaves of this tree are an excellent backdrop to flower or shrub borders; site so that debris does not land in the garden.

SELECTIONS *A. menziesii,* Pacific madrone, grows to 75 feet tall.

A. unedo, strawberry tree, is much smaller (usually growing only to 10 feet, but sometimes to 30) and is usually considered a shrub. Native to Europe, it is grown for its bright red strawberrylike fruits.

ASIMINA TRILOBA PAWPAW, INDIANA BANANA *Annonaceae (Annona family)*

Native to eastern and central North America, pawpaw has the largest of all native fruits. They are edible, about 3-6 inches long and may weigh 8-12 ounces. Over 60 cultivars have been named for fruit production. Current research at Purdue University has isolated an anti-cancer drug which drains cell energy rather than inhibiting cell growth. As an ornamental, pawpaw has a straight trunk to 15-20 feet tall and a pyramidal habit.

Betula pendula 'Dalecarlica'.

BEST CONDITIONS Pawpaw tolerates partially shaded positions as an understory tree, but to maximize fruit production full sun is required. Soil should be deep, moist, and fertile; acid soil is usually recommended but at Chicago Botanic Garden a specimen has thrived in a soil of pH 7.8, surrounded by pavement and a building, for 12 years. Not a heavy feeder, but a high phosphorus fertilizer may help fruit production.

PLANTING Large plants are difficult to transplant; select young plants about 5-6 feet tall. Spring planting of container-grown stock has the best success. The root-ball should remain at the same level. Keep well watered and mulch to reduce water loss.

ROUTINE CARE Keep well watered. Annual addition of a high-phosphorous fertilizer improves fruit production.

PRUNING Prune only to eliminate crossing branches and to open up the center of the plant. Routinely remove suckers from the base of the plant. These may appear in sandy soils with underlying clay. Water deeply during dry periods.

PESTS, DISEASES, OTHER PROBLEMS None serious.

PROPAGATION Sow seed in fall or stratify at about 40° F for 60-100 days prior to spring planting. Improve germination with bottom heat of 80° F. The cultivars are chip-budded by nurseries.

USE The large leaves, which turn yellow to gold in fall, create a certain unique tropical effect. The small stature suits today's smaller properties well, and the sweet, bananalike fruits are nutritious and exotic. Certainly an underused native.

SELECTIONS Some selections made for fruit quality include **'Davis'**, **'Prolific'**, and **'Rebecca's Gold'**. The fruits of **'Overleese'** may top 1 pound in weight.

BETULA BIRCH *Betulaceae (Birch family)*

Birches are found growing in north temperate and arctic regions of the world and several of our native species make fine ornamentals. Although they generally live only 50-100 years, they are fast-growing deciduous trees of elegant habit, with fine-textured foliage. Several species have attractive white bark marked with black and provide excellent fall color. Where site or species selection is poor, birches are subject to many insect pests. Birch wood is durable unless allowed to get wet and rot. Birch lumber is popular for making furniture and for flooring.

BEST CONDITIONS Plant in full sun or light shade. Birches enjoy having their roots in cool shade and their crowns in the sun. They do best where the soil is acidic to neutral and moist, but drains well. They are especially well-suited to damp sites near water, in or on the edge of a forest setting.

PLANTING Plant at the same depth as in the field or container. Mulch routinely. Select a site that meets the particular needs of the species.

ROUTINE CARE Keep well watered during dry weather. Apply a mulch 2-4 inches thick in a 3-foot ring on young trees. A balanced fertilizer program helps to maintain vigor and vitality.

PRUNING Prune routinely in summer to remove dead branches and major crossing branches.

PESTS, DISEASES, OTHER PROBLEMS Birches are susceptible to a number of diseases, including canker and mildew. Some of the pests that are attracted to birches are bronze birch borer, birch leaf miner, and skeletonizers. Twig dieback is common.

ASIMINA TRILOBA (PAWPAW) Deciduous. 10 years: 10 feet; 20 years: 20 feet; 50 years: 30-35 feet; maturity: to 40 feet. Pyramidal form. Dark green oblong leaves, to 1 foot long, edible fruits weighing up to 12 ounces. Moist fertile soil, full sun. Zones 5-8.

BETULA LENTA (SWEET BIRCH, CHERRY BIRCH) Deciduous. 10 years: 20 feet; 20 years: 40 feet; 50 years: 60-70 feet; maturity: to 80 feet. Dark reddish brown bark becomes nearly black at maturity; dense dark green leaves turn golden yellow in autumn. Light shade to full sun and very acidic, moist, loamy soil; does not tolerate flooding. Zones 4-9.

BETULA NIGRA 'LITTLE KING' (FOX VALLEY™ RIVER BIRCH) Deciduous. 10 years: 10 feet; 20 years: 20 feet; 50 years: 35-40 feet; maturity: to 55 feet. Simple serrated green leaves, open habit, beautiful light peeling bark. Well-drained acidic soil, tolerates flooding, clay soil, and summer drought. Full sun or partial shade. Zones 4-9. A Chicagoland Grows® Program introduction.

BETULA NIGRA 'CULLY' (HERITAGE® RIVER BIRCH) Deciduous. 10 years: 20 feet; 20 years: 40 feet; 50 years: 60-70 feet; maturity: to 85 feet. Beautiful peeling, light bronze/salmon bark. Well-drained acidic soil, tolerates flooding, clay soil, and summer drought. Full sun or partial shade. Zones 4-9.

In an infant state of society, in regard to the fine arts, much will done in violation of good taste; but here, where nature has done so much for us, there is scarcely a large country residence in the Union from which useful hints in landscape gardening may not be taken. A natural group of trees, an accidental pond of water, or some equally simple object, may form a study more convincing to the mind of a true admirer of natural beauty than the most carefully drawn plan, or the most elaborately written description.

ANDREW JACKSON DOWLING,
A Treatise of the Theory and Practice of Landscape Gardening, 1841.

PROPAGATION Seeds collected from gardens often produce hybrid offspring.
USE Birches look wonderful in a naturalized setting. Their attractive bark provides strong winter interest.

BETULA ALLEGHANIENSIS [B. LUTEA] YELLOW BIRCH *Betulaceae (Birch family)*

Native from the northern Midwest and eastern U.S. north to southern Canada, yellow birch is important more as a timber tree than as an ornamental. Its wood is valued for fine furniture and cabinet-making. It may reach 100 feet or more in the wild where mature trees may live to be 150-200 years old. When young, the amber to silver-gray bark peels in curling strips but adheres to the trunk; it darkens with older specimens and remains attached in ragged plates.
BEST CONDITIONS This woodland understory, small-canopied tree requires some shade, but tolerates deeply shaded sites. It is adapted to a range of soils from fine clay to coarse sand with a pH range of 4.5-8.0. Ideal soil conditions are moist and well-drained; not tolerant of drought or flooding.
PLANTING Select plants with a healthy-looking trunk and leaves. At Holden Arboretum a good-sized tree was transplanted in mid-spring in full leaf with good results. A specimen on another part of the property was moved only a few feet to where the drainage was better and has responded with faster and apparently healthier growth.
ROUTINE CARE Water deeply during dry weather and mulch 2-4 inches deep in a 3-foot ring around young trees. Fertilize routinely.
PRUNING Prune routinely in summer to remove dead branches and major crossing branches.
PESTS, DISEASES, OTHER PROBLEMS In the upper Midwest, if sited well this species has minimal pest and disease problems.
PROPAGATION Seed requires cold stratification for 60 days.
USE Best in the larger landscape in woodlands, along streams, and in natural areas. Rated very high in wildlife value, and suitable in wildlife preserves. Oil of wintergreen may be distilled from the bark.

BETULA LENTA SWEET BIRCH, CHERRY BIRCH *Betulaceae (Birch family)*

Sweet birch is found throughout the northeastern U.S., through the Appalachian Mountains and south to northern Alabama. Its nonpeeling, dark reddish brown bark (reminiscent of cherries) is almost black at maturity. Pyramidal when young, sweet birch develops a rounded crown at maturity and may reach 40-50 feet in cultivation, but up to 80 feet in the wild. Its golden fall color is the best of all birches. The sap was used for birch beer.
BEST CONDITIONS Sweet birch does best in light shade to full sun. A moist loamy soil with a pH of 4.5-5.0 is ideal, but the tree does well in a soil with pH up to 6.5. Does not tolerate flooding.
PLANTING Somewhat difficult to transplant. Select damage-free balled-and-burlapped material and plant in early spring. Water well and mulch.
ROUTINE CARE Water deeply during dry weather and mulch 2-4 inches deep in a 3-foot ring around young trees. Fertilize routinely.

Opposite: River birches.

I'd like to go by climbing a
birch tree,
And climb black branches up a
snow-white trunk
Toward heaven, till the tree
could bear no more,
But dipped its top and set me
down again.
That would be good both going
and coming back.
One could do worse than be a
swinger of birches.
ROBERT FROST, "BIRCHES"

PRUNING Prune routinely in summer to remove dead branches and major crossing branches.

PESTS, DISEASES, OTHER PROBLEMS To reduce serious pest and disease problems, choose a perfect site, mulch, and fertilize routinely to encourage strong healthy growth without undue stress. Leaf miners are prevalent in New England. Aphids and birch leaf miner may become severe, but numerous other pests are also attracted to sweet birch. Resistant to bronze birch borer.

PROPAGATION Seed germinates poorly but responds better to one month of cold stratification, or shallow seeding with exposure to light. Cuttings and tissue culture are also used effectively.

USE Sweet birch is best suited to large areas such as golf courses, parks, campuses, and estates. Use it in a natural setting; it is rated very high in wildlife value.

BETULA MAXIMOWICZIANA MONARCH BIRCH *Betulaceae (Birch family)*

Monarch birch reaches 40-50 feet tall in cultivation and has amber to gray bark which darkens with age. It has the largest leaves of any birch and its catkins may reach 6 inches in length. Native to northern Japan. The specimens of this tree at Holden Arboretum may be hybrids rather than the true species. There is, however, a fine 17-year-old specimen at the David G. Leach Research Station in Madison, Ohio. It is 25 feet tall with a spread of 20 feet. This specimen has not been affected by borers, in spite of nearby damage to *B. platyphylla*. The Ohio Agricultural Research and Development Center at Wooster, Ohio, lists this species as being susceptible to bronze birch borers, and young trees at Arnold Arboretum have been affected by them.

BEST CONDITIONS Full sun, and a moist acidic to slightly acidic soil.

PLANTING Plant at the same depth as in the field or container. Mulch routinely.

ROUTINE CARE Keep well watered during dry weather. Apply a mulch 2-4 inches thick in a 3-foot ring on young trees. A balanced fertilizer program helps to maintain vigor and vitality.

PRUNING Prune routinely in summer to remove dead branches and major crossing branches.

PESTS, DISEASES, OTHER PROBLEMS Birches are susceptible to a number of diseases, including canker and mildew. Some of the pests that are attracted to birches are bronze birch borer, birch leaf miner, and skeletonizers. Twig dieback is common.

PROPAGATION Seeds collected from gardens often produce hybrid offspring.

USE Best in a natural setting.

BETULA NIGRA RIVER BIRCH *Betulaceae (Birch family)*

River birch is the most reliable and adaptable of all birches and is accordingly the most widely grown. It is native along stream banks in the eastern U.S. and Midwest.

BEST CONDITIONS River birches do best in sun or in positions that have sun for part of the day. They do not tolerate full shade. The ideal soil is well drained and acidic (pH no higher than 6.5), cool and moist, but even hot, dry soils are tolerated, as are summer droughts, clay soils, and even flooding.

PLANTING Transplants readily. Select material with healthy trunks and leaves.

Plant balled-and-burlapped stock in early spring or in autumn. Water well and mulch.

PESTS, DISEASES, OTHER PROBLEMS Resistant to bronze birch borer. Few pest and disease problems at Holden Arboretum. In the Midwest iron chlorosis is frequently widespread in alkaline soils.

ROUTINE CARE Keep well watered during dry weather. Apply a mulch 2-4 inches thick in a 3-foot ring on young trees. A balanced fertilizer program helps to maintain vigor and vitality.

PRUNING Prune routinely in summer to remove dead branches and major crossing branches.

PROPAGATION Seed as soon as it ripens in summer. Press into the seed mix and keep moist.

USE A magnificent tree for large landscapes, especially on difficult sites that drain poorly in winter but dry out in summer. Good in hot climates.

SELECTIONS 'Heritage' is a superior fast-growing cultivar which has gained widespread acceptance in the trade. Its bark exfoliates even on young plants; it is white to pinkish white darkening to a blackish brown with age; it does not peel.. Excellent yellow fall color in most seasons in some areas, but fall color is not reliable in Chicago. Thrives in Zones 3-8, and tolerates summer heat and humidity. **'Little King'** a smaller river birch, grows 20-25 feet tall; small-statured trees like this one are invaluable in today's limited-size gardens.

BETULA PAPYRIFERA PAPER BIRCH, CANOE BIRCH, WHITE BIRCH Betulaceae (Birch family)

Widespread from Canada and New England across the Midwest to the mountains of Washington and Montana, paper birch is one of the most beautiful of the white-barked species. The chalky white bark peels in thin strips and turns black with age. The trees mature at about 60-75 years old and exceptional specimens have been known to reach 100 feet or more tall. The wood was used by the American Indians for making canoes, and the bark for covering wigwams and making utensils.

BEST CONDITIONS Plant in a sunny position; not tolerant of shade. Paper birch also does not tolerate wet soil, heat, or pollution. Thrives in a range of soil pH from 5.0-8.0.

PLANTING Somewhat difficult to transplant. Spring planting of healthy balled-and-burlapped material is best. For maximum hardiness, try to procure seed-grown plants from a close geographical source.

ROUTINE CARE Keep well watered during dry weather. Apply a mulch 2-4 inches thick in a 3-foot ring on young trees. A balanced fertilizer program helps to maintain vigor and vitality.

PRUNING Prune routinely in summer to remove dead branches and major crossing branches.

PESTS, DISEASES, OTHER PROBLEMS Frequent problems include canker, mildew, and dieback. Fairly resistant to bronze birch borer and very resistant to leaf miners. At Holden the summers are really too hot for best growth, causing decline and susceptibility to pests and diseases.

PROPAGATION Seed may be stratified at 41° F for two to three months or sown and

Daffodils grow under a birch tree (*Betula albo-sinensis* var. *septentrionalis*) before it leafs out in early spring.

BETULA PAPYRIFERA (PAPER BIRCH, WHITE BIRCH) Deciduous. 10 years: 18 feet; 20 years: 35 feet; 50 years: 55-65 feet; maturity: to 80 feet. Very white, chalky peeling bark, small bright green leaves, open habit. Stony to loamy soil, full sun; does not tolerate shade, heat, or pollution. Zones 2-6.

BETULA PENDULA 'YOUNGII' Deciduous. 10 years: 8 feet; 20 years: 15 feet; 50 years: 30-35 feet; maturity: to 50 feet. A compact, weeping birch with an open habit and small bright green leaves. Acidic, moist, well-drained soil; full sun but keep roots cool, moist, and shaded. Zones 3-8.

BETULA UTILIS VAR. JACQUEMONTII (JACQUEMONT BIRCH, WHITE-BARKED HIMALAYAN BIRCH) Deciduous. 10 years: 8 feet; 20 years: 30 feet; 50 years: 45-50 feet; maturity: to 70 feet. Whitest of the white-barked birches, with thick, tough, dark green foliage. Full sun, well-drained soil. Zones 6-9.

CAMELLIA JAPONICA 'ALBA' (CAMELLIA) Evergreen. 10 years: 7 feet; 20 years: 15 feet; 50 years: 25-30 feet; maturity: to 40 feet. Lustrous dark green foliage, 2-inch single white flowers with yellow centers. Moist, well-drained acidic soil, partial shade (tolerates full sun or deeper shade). Zone 7.

exposed to light for nine hours daily. The simplest way to germinate is to sow in fall and overwinter outside for spring germination. Difficult from cuttings.
USE The beautiful white bark makes a striking accent in the winter landscape, especially when seen against a backdrop of evergreens. Suitable for large parks, golf courses, and estates.
SELECTIONS *B. papyrifera* var. *commutata,* Western paper birch. At Holden, 30-year-old trees planted in full sun with good drainage are now 40-50 feet tall. They are treated routinely for leaf miner.

BETULA PENDULA [B. ALBA] EUROPEAN WHITE BIRCH
Betulaceae (Birch family)
The European white birch makes a nice specimen plant but is too prone to insects and diseases in much of the country to deserve its widespread popularity. It is native throughout Europe and Britain, and in parts of Asia, especially at high altitudes. It has been cultivated for centuries, and is prized for its white peeling bark, which darkens at maturity; it does not peel as much as that of the paper birch. A medium-fast-growing tree with good fall color in cold regions, but of limited use in much of the country.
BEST CONDITIONS Not shade tolerant, but moderately wet or dry soil conditions are acceptable.
PLANTING Easily transplanted, preferably in spring.
ROUTINE CARE A regular spray program is recommended. Keep well watered during dry weather. Apply a mulch 2-4 inches thick in a 3-foot ring on young trees. A balanced fertilizer program helps to maintain vigor and vitality.
PRUNING Avoid pruning in spring as severe "bleeding" results. Prune routinely in summer to remove dead branches and major crossing branches.
PESTS, DISEASES, OTHER PROBLEMS At Holden, this tree cannot be grown without maintaining a spray program for bronze birch borer.
PROPAGATION Graft cultivars onto seedling stock. Seeds collected from gardens often produce hybrid offspring.
USE Although very popular for residential gardens, this is not an ideal tree for homeowners due to its susceptibility to pests and diseases. Often seen in cemeteries and parks.
SELECTIONS 'Youngii' is a small weeping form often grafted onto a standard form. **'Dalecarlica'** has deeply cut leaves to 3 inches long, and a distinctive pendulous habit. Widely grown.

BETULA PLATYPHYLLA MANCHURIAN BIRCH, ASIAN BIRCH
Betulaceae (Birch family)
Several varieties of this birch, from Japan and western China, are offered on the market in the U.S. The typical species grows into a large tree to 70 feet or so in height, and has good white bark.
BEST CONDITIONS Plant in full sun in soil that remains moist throughout the year.
PLANTING Plant at the same depth as in the field or container. Mulch routinely.
ROUTINE CARE Keep well watered during dry weather. Apply a mulch 2-4 inches thick in a 3-foot ring on young trees. A balanced fertilizer program helps to maintain vigor and vitality.

Betula nigra.

PRUNING Prune routinely in summer to remove dead branches and major crossing branches.
PESTS, DISEASES, OTHER PROBLEMS Susceptible to bronze birch borer and birch leaf miner.
PROPAGATION Seed as soon as it ripens in summer. Press into the seed mix and keep moist.
USE As for other large birches.
SELECTIONS 'Whitespire' is heat tolerant and grows in a wide range of soils. It is reputed to be resistant to bronze birch borer, but this may be linked to its heat tolerance, which results in less stress, and therefore diminished insect resistance, in hot climates. Not reliably resistant, but usually so. Should be propagated vegetatively from original selection.
B. platyphylla **var.** *japonica* is native to Japan and grows in the wild there to 85 feet tall. However, in cultivation it seldom tops 50 feet. It has pure white bark and a dominant central leader. Better leaf miner resistance than the following.
B. platyphylla **var.** *szechuanica,* from western China, tolerates wetter soils than the above and has a more open, spreading habit. It has peeling silvery white bark.

BETULA POPULIFOLIA GRAY BIRCH *Betulaceae (Birch family)*

In spite of its common name, gray birch has dull white bark which does not peel. Below each branch, the trunk is punctuated by a dark triangular patch. This native is found in New England, Nova Scotia, and Newfoundland, and its fast-growing habit enables other less hardy plants to become established under its light protective shade. It seeds and suckers freely, forming clumps or thickets.
BEST CONDITIONS Plant in sun, where the soil is neutral to acid, and moist. Intolerant of shaded positions, but accepts clay or dry soils.
PLANTING Plant at the same depth as in the field or container. Mulch routinely.
ROUTINE CARE Keep well watered during dry weather. Apply a mulch 2-4 inches thick in a 3-foot ring on young trees. A balanced fertilizer program helps to maintain vigor and vitality.
PRUNING Prune routinely in summer to remove dead branches and major crossing branches.
PESTS, DISEASES, OTHER PROBLEMS Resistant to bronze birch borer at Holden, but may be attacked severely by birch leaf miner (more than any other birch). This species has a short life span in the upper Midwest due to the summers being too hot. They may suddenly die after 12 or so years.
PROPAGATION Rapidly reseeds itself. Young shoots grow quickly by root suckering.
USE A short-lived tree, useful for only 10-15 years. It is good for quick colonizing of areas where the soil is poor, and other species have difficulty. Certainly not the best ornamental species.

BETULA UTILIS VAR. JACQUEMONTII JACQUEMONT BIRCH,
WHITE-BARKED HIMALAYAN BIRCH *Betulaceae (Birch family)*

This birch from the western Himalayas is known as the whitest of the white-barked birches. However, not all specimens exhibit this beautiful feature to the same degree. Also there seems to be some confusion about the nomenclature, some considering it to be a species of its own. In any case, the best specimens display very white bark even when young and rapidly grow to 25 feet or so in height. The leaves are thick, tough, and dark green.

BEST CONDITIONS Must have full sun and a well-drained soil.

PLANTING Plant at the same depth as in the field or container. Mulch routinely.

ROUTINE CARE It is important to avoid drought conditions. Keep well watered.

PRUNING Prune routinely in summer to remove dead branches and major crossing branches.

PESTS, DISEASES, OTHER PROBLEMS Once thought to be resistant to bronze birch borer but now it appears to be susceptible. However, it does show some resistance to birch leaf miner.

PROPAGATION Take cuttings in late summer to early fall.

USE Valued for its beautiful white bark, this birch is perfect for small gardens and can be planted in a container for use on patios and terraces. It is an excellent, and easily found, tree in the Pacific Northwest.

CAMELLIA CAMELLIA *Theaceae (Tea family)*

Popular as shrubs, many camellia selections reach tree proportions over time in the proper site. Although they require a good deal of care to keep soil properly fertile and to control pests, these lovely plants provide irresistibly beautiful flowers and glossy foliage.

BEST CONDITIONS Camellias thrive in moist, well-drained acidic soil (with a pH of about 6.0) that has been well enriched with organic matter. Though they prefer partial shade, they will often tolerate deeper shade as well as full sun. Camellias are reliably hardy only to Zone 7, though they can be grown with protection in Zone 6.

PLANTING Plant anytime, making sure to provide a layer of mulch to protect the camellia's shallow roots.

ROUTINE CARE Keep evenly moist, especially during establishment. Provide additional fertilizer until the plant is well established, and annually unless the soil is naturally fertile.

PRUNING Most camellias need little pruning; if grown as hedges or espaliers, prune during or immediately after flowering. If grown as foundation plants, prune back annually. Remove spent flowers to neaten.

PESTS, DISEASES, OTHER PROBLEMS Red spider mites; scale; sometimes dieback.

PROPAGATION Propagate by seeds, cuttings, or grafting.

USE Their brilliant blooms and striking foliage make camellias a natural for specimen as well as border plantings, and many make fine tall hedges.

SELECTIONS *C. hiemalis*, often grown as a small tree, has pink or white flowers and grows to 20 feet tall.

C. japonica grows to 45 feet tall and has dark green evergreen foliage. Among the best of the many cultivars available are **'Adolphe Audusson'**, with 4-inch semidouble flowers in several shades of red; **'Debutante'** with carmine red semidouble flowers up to 3 inches in diameter; and **'Shira-giku'** with longlasting double white flowers.

CARPINUS HORNBEAM, MUSCLEWOOD *Betulaceae (Birch family)*

American hornbeam has been valued since Colonial times for its dense wood, well suited for making household utensils, levers, and hammer handles, as well as being used for fuel and timber. As an ornamental, this intermediate-sized native has gray, often fluted bark, reminiscent of a well-muscled forearm: hence "mus-

Carya ovata.

clewood." The other common name is derived from "horn," or tough, and "beam," which is similar to the German *baum* for tree. Its spring-blooming catkins mature into small ribbed nuts that ripen in the fall. It often lives to 150 years old.

BEST CONDITIONS Although a shade-tolerant, understory plant in the wild, its best fall color is displayed in full sun. American hornbeam tolerates a wide range of soil pH, and does best in deep, moist soils.

PLANTING Plant balled-and-burlapped or from container stock in spring. Mature plants will reach 20-30 feet tall and as wide, so should be sited with that in mind. Water deeply and mulch until established.

ROUTINE CARE Mulch routinely. Provide water and nutrients if soil is poor or in times of drought.

PRUNING Prune to remove crossing branches. Encourage good branching habit to show off the attractive undulated branches. Does not take shearing as well as the European hornbeam in formal settings.

PESTS, DISEASES, OTHER PROBLEMS Severe stress caused by very difficult environmental conditions may result in canker, leaf spot, and twig blight. Parking area trees are especially vulnerable.

PROPAGATION Most cultivars are grafted in the nursery.

USE American hornbeam makes an attractive medium-sized tree useful for hedging and in naturalized areas. Its ornamental bark and good fall color are valued in autumn and winter gardens.

SELECTIONS *C. betulus* grows from a pyramidal to rounded shape as it matures, reaching 40-50 feet tall with a spread of 25-35 feet. In Europe it is a popular specimen and hedging plant. *C. b.* **'Fastigiata'** is more uniform and egg-shaped than the species. Planted as a screen, its dense branches make it effective throughout the summer and to some degree in winter.

C. caroliniana has a wide-spreading habit on multistemmed or single-stemmed trees, making it best suited to naturalistic landscapes. In the fall it displays great yellow, orange, and red foliage color, and maintains interest with its muscular-looking bark in winter.

CARYA OVATA SHAGBARK HICKORY *Juglandaceae (Walnut family)*

Shagbark hickory, unfortunately, is not widely available in the trade because it is hard to propagate and transplants poorly. However, they are found in the wild over a large area from Quebec to Minnesota and south to Alabama, Georgia, and Texas. Its hard wood is burned to cure hickory-smoked hams and used to add flavor to barbecued meals. It is also grown for its edible nuts. For ornamental purposes, fall color and shaggy bark are the most interesting features.

BEST CONDITIONS Although wild trees are found in woodland conditions, a full-sun position is best for ornamentals. Tolerant of a wide range of soil conditions. Lawn fertilizer is usually sufficient.

PLANTING Plant balled-and-burlapped or container-grown stock in spring. Water well and mulch.

ROUTINE CARE Addition of water or fertilizer is necessary only in extreme situations, especially if mulched routinely. The fallen nuts are mostly eaten or buried by squirrels. Sometimes plates of bark fall off and should be picked up.

PRUNING Pruning is seldom necessary.

CARPINUS CAROLINIANA (AMERICAN HORNBEAM, MUSCLEWOOD)
Deciduous. 10 years: 10 feet; 20 years: 20 feet; 50 years: 25-30 feet; maturity: to 40 feet. Wide-spreading multistemmed or single-trunked habit, bright green leaves turn red, orange, or yellow in fall. Tolerates shade and wide range of soil; best in moist, well-drained soil, full sun. Zones 2-10.

CARPINUS BETULUS 'FASTIGIATA' (EUROPEAN HORNBEAM)
Deciduous. 10 years: 10 feet; 20 years: 20 feet; 50 years: 25-30 feet; maturity: to 40 feet. Graceful form, dark green leaves turn clear yellow-orange in fall. Tolerates shade and wide range of soil; best in moist, well-drained soil, full sun. Zones 4-9.

CARYA ILLINOINENSIS (PECAN) Deciduous. 10 years: 15 feet; 20 years: 30-40 feet; 50 years: 7-80 feet; maturity: to 120 feet. Broad oval crown with dark green serrated leaves; produces pecan nuts. Full sun, moist well-drained soil. Zones 6-8.

CARYA OVATA (SHAGBARK HICKORY) Deciduous. 10 years: 12 feet; 20 years: 25 feet; 50 years: 50-55 feet; maturity: to 90 feet.Usually single trunk, bright green leaves, interesting shaggy brown bark. Full sun, wide variety of soils. Zones 4-8.

CATALPA SPECIOSA (HARDY CATALPA) Deciduous. 10 years: 15 feet; 20 years: 30-35 feet; 50 years: 60-70 feet; maturity: to 90 feet. Narrow tree with large green leaves and ornamental flowers in early summer. Deep, moist, fertile soil, full sun. Zones 5-8.

CEDRELA SINENSIS (CHINESE TOON TREE) Deciduous. 10 years: 10 feet; 20 years: 20 feet; 50 years: 35-40 feet; maturity: to 55 feet. Compound leaves, similar to ailanthus, small white flowers in foot-long panicles. Moist alkaline soil, full sun but adapts to shade. Zones 5-9.

CEDRUS ATLANTICA 'GLAUCA PENDULA' (BLUE ATLAS CEDAR) Evergreen. Grows an average of 2 feet per year; must be trained as a tree to desired height on appropriate structure. Initially pyramidal, its pendulous branches begin branching horizontally. Dark green needles. Moderately moist, fertile soil, full sun. Zone 6-9.

CEDRUS DEODARA (DEODAR CEDAR) Evergreen. 10 years: 10 feet; 20 years: 20-25 feet; 50 years: 50-60 feet; maturity: to 80 feet. Pyramidal form, graceful pendulous branches. Moderately moist, fertile soil , full sun; do not expose to drying winds. Zones 6-8.

PESTS, DISEASES, OTHER PROBLEMS Seldom serious, although canker may result from severe drought conditions.

PROPAGATION Start nuts in deep containers or tubepots to accommodate the long tap root. The tap root may grow 2-3 feet deep the first year and resents transplanting damage.

USE The narrow upright habit of shagbark hickory makes it valuable for small residential gardens. It develops its yellow fall color early and remains interesting in the winter when its ornamental bark shows off. This bark has been thought to be a deterrent to squirrels, which find the nuts much to their liking.

SELECTIONS *C. illinoisensis* is the pecan nut tree. It is grown for nut production and should be given well-drained, deep rich soil and a sunny position with good air circulation. It commonly lives for 300 years and is hardy in Zone 6.

C. tomentosa, mockernut hickory, has fragrant foliage that takes on golden yellow shades in fall. Its habit is narrow to broadly rounded; reaches 50-60 feet or more and lives over 150-250 years. Seldom encountered in the trade.

CATALPA CATALPA, CATAWBA, INDIAN BEAN *Bignoniaceae* (Bignonia family)

Catalpa are often found alongside ponds and streams in the South where it is the only host of the 3-inch-long green and yellow-and-black striped caterpillar of the catalpa sphinx. This caterpillar makes excellent fish bait. They can completely defoliate the trees, but refoliation takes place within a month. Panicles of showy white flowers give way to hanging bunches of long capsules containing the seeds.

BEST CONDITIONS Catalpas do well in sun or shade. Southern catalpa, a widely adapted tree, tolerates varying light conditions, acid to neutral and wet or dry soils, and thrives in heat or cold conditions. Northern catalpa withstands hot, dry conditions well and is resistant to soil compaction; pH 6.1-8.0. Although tolerant of wet or dry soils, the ideal is deep, moist and fertile.

PLANTING Plant balled-and-burlapped or container stock in early spring or fall. The plantings done at Holden Arboretum in the fall have been successful. In northern climates plant by September 15 and mulch. Select healthy looking plants. Water well and mulch.

PRUNING Prune to remove dead branches.

PESTS, DISEASES, OTHER PROBLEMS On southern catalpa, catalpa sphinx caterpillars can defoliate the trees if a large infestation is allowed to build up. The trees are not really hurt as they produce a new crop of leaves within a short time. Disease problems are infrequent on northern catalpa, but leaf spots, powdery mildew, root rot, and verticillium wilt sometimes attack. Be alert for catalpa midge, catalpa sphinx, and mealybugs.

PROPAGATION For southern catalpa, soft or hardwood cuttings are successful. Seeds germinate without pretreatment. For northern catalpa, take root cuttings and hardwood cuttings in December; softwood cuttings in early summer. Seeds do not require pretreatment.

USE Used as shade or specimen trees. Some consider them to be too messy as ornamentals, due to the dropping of the fruits.

SELECTIONS *C. bignonioides* (southern catalpa, common catalpa, Indian bean) Native in the southeastern states of the U.S., common catalpa is not as tall as the north-

VIEWPOINT
PRUNING CONIFERS

The natural look is in for conifers in the Pacific Northwest where cities and towns are surrounded by forests. Dead wood and crossing branches are pruned out. The only other pruning we do is thinning branches to allow better air movement through the tree, reducing breakage and disease problems.
SUSAN THOMAS,
HOYT ARBORETUM, PORTLAND

I don't prune conifers unless I am making a hedge or arborvitae or hemlock; then I prune so bottom is wider than top so lower branches can get light for good growth. I also limit growth on pines by pinching out or back the candles in late spring.
JULIE MORRIS, BLITHEWOLD MANSION AND GARDENS, RHODE ISLAND

I strongly believe in letting conifers retain their natural shape. Don't prune the leader off. Candle-prune them–remove ½ of the new shoots in spring–to get thicker, bushier plants.
DORTHE HVIID,
BERKSHIRE BOTANICAL GARDEN

Unless a conifer is being grown as a hedge, I prefer to avoid pruning and allow the plant to retain its natural form. Some species, like pines, are difficult for professionals to prune, so homeowners should avoid. Others, like junipers and false cypresses, are fairly easy as long as homeowners do cut only wood that has no leaves on the interior. Proper selection of species for size should drive the choice of conifer, unless the homeowner is looking for extra work.
RICK LEWANDOWSKI, MORRIS ARBORETUM , U. OF PENNSYLVANIA

I like to see all trees grown naturally. The exception is when trees like *Thuja occidentalis, T. plicata,* or *Chamaecyparis lawsoniana* are sheared as hedges.
GERALD STRALEY, U. OF BRITISH COLUMBIA BOTANICAL GARDEN

If the right plant is placed properly with mature size in mind, little if any pruning is necessary. Candling helps keep plant in desired shape. Don't remove lower branches of evergreens.
GALEN GATES, CHICAGO BOTANIC GARDEN

Cedrus deodara.

ern species, generally only reaching 30-40 feet but at least as wide. The light green leaves are 4-8 inches long, and slightly pubescent beneath. The white flowers, spotted in yellow and purple, cluster into wide panicles up to 10 inches long, and open in early summer. Pendulous, slender pods follow, ranging from 6-15 inches in length; these persist on the tree for several months. It was introduced in 1726. At Holden Arboretum, the specimen representing the species in the catalpa collection has been there since 1956. It is still fairly small, but the pods grow quite long and mature to a light brown which contrasts well with the bark. The young leaves of 'Aurea' are bright yellow, but change to green after midsummer. At Holden, the specimens planted in the fall of 1964 have grown into perfect examples of size and shape. They are smaller than the species, much wider than tall, with full crowns. The pods persist through the winter. **'Nana'** is grown for its unusual dwarf form.

C. speciosa (northern catalpa, western catalpa, hardy catalpa) This native from southern Illinois and Indiana to western Texas and northern Arkansas may reach 130 feet tall in the wild. In cultivation, however, 40-60 feet is more common with a spread of 20-40 feet. The rot-resistant wood has been used for railroad ties. At Holden three specimens were planted 10-15 feet apart in the 1950s. They are in excellent condition, but can be expected to survive for 50-75 years. The interesting coarseness of the tree in winter is in striking contrast with the softness of the large leaves in summer. This species does not hold its fruit through winter. A useful tree for difficult terrain.

CEDRELA SINENSIS CHINESE TOON TREE *Meliaceae (Mahogany family)*

This Chinese native resembles *Ailanthus altissima* except that the pinnately compound leaves are dark red when young. The leaves may reach 20 inches in length. Both the new shoots and leaves have a pungent onion smell and are pickled and eaten in China. The small, white, bell-shaped flowers are borne in foot-long panicles in summer and are followed by very ornamental 1-inch-long seed capsules, that resemble flowers themselves. The cedrelas growing at Blithewold caused great excitement when they bloomed for the first time in the 1920s. Flowers taken to the Arnold Arboretum for identification brought Alfred Rehder and Ernest Henry Wilson (Chinese Wilson) to see the trees in bloom at Blithewold. They believed them to be the first to bloom in the U.S. The trees were about 50 years old at the time.

BEST CONDITIONS Ideally plant in full sun, but these are adaptable trees and do not demand sun. They prefer alkaline soils that do not dry out, but are native to dry regions and are extremely drought tolerant. Zones 6-9.

PLANTING Plant balled-and-burlapped stock in spring. Not widely available in the trade, but worth seeking.

ROUTINE CARE Water during dry spells.

PRUNING Prune in winter to remove crossing branches. At the Morris Arboretum, a large grove of Chinese toon trees often requires removal of broken branches, particularly after a harsh winter.

PESTS, DISEASES, OTHER PROBLEMS None serious.

PROPAGATION Seeds germinate easily. Suckers from established plants may be removed. In the wild the suckers form a colony or grove of trees.

USE More or less a curiosity, but should be more widely grown. It assorts well with other large trees. At Blithewold it is in the nut grove with Chinese chestnuts and Manchurian walnuts. It makes a fine shade tree and is effective in parks, on lawns, and as street and avenue trees where there is space.

CEDRUS CEDAR *Pinaceae (Pine family)*

A cedar grown in an appropriate site is among the most attractive of conifers. Its branches are well spaced and dense, its color is vivid, and it imparts a distinct, but not overpowering, fragrance to the air. These evergreen conifers grow to towering heights. Many important and even historic groves of cedar have been destroyed for their lumber.

BEST CONDITIONS Cedars are not particularly coldhardy; most are hardy only in Zones 6 or 7. They need moderately moist, fertile soil and full sun and should not be exposed to drying winds. Most cedars do not tolerate wet soils.

PLANTING Most cedars are not easy to transplant. Transplant containerized or balled-and-burlapped trees in spring. *C. deodara* often needs to be staked for the first year or two.

ROUTINE CARE Provide enough water to keep soil evenly moist. Do not overfeed, or soft growth that promotes disease will occur.

PRUNING Prune cedars when young to establish a single leader. Once the basic shape is established, pruning becomes unnecessary.

PROPAGATION Propagate by seeds sown in fall, grafting in the spring, or cuttings taken in summer.

Cedrus atlantica 'Glauca Pendula' at The National Arboretum.

Cercidiphyllum japonicum in autumn.

PESTS, DISEASES, OTHER PROBLEMS None serious. but most cedars are intolerant of wet soils.

USE They need lots of room to grow and are not at their best when crowded by other trees, but a well-grown specimen cedar is unbeatable.

SELECTIONS *C. atlantica* (atlas cedar) is hardy in Zones 6-9. It grows in a pyramidal form for several years, then branches out horizontally, eventually reaching a height of 120 feet. The cultivars **'Argentea'** and **'Glauca'** have bluish needles. **'Glauca Pendula'** has drooping branches; a magnificent specimen in the Gottelli collection at The National Arboretum has a unique sculptural quality. This species is somewhat difficult to transplant and should be purchased containerized. Although it prefers moist deep loam, atlas cedar will accept sandy or clay soils; it will not, however, thrive with wet feet.

C. deodara grows to 150 feet and is hardy only to Zone 7. It has a natural pyramidal form and pendulous branches that are particularly graceful. The cultivar **'Limelight'** has attractive yellow-green foliage. **'Shalimar'** and **'Kingsville'** are hardier than the species, with silvery foliage; reliably hardy to Zone 6. This species transplants more easily than other cedars, especially if root pruned and planted in a sunny, fairly dry site.

C. libani (cedar of Lebanon) is hardy to Zone 6; its wood was used in the building of Solomon's temple and it has been used in this country since colonial times. It grows to 120 feet tall and has a stiff, horizontal shape. It does not tolerate shade or pollution and needs sun, space, and well-drained loam.

CELTIS OCCIDENTALIS COMMON HACKBERRY *Ulmaceae (Elm family)*

Hackberry is one of the best choices for difficult positions because of its tolerance of many soil conditions and to urban pollution. It develops rapidly into a medium to large tree, and is found growing throughout a wide range of temperate regions of the northern hemisphere; in North America it grows from Quebec to North Carolina and Alabama.

BEST CONDITIONS Partial shade is sufficient for young trees, but as they mature a full-sun position is preferable. Hackberry adapts well to both acid and alkaline soils (pH 8.0), and tolerates wet, compacted conditions as well as much drier ones.

PLANTING Plant in spring so that it is established before the stress of summer heat. Plant at the same level as the root ball and keep well watered to encourage a deep root system. Site where there is plenty of space for future growth.

ROUTINE CARE Mulch routinely. Lawn fertilizer is sufficient for this fast grower. Mature specimens should be examined by a bonded and certified arborist occasionally to evaluate for structural strength. The trees may live 100-200 years.

PRUNING Prune for a central leader and to eliminate crossing or rubbing branches.

PESTS, DISEASES, OTHER PROBLEMS Usually not serious. Witches brooms are unsightly rather than crippling; nipple gall (small bumps on the leaves) is also disfiguring.

PROPAGATION Seed must be stratified at 41° F for 60-90 days. Best to purchase nursery-grown stock.

USE Hackberry is best utilized in the large landscape in parks, streets and open spaces, although it has value as a specimen shade tree. Excellent under city conditions, and where it is dry, wet, or windy. It is widely grown in the exposed Plain

CEDRUS DEODORA 'AUREA' (CEDAR) Evergreen. 10 years: 8 feet; 20 years: 18 feet; 50 years: 40-45 feet; maturity: to 60 feet. Pyramidal form, graceful pendulous branches, yellow-green needles. Moderately moist, fertile soil , full sun; do not expose to drying winds. Zones 6-8.

CEDRUS LIBANI (CEDAR OF LEBANON) Evergreen. 10 years: 10 feet; 20 years: 20-25 feet; 50 years: 50-60 feet; maturity: to 80 feet. Stiff horizontal shape, dark green needles. Moderately moist, fertile soil, full sun; do not expose to drying winds. Zones 6-8.

CELTIS OCCIDENTALIS (COMMON HACKBERRY) Deciduous. 10 years: 12 feet; 20 years: 25 feet; 50 years: 55-65 feet; maturity: to 90 feet. Pointed leaves often turn warm yellow in fall; bark on mature trees has interesting ridges. Full sun (young plants tolerate partial shade), acid or alkaline soil; tolerates wet soil and some dryness, as well as city conditions. Zones 3-8.

CERCIDIPHYLLUM JAPONICUM (KATSURA TREE) Deciduous. 10 years: 10 feet; 20 years: 20 feet; 50 years: 40-45 feet; maturity: to 60 feet. Heart-shaped gray-green leaves (spring growth is pink to purple); tree develops horizontal plates of foliage. Full sun, moist, rich, well-drained soil. Zones 5-9.

I never before knew the full value of trees. My house is entirely enbosomed in high plains trees, with good grass below and under them I breakfast, dine, write, read, and receive my company. What would I not give that the trees planted nearest round the house at Monticello were full grown.

THOMAS JEFFERSON

states as well as the moist Great Lakes states. Zones 2-9. Older specimens develop interesting gray, articulating ridges on the bark; fall color is a warm yellow.

SELECTIONS 'Chicagoland' is a fast-growing selection from Roy Klehm. It develops a strong central leader. **'Prairie Pride'** is not as imposing as the species. It makes a compact broadly globe-shaped tree 40 feet tall and wide. Zone 3.

C. reticulata, native to southern U.S. is widely used in the South and Southwest.

C. pallida is somewhat rare, but is a good small tree for the desert.

CERCIDIPHYLLUM JAPONICUM KATSURA TREE *Cercidiphyllaceae (Katsura tree family)*

This Asian native makes a handsome ornamental specimen for American gardens, but in China and Japan, where it is the largest deciduous tree, its wood is prized for cabinetry and panelling. Like ginkgo, it has been extinct in Europe and North America since the Pleistocene era, but fortunately survived in Asia.

BEST CONDITIONS Plant in full sun for best development. Tolerant of humid conditions. Katsura tree prefers a rich, well-drained acid soil. Water often in dry weather, and fertilize to maintain rapid growth.

PLANTING Katsura tree is easy to transplant. It is shallow-rooted and must be watered well and mulched for at least two years, before it becomes established. Select and plant healthy, container-grown or balled-and-burlapped plants in spring and early summer for best results; container stock may be planted through the fall.

ROUTINE CARE Stressed plants do not thrive; provide additional water during dry spells and fertilize annually if soil is not rich.

PRUNING Prune routinely to remove crossing or damaged limbs.

PESTS, DISEASES, OTHER PROBLEMS Seldom bothered by pests and diseases, although canker is sometimes a problem. Stressed plants may be subject to sun scald.

PROPAGATION Sow seed with protection in early winter, or take cuttings. Seeds germinate like grass without any treatment; Rick Lewandowski of the Morris Arboretum finds them as easy to work with as marigolds and has often started seeds in March that produce 3- to 5-foot-tall plants by October.

USE This exceptional four-season landscape tree is excellent for residential gardens, as well as for large public places. In spring its heart-shaped leaves emerge red or purple, changing to blue-green as they mature; tiny flowers have an effect similar to red maple. In autumn they display brilliant yellow or orange fall color, especially effective when back lit by the morning or setting sun. This color is somewhat variable in some regions, but the tree also releases an interesting scent, reminiscent of burnt cotton candy. The winter silhouette is of strong main branches and delicate side branch tracery.

SELECTIONS *C. j.* **'Pendulum'** makes a small tree which is stunning in and of itself. There are two forms, but both appear as fountains of blue-green foliage in summer. The fuller plant may be *C. magnificum* **'Pendulum'.** Two remarkable specimens are on display at Spring Grove Cemetery in Cincinnati, Ohio, and Mount Auburn Cemetery outside Boston.

CERCIS CANADENSIS EASTERN REDBUD *Fabaceae (Pea family)*

A welcome sight in early spring, the native *C. canadensis* blooms with purple-pink flowers on woody branches and even the trunks of old specimens. In the wild it is

CERCIS CANADENSIS (EASTERN REDBUD) Deciduous. 10 years: 8 feet; 20 years: 15 feet; 50 years: 20-25 feet; maturity: to 30 feet. Small purple-pink pea-shaped flowers. Moderate shade or sun, prefers rich soil, but tolerates a wide range of soils, humidity, drought, and heat. Zones 5-9.

CHAMAECYPARIS LAWSONIANA (LAWSON FALSE CYPRESS) Evergreen. 10 years: 8 feet; 20 years: 16-20 feet; 50 years: 40-50 feet; maturity: to 90 feet. Irregular columnar form, dark green foliage (sometimes gray-green). Moist, slightly acid soil and full sun; no tolerance for heat, wet soils, and drought. Zones 6-8.

CHAMAECYPARIS NOOTKATENSIS 'PENDULA' (WEEPING NOOTKA FALSE CYPRESS) Evergreen. 10 years: 8 feet; 20 years: 16-20 feet; 50 years: 40-50 feet; maturity: to 90 feet. Blue- or gray-green needles, conical form with very horizontal drooping branches. Moist, slightly acid soil and full sun; no tolerance for heat and drought. Zones 4-9.

CHAMAECYPARIS OBTUSA 'CRIPSII' (HINOKI FALSE CYPRESS) Deciduous. 10 years: 7 feet; 20 years: 15 feet; 50 years: 30-35 feet; maturity: to 60 feet. Golden leaves, in flattened fans, turns dark green at maturity, pyramidal form with pendulous branches. Moist, slightly acid soil and full sun; no tolerance for heat and drought. Zones 4-9.

an understory tree, but under garden conditions may reach 15-40 feet tall. Although it does well in lightly shaded positions, it also makes a fine specimen in full sun. The North Carolina State University Arboretum in Raleigh has one of the largest collections of redbud species and cultivars in the world.

BEST CONDITIONS Eastern redbud adapts to both light shade and full sun in northern climates. In the wild it is found growing mostly in rich soils along river banks, but in the Prairie states it thrives in the forest duff of oak and hickory. In cultivation it needs well-drained soil with adequate moisture to become established but as it matures it will take drier conditions. It tolerates a broad range of pH, including very alkaline soils; heat, drought, and high humidity are no problem. Extremely susceptible to herbicides used on lawns.

PLANTING Plant balled-and-burlapped plants in spring or fall; container stock may be planted throughout the season. Keep well watered and mulch.

ROUTINE CARE Although an annual application of fertilizer will benefit redbud, in a proper site it needs little care.

PRUNING Prune to shape and to create an open framework.

PESTS, DISEASES, OTHER PROBLEMS Verticillium wilt is sometimes a problem, especially in heavy, poorly drained soils. Canker is sometimes seen on mature stems.

PROPAGATION Difficult from seed. Some cultivars are budded onto seedling stock.

USE This spring-blooming native is an excellent tree for residential gardens. Its relatively small stature, tolerance of a wide range of growing conditions, and often yellow fall color put it high on the list of favored plants. Depending on how it is pruned, it is an excellent large shrub or small tree.

SELECTIONS The white-flowered **'Alba'** seems not as long-lived or hardy as the species at the Chicago Botanic Garden. **'Forest Pansy'**, Zones 5-6, has purplish leaves throughout the season, but does not hold its color well in hot summer climates. **'Pinkbud'** is a spectacular plant with clear pink flowers. The Wisconsin Arboretum has distributed the "Columbus strain," which has superior hardiness. The western redbud, **C. occidentalis,** from California, may reach 20 feet tall and grows in the wild in dry, gravelly, or moist soils.

The larger-flowered Chinese species, **C. chinensis,** is a multistemmed shrub for Zone 6. It grows up to 10 feet tall.

CHAMAECYPARIS FALSE CYPRESS *Cupressaceae (Cypress family)*

The false cypresses are very ornamental evergreen conifers. They exhibit particularly good coloration, ranging from very dark green to very bright gold and their leaves are intricate and often fanlike and flattened against themselves.

BEST CONDITIONS False cypresses need moist, slightly acid soil and full sun. They are hardy in Zones 4-9. Hot, dry areas are unsuitable, as are windy areas.

PLANTING These trees do not transplant easily; containerized trees are most successful.

ROUTINE CARE Provide extra water for young plants; established plants do not need extra water. A mulch will help keep soil moist and fertile.

PRUNING Prune to shape when young; mature trees need pruning only to remove dead branches. False cypresses look unkempt if dead branches are not removed.

PROPAGATION Propagation can be accomplished by seeds, but they do not germinate well without stratification and do not reproduce true to form. Hardwood and softwood cuttings taken in the fall root reasonably well.

Chamaecyparis pisifera 'Filifera Aurea'.

PESTS, DISEASES, OTHER PROBLEMS Usually problem free, but sometimes attacked by *Phytophthora lateralis,* a serious fungus disease. Inspect frequently and remove infected parts immediately, since it can spread to the roots and kill the tree.
USE False cypresses are unbeatable specimen plants and combine well with other trees; try a gold variety with a bright red Japanese maple. They are also useful as backdrops to perennial borders, hedges, screens, and border plants.
SELECTIONS *C. lawsoniana,* Lawson false cypress, grows to an irregular column, covered in bright or gray-green foliage, 120 feet tall; it prefers a humid climate and high atmospheric pressure. Hardy to Zone 6.
C. obtusa, Hinoki false cypress, is broadly pyramidal and has an attractive peeling bark and dense, ferny foliage. It is the best of the genus for the Midwest. **'Cripsii'** has yellow foliage when young, dark green when mature. **'Nana'** is a very slow-growing cultivar that rarely exceeds 3 feet tall. Zone 6.
C. nootkatensis, Nootka false cypress, western cedar, Alaska yellow cedar, has a particularly dramatic habit composed of a conical crown and pendulous branches that curve down at the tips. It grows 30-45 feet in cultivation, twice that in the wild. **'Pendula'** is an excellent weeping form.
C. pisifera is a valuable tree, though sometimes overused. Cultivars have been selected for gold, blue-green, and dark green foliage. **'Filifera'** has very fine-textured, lacy foliage in chartreuse; **'Filifera Aurea'** is similar, but bright yellow. **'Golden Spangle'** is an even brighter yellow, with a soft, fluffy effect.

CHIONANTHUS VIRGINICUS WHITE FRINGE TREE *Oleaceae (Olive family)*

Also known as old man's beard, chionanthus is a small tree or shrub found from New Jersey south to Florida, and west to Missouri, Oklahoma, and Texas. Although it has virtually no visible flowerbuds, each produces fragrant 6- to 8-inch-long flowers that in mass create a cloudlike appearance that covers the tree in late spring. On female plants, these are followed in late summer by olive-shaped, dark blue 1-inch fruits, which the birds find attractive; male trees have showier flowers. Good yellow fall color in sun. One of the best small trees around patios, decks, and terraces.
BEST CONDITIONS Though fringe tree will bloom in sun or shade, it does best in bright light in a moist, fertile, slightly acid soil.
PLANTING Plant containerized or balled-and-burlapped plants in spring or fall.
ROUTINE CARE Keep evenly moist; an annual application of fertilizer is beneficial.
PRUNING Prune to shape immediately after blooming; blooms on old wood.
PESTS, DISEASES, OTHER PROBLEMS None serious except for occasional infestations of scale, powdery mildew, or canker.
PROPAGATION Propagate by layering, cuttings, or seed.
USE These small trees can be used as specimens or as anchors or focal points in a shrub or mixed border.
SELECTIONS *C. retusus,* Chinese fringe tree, boasts small leathery leaves, clusters of white flowers in May and June, and blue fruits, resembling blueberries, in late summer, and golden exfoliating bark. Flowers are borne on new wood, so any pruning to shape should be done in late winter or early spring. Zones 5-8; grows 15-25 feet tall, 20 feet wide.

LONG-LIVED TREES
The oldest tree in the world–thus also the oldest living thing on earth–is today believed to be a bristlecone pine in California named Methuselah, estimated to be 4,700 years old. Before that tree was discovered by botanists in the last century, other trees in other lands had the honor of being declared oldest, at least by locals. Around the time of the American Civil War a cypress tree in Lombardy in northern Italy was thought by some to be the world's oldest tree; according to one contemporary account it had been "forty years old when Christ was born." It had competitors, however, including the so-called Chapultepec cypress of Mexico; a grove of chestnut trees on the slopes of Sicily's Mount Etna; and eight olive trees on the Mount of Olives, said to have already been old "when the Turks took Jerusalem."

CHAMAECYPARIS PISIFERA 'GOLDEN SPANGLE' (JAPANESE FALSE CYPRESS) Evergreen. 10 years: 6 feet; 20 years: 15 feet; 50 years: 30-35 feet; maturity: to 60 feet. Expansive tree with loose, open form, feathery yellow foliage. Moist, slightly acid soil and full sun; no tolerance for heat and drought. Zones 3-7.

CHIONANTHUS VIRGINICUS (WHITE FRINGE TREE) Deciduous. 10 years: 6 feet; 20 years: 10-15 feet; 50 years: 15-25 feet; maturity: to 30 feet. Shrubby habit, covered in white flowers in late spring; good yellow fall color. Full sun for best color, but will bloom in shade; moist, fertile soil. Zones 4-10.

CLADRASTIS KENTUKEA (AMERICAN YELLOWWOOD) Deciduous. 10 years: 13 feet; 20 years: 25-30 feet; 50 years: 50-60 feet; maturity: to 70 feet. Showy fragrant white flowers; leaves open yellow green, turn bright green in summer and yellow in fall. Full sun, moist acid or alkaline soil. Zones 4-8.

CORNUS ALTERNIFOLIA (PAGODA DOGWOOD) Deciduous. 10 years: 8 feet; 20 years: 15 feet; 50 years: 20-30 feet; maturity: to 35 feet. Creamy white flowers in late spring, black and blue fruit in late summer. Medium green foliage on horizontal branches. Sun or light shade, organic, moist well-drained soil with acidic pH. Zones 4-8.

CLADRASTIS KENTUKEA [LUTEA] AMERICAN YELLOWWOOD

Fabaceae (Pea family)

Chionanthus virginicus.

American yellowwood was named by the French botanist Andre Michaux, for the yellow internal wood, which was a favorite for gunstocks. It reaches 35-50 feet tall with an equal spread and is grown as an ornamental for its showy panicles of fragrant, white pealike flowers. Heavy bloom occurs every second or third year on vigorous trees; stressed trees may bloom profusely every year.

BEST CONDITIONS For the development of flowers, fruit, and fall color, best growth occurs in full sun. It grows in the wild on moist limestone soils; tolerant of soils between pH 6.0-8.0. Lawn fertilizer is usually sufficient, but in grass avoid herbicidal sprays containing 2,4-D.

PLANTING Plant young balled-and-burlapped stock in spring. Water thoroughly. Look for plants with good crotch angles of about 45° from the main trunk. Poorly angled branches (less than 45°) are susceptible to heavy ice and wind damage as they age.

ROUTINE CARE Mulch routinely and maintain sufficient moisture for at least the first year. Removal of the seed pods may increase flower production the following year, but the winter interest is lost.

PRUNING Prune to create wide crotch angles up to 90°. Do not prune live wood in spring, as trees will bleed sap at that time.

PESTS, DISEASES, OTHER PROBLEMS Verticillium is sometimes a problem, but otherwise pest and disease free.

PROPAGATION Best to buy nursery stock. Seed is difficult and requires stratification or scarification.

USE American yellowwood is a good choice for limited- size residential lots. It makes a fine shade tree, and has attractive gray beechlike bark for year-round interest. Its fragrant flowers open in late spring or early summer and the leaves often turn warm yellow in fall. In bleak northern winters the persistent seed pods also provide interest. In the wild these trees may survive for 120-150 years.

SELECTIONS 'Rosea' is a pink-flowered form, but is scarce in the trade.

The Japanese yellowwood, **C. platycarpa,** blooms later, on trees 20-40 feet tall. The Chinese yellowwood, **C. sinensis,** grows 30-50 feet tall, and bears panicles of pinkish white flowers in midsummer.

CORNUS DOGWOOD Cornaceae (Dogwood family)

This well-known genus is largely native in temperate parts of the northern hemisphere, and includes several of the best deciduous small trees and shrubs for ornamental use. They bloom in spring and early summer, sometimes even before the leaves emerge, and the most showy ones have their flower clusters surrounded by white, pink, or red flowerlike bracts.

BEST CONDITIONS Dogwoods prefer light shade to a full-sun position where the soil is moist but well drained, with a high organic content; some prefer acid, others prefer alkaline soils. They do best where the climate is relatively cool and where air movement is good.

PLANTING Plant at the same level as the root collar, or a little above. Water well after planting. Mulching is important on a routine basis.

ROUTINE CARE Water during dry weather. A 3-inch-deep mulch in a 3-foot-diameter ring around the plants helps to keep the roots cool and cuts down on surface evaporation. Be sure that the mulch is not touching the trunk, as this leads to rot. Fertilize lightly with 3:2:1 in the fall, to help keep the plants growing strongly.

PRUNING Prune to remove crossing branches and to shape if necessary.

PESTS, DISEASES, OTHER PROBLEMS Many diseases attack dogwoods. To combat these, keep the trees healthy and growing vigorously. Site selection is important particularly in terms of soil and drainage. Plant resistant Asian species to reduce disease problems; remove leaf and twig debris to reduce fungal disease.

PROPAGATION Both seeds and softwood cuttings work well. Look for a seed source in your area for offspring of reliable hardiness.

USE The bark and branch structure of several of the dogwoods is interesting in winter, and the flowers are often quite showy. Red, blue, or black berries follow and these attract birds to the garden. Dogwoods are excellent small trees for residential gardens, even where space is limited. Unfortunately they do not tolerate urban conditions well.

CORNUS ALTERNIFOLIA PAGODA DOGWOOD Cornaceae

Pagoda dogwood, so named for its interesting tiers of branches, grows from New Brunswick to Minnesota and south to Georgia and Alabama. It has flattened clusters of small, creamy white flowers in late spring, but these are more notable for their cloying fragrance than for their brilliant floral display. Clusters of black fruits turn to blue as they ripen. The foliage is medium to dark green and turns a dull reddish purple in fall.

BEST CONDITIONS A moist site in partial shade is acceptable but full sun is preferable. Site in a protected place as wind and ice damage can be serious.

PLANTING Transplant balled-and-burlapped or container-grown stock in spring. Water well and mulch to protect the wide-spreading, fibrous roots.

ROUTINE CARE Water well during dry weather to avoid undue stress. Apply 2-3 inches of mulch annually.

Flowering dogwood (*Cornus florida*) is available in many shades of white, cream (above), red, and pink (opposite).

PRUNING Prune off any damaged stems, resulting from ice or wind damage.

PESTS, DISEASES, OTHER PROBLEMS Leafspot and cankers may become serious, but several problems can be avoided by good growing practices and conditions.

PROPAGATION Clean and sow ripe seeds as soon as they mature in late summer. Softwood and hardwood cuttings root fairly easily. Allow cuttings to overwinter in the propagation unit, before potting individually.

USE This dogwood is especially good in a natural setting. It is of great value to wildlife and is suitable for native plant and wildlife gardens. Although not as showy in bloom as *C. florida,* its strongly layered, horizontal branching habit is an attractive and unique feature.

SELECTIONS *C. alternifolia* **'Argentea'** has interesting variegated foliage.

C. controversa, the giant dogwood, is a Far-East native, which grows rapidly to reach 30-45 feet in cultivation. It is also horizontally branched and has creamy white flowers in late spring. It becomes spectacular in fall, as its fruits ripen and its stems turn dark burgundy or red; birds love this fruit. Zone 5.

C. c. **'Variegata'** is one of the most sought-after variegated trees, magnificent when mature. It prefers partial shade or evenly moist soils and does not do well in dry, hot locations.

CORNUS FLORIDA FLOWERING DOGWOOD *Cornaceae*

An understory tree in woodlands throughout much of the eastern United States, flowering dogwood is perhaps the best known and loved of our native trees. In spring the showy flower bracts, which may be white, pink, or red, surrounding the true flowers, appear before the tree is in leaf. The foliage leafs out light green

CORNUS FLORIDA (FLOWERING DOGWOOD) Deciduous. 10 years: 8 feet; 20 years: 15-20 feet; 50 years: 25-35 feet; maturity: to 45 feet. White, pink or red flowers appear before dark green leaves; spreading crown. Sun or light shade, organic, moist, well-drained soil with acidic pH. Zones 4-9.

CORNUS MAS (CORNELIAN CHERRY) Deciduous. 10-20 feet. Delicate small yellow flowers in very early spring, dark green leaves in summer; birds enjoy the fruit. Sun or light shade, organic, moist, well-drained soil with acidic or alkaline pH. Zones 3-7.

CORYLUS MAXIMA 'ATROPURPUREA' (GIANT FILBERT) Deciduous. 10 years: 8 feet; 20 years: 15 feet; 50 years: 30-35 feet; maturity: to 40 feet. Purplish red leaves, 5-6 inches long, large nuts. Moist or dry acid to alkaline soil. Zones 4-8.

COTINUS OBOVATUS (AMERICAN SMOKETREE) Deciduous. 10 years: 6 feet; 20 years: 16 feet; 50 years: 20-30 feet; maturity: to 40 feet. Spreading or rounded habit; excellent yellow-orange to red fall color. Full sun, adapts to many soils, including dry and rocky. Zones 5-8.

or bronze, deepens to dark green in summer and mostly turns vibrant red or reddish purple in fall. The interesting branching habit, gray bark, and small onion-shaped winter buds make this an effective four-season tree.

BEST CONDITIONS Best with morning sun, but afternoon shade. Site where air circulation is good to avoid anthracnose problems. At The New York Botanical Garden, *C. florida* does best in full sun with no competition from other trees. Does not tolerate pollution well.

PLANTING Select balled-and-burlapped plants 3-4 feet tall and plant in spring. Try to determine the seed source of the stock, and choose according to your region. Southern stock may not be as hardy in cold winter regions as plants raised from northern seed sources. Acid, moisture-retentive, organic soil is ideal. Water well and mulch.

ROUTINE CARE Water during dry weather. Apply 3 inches of mulch in a 3-foot ring around young trees, being careful not to suffocate the trunk. At The New York Botanical Garden, this tree is fertilized annually in early spring.

PRUNING Prune to remove crossing branches and to shape.

PESTS, DISEASES, OTHER PROBLEMS Regrettably, flowering dogwood is subject to many diseases and also attracts borers. Anthracnose, borers, and severe droughts have killed a huge number of wild specimens over the last ten years or so. Keeping the trees healthy and actively growing without undue stress goes a long way to helping the plants avoid such serious problems.

PROPAGATION Seeds should be stratified at 41° F for 100-130 days. Take softwood cuttings just after flowering. Allow rooted cuttings to go through a period of dormancy before planting.

USE Ideal for native plant and wildlife gardens. A spectacular small tree planted as a specimen, perhaps near a terrace or patio, or in a lawn; often planted on the corner of a house to act as a design anchor. Flowering dogwoods are also unmatched in light woodlands, either singly or grouped in mass plantings. With good care, a healthy, well-sited tree will live 15-20 years.

SELECTIONS **'Apple Blossom'** has light pink bracts, which fade to white in the center.

'Cherokee Chief' is among the most popular red-bracted cultivars.

'Cloud 9' begins flowering at a young age, with showy white bracts. It has a spreading habit and grows slowly. One of the hardiest in bud.

'Fastigiata' is an upright grower, but may lose its definitive shape with age. White bracts.

'Rainbow' has variegated light green, pink, and white foliage, which turns red in fall. White bracts.

'Eddie's White Wonder' (*C. nuttallii* x *C. florida*) is a better garden plant than either of its parents in the Pacific Northwest; the best of the early-flowering dogwoods in Zone 8, it is rivaled only by the later *C. kousa*.

CORNUS KOUSA KOUSA DOGWOOD *Cornaceae (Dogwood family)*

This Asian species is valuable in American gardens for its later and longer blooming time, some three weeks or so after our native flowering dogwood has passed, with blooms for three to four weeks. The flowers are borne above the foliage on short stalks, surrounded by creamy white, pointed bracts which frequently fade to pink. Large, strawberrylike fruits follow; the best fruiting occurs when at least two plants are growing in proximity. Fall color is reddish purple or scarlet but

SPECIALTY WOOD

The Greeks and Romans prized the cornelian cherry (*Cornus mas*) for its hard wood and used it to make lances. (Some scholars believe it was the wood used to fashion the Trojan horse.) The yew (*Taxus baccata*) was the tree preferred for making the longbows used by English archers (although the imported variety was preferred to the domestic). The range of the black locust (*Robinia pseudoacacia*) was extended by native Americans of the eastern woodlands because they preferred its wood in the making of bows. More recently, a species of willow (*Salix alba* var. *caerulea*), has achieved popularity in Britain for a special use: it is commonly known as the cricket bat willow.

The showy white bracts of *Cornus kousa* flowers are pointed.

varies widely. In winter, the habit and branching pattern are evident. Young trees are vase-shaped but as they mature they develop a strong horizontal pattern, and the bark begins to exfoliate, revealing a mosaic of tan and brown patches.

BEST CONDITIONS Mostly sun or light shade. Kousa dogwood tolerates more heat and sun than does flowering dogwood, but is less tolerant of shaded conditions. It does not perform well in heavy clay soils. At Holden some specimens have declined and died under these soil conditions. An acid sandy or well-drained alkaline soil, well enriched with organic matter is ideal.

PLANTING Plant young, balled-and-burlapped stock. Select healthy, fast-growing trees; some seedlings are of low vigor, probably due to the small gene pool available in the nursery trade. Mulch routinely after watering.

ROUTINE CARE Less susceptible to drought conditions than *C. florida,* but do not allow to become unduly stressed. Mulch routinely.

PRUNING Prune out dead, damaged, or crossing branches.

PESTS, DISEASES, OTHER PROBLEMS In the Midwest, *C. kousa* is relatively free from pests and diseases. Watch for occasional borer problems and control at once.

PROPAGATION Seed should be stratified at 41° F for three months. Cuttings do not root as readily as those of *C. florida.* Take cuttings after flowering time and treat with a rooting hormone. Delay planting until the following spring.

USE A showy ornamental tree excellent near buildings or on the corner of a house to break up the regularity of foundation plantings. The horizontal branching habit is attractive at all seasons, and the exfoliating bark of mature specimens adds an unusual dimension to the winter garden. Handsome as a specimen plant in lawns, but also useful in shrub collections and even in large mixed borders with shrubs and perennials.

SELECTIONS 'Summer stars' flowers for up to ten weeks in some areas.

C. k. **var.** *chinensis* is very similar to the species but has better flower production. Bracts are green at first, changing to white.

C. k. **var.** *chinensis* **'Milky Way'** is a heavy flower producer. Be aware that not all specimens of this cultivar are alike; there are many seed sources.

C. k. **x** *C. florida* (hybrid dogwood) This hybrid series shows great promise. It is the result of a breeding program by Dr. Elwin Orton of Rutgers University in 1965. His aim was to breed increased vigor and resistance to borers into flowering dogwoods. He was also interested in pink-bracted trees. Six hybrids are on the market, five with white bracts and one with pink bracts. These are known as the "Stellar" series. Some display hybrid vigor and are highly resistant to borers. Their habit is generally upright while young and the bract shape is intermediate between the parents. They are also intermediate in terms of hardiness, performing well in Zones 6-8. Culture is as for the genus; avoid overwatering and remove the lower branches on mature specimens for increased longevity. These hybrids resist dogwood borer and anthracnose. Many cultivars are available. **'Ruth Ellen'** is one of the first to bloom. It grows into a broad, spreading tree. **'Stardust'** has a similar shape but is a dwarf edition; it begins to bloom one day later than 'Ruth Ellen'. **'Constellation'** blooms yet another day later. It has large, overlapping bracts. Low branching but uniform. **'Aurora', 'Galaxy'** and **'Stellar Pink'** all bloom about four to five days after 'Ruth Ellen'. They all branch low but are uniform all the way up. Their flowers are similar to *C. florida,* ('Stellar Pink' has soft pink bracts), but the flowers are abundant and almost entirely cover the leaves.

CORYLUS COLURNA FILBERT, HAZELNUT *Betulaceae (Birch family)*

This genus includes many useful small trees–most notably the fascinatingly contorted Harry Lauder's walking stick–as well as a very hardy and shapely tree, *C. colurna* (Turkish filbert), which produces nuts under the right conditions. Its ornamental elements are its pyramidal shape and the catkins it produces in early spring.

BEST CONDITIONS *C. colurna* is hardy to Zone 4 and does well even in very dry conditions, though it does best in deep, loamy slightly acid to alkaline soil, and it colors best in full sun.

PLANTING Follow general planting procedures.

ROUTINE CARE Fertilize only in poor soil; after establishment, water during dry periods.

PRUNING Prune lightly to shape; take care not to disturb natural pyramidal shape.

PROPAGATION Propagate by seeds, grafting, layering, or medium-hardwood (firm but not totally hard) cuttings taken in summer.

PESTS, DISEASES, OTHER PROBLEMS None serious.

USE Often grown for its nuts, *C. colurna* is a good shade tree for dry areas.

SELECTIONS *C. maxima* 'Atropurpurea' has dark purple leaves that fade to dark green. *C. avellana,* European filbert, is usually grown as a shrub but can also be trained to tree form, up to 20 feet tall.

COTINUS OBOVATUS [C. AMERICANUS] AMERICAN SMOKETREE
Anacardiaceae (Cashew family)

There are two species of smoketree in cultivation; *C. obovatus* [*C. americanus*], American smoketree, is native to North America; *C. coggygria* is native to Eurasia. Ranging in height from 15-30 feet and possessing ornamental foliage flowers, and fruit, American smoketrees are underutilized but valuable trees with excellent fall color. The common name smoketree results from feathery, plumelike flowers and seedheads. The soft but durable interior wood yields a dye that was in great demand during the Civil War. In youth, this species has an upright oval or slightly irregular shape and develops a beautiful oval upright rounded habit in maturity.

BEST CONDITIONS Smoketrees prefer full sun and are virtually intolerant of shade in nature. They are very well suited to gravelly soils with high pH (8.0) but are sensitive to soil compaction that can be caused by heavy traffic on clay soils. They prefer soil that is dry and infertile to that which is moist and rich. They are also tolerant of humidity. Zone 4.

PLANTING Plant young balled-and-burlapped plants in spring.

ROUTINE CARE Watering can be detrimental and is almost always unnecessary. Avoid standing water around the tree. No fertilization is needed. Mulching during establishment is beneficial and unnecessary thereafter.

PRUNING Watch branch angles as the tree matures. Cutting back shrubby *C. coggygria* may be necessary after a severe northern winter, but it comes back readily.

PESTS, DISEASES, OTHER PROBLEMS Usually none; rarely, scale or leafspot.

PROPAGATION Smoketrees can be grown from seeds, but even professionals find it difficult; it is best to purchase plants.

USE This rugged small-scale tree has an upright habit that allows it to fit in many narrow spaces, such as small yards, walkways, street parkways without powerlines. The gray bark is attractive in winter, developing a unique scaley appearance

Tulips and other spring bulbs can be grown under *Crataegus viridis* 'Winter King' while it is young and before it leafs out; later, the tree provides too much shade for these plants.

with age. American smoketree's strongest characteristic is its foliage, which is bluish green through summer and a remarkable range of yellow, red, orange, and purple in fall.

SELECTIONS *C.* **'Grace'**, a hybrid between *C. coggygria* and *C. obovatus* introduced by Hillier Nurseries in England is a vigorous form with larger leaves and pink flowers. At Chicago Botanic Garden, its fall color is effective later than *C. obovatus*.

C. coggygria, smokebush, is a smaller plant, usually not exceeding 10-18 feet; it too thrives in alkaline soil. It is usually sold in its purple-foliage form under a number of cultivar names; **'Royal Purple'** is one of the best. This cultivar is pruned severely every spring in the perennial garden at The New York Botanical Garden.

CRATAEGUS PHAENOPYRUM WASHINGTON HAWTHORN

Rosaceae (Rose family)

This thorny, deciduous small (12-40 foot) tree is native to the North temperate zone. In North America it can be found from Pennsylvania to Florida and west to Missouri and Arkansas. It is valued for its white flowers in early summer, long-lasting red or orange fruits, and fall color.

BEST CONDITIONS A full sun position where the air circulates freely and there is sufficient space is best. Washington hawthorn tolerates a wide range of soil pH, both acid and alkaline, and does surprisingly well where drainage is poor. Humidity seems to be no problem. Site in front of an evergreen background for good effect.

PLANTING Spring planting of balled-and-burlapped stock is best. Bear in mind the eventual size of the tree. Water well and mulch.

PESTS, DISEASES, OTHER PROBLEMS Rust is often seen on the leaves; though unsightly, it does not seem to affect the health of the tree. Get recommendations from your local extension agent, botanic garden or arboretum before spraying.

ROUTINE CARE Mulch routinely. Keep well watered during dry weather; turf fertilizer is usually sufficient.

PRUNING Prune only to remove crossing branches. Remove lower limbs on specimen trees to avoid the dangerous thorns on low branches.

PROPAGATION Grow plants from seed.

USE Useful as a street tree, a specimen or grouped for hedging or a thorny barrier. One of the best hawthorns due to its upright but spreading horizontal branching habit and multi-seasonal interest. It blooms after the bulk of the spring flowering shrubs, thereby extending the season. Displays good red to orange fall color and retains its red fruits well into the winter for consumption by birds.

SELECTIONS *C. viridis* **'Winter King'** is an award winning selection of the species with strong horizontal habit to 35 feet and as wide. The mottled and multicolored bark improves with age. It also has white flowers, and orange fruit which turns red with decreasing temperatures. In the Chicago area, cedar waxwing birds grace this tree with their presence in December-January, methodically moving from one area of the tree to the next devouring the fruit. Site towards the back of the border or garden where there is sufficient room for the low branches.

C. crus-galli **var. *inermis*,** the thornless cockspur hawthorn, is more desirable in a "friendly" ornamental garden, since the 2-inch thorns of the species are absent. Regrettably the white flowers are malodorous, so site the tree away from high traffic areas. Very attractive glossy foliage but little fall color.

CRATAEGUS CRUS-GALLI (COCKSPUR HAWTHORN) Deciduous. 10 years: 7 feet; 20 years: 15 feet; 50 years: 20-25 feet; maturity: to 30 feet. Rounded head, horizontal branching. Foliage unfurls in red, turns green, small white flowers, red fruit in fall and winter. Full sun, moist to dry acid and alkaline soils. Zones 4-8.

CRATAEGUS PHAENOPYRUM (WASHINGTON HAWTHORN) Deciduous. 10 years: 8 feet; 20 years: 16 feet; 50 years: 20-25 feet; maturity: to 35 feet. Columnar; develops a rounded head in maturity. Lustrous lobed green leaves turn red in autumn, clusters of white flowers in spring, bright red fruit in fall. Full sun, moist to dry acid and alkaline soils. Zones 4-8.

CRATAEGUS VIRIDIS 'WINTER KING' (GREEN HAWTHORN)
Deciduous. 10 years: 10 feet; 20 years: 20 feet; 50 years: 30-35 feet; maturity: to 40 feet. Spreading tree with very dense foliage and clusters of small white flowers. Full sun, moist to dry acid and alkaline soils. Zones 4-8.

CRYPTOMERIA JAPONICA 'ELEGANS' (JAPANESE CEDAR)
Evergreen. 10 years: 9 feet; 20 years: 18 feet; 50 years: 40-45 feet; maturity: to 80 feet. Pyramidal tree with spreading branches, shredding reddish brown bark. Full sun on coast, some shade inland, light well-drained moist acidic soil. Zones 6-9.

Cryptomeria japonica is an excellent subject for bonsai treatment.

CRYPTOMERIA JAPONICA JAPANESE CEDAR *Taxodiaceae (Taxodium family)*

In Japan, this lumber and forest tree grows 50-60 feet tall. It has been cultivated for centuries, but was introduced into the U.S. in 1861. Its awllike needles produce a soft appearance and are bright bluish green in summer, turning bronze in winter. In older trees the reddish brown bark is interesting. Cone production varies; about 1 inch in diameter and green when young, they mature to brown and stay on the trees for several years.

BEST CONDITIONS Japanese cedar is an easy evergreen for full sun positions in coastal gardens, where they appear to be salt tolerant. Inland, avoid drying winds and provide shade to protect the foliage from dehydration and early breaking of dormancy. Dwarf forms are hardier than the species.

PLANTING Transplanting may be done in spring or fall, and even large specimens move readily.

PRUNING Only required to remove dead foliage.

PESTS, DISEASES, OTHER PROBLEMS In colder parts of Zones 6-9, susceptible cultivars may be attacked by red fire ants. Leaf spot and leaf blight may need control. The best control is to keep the plants growing vigorously to prevent fungal susceptibility.

PROPAGATION To germinate, the seeds require three months of warm temperatures followed by three months of cold stratification to break dormancy. Hardwood cuttings may be taken from summer through until the winter.

USE Excellent as a screen or coastal windbreak, Japanese cedars are also elegant specimen plants. They tolerate shearing and can be planted close as a hedge; the dwarf cultivars are suitable in rock garden settings.

SELECTIONS 'Yoshino' has an attractive form and fine-textured, bright blue-green foliage. It grows rapidly and may eventually reach 60 feet or more. Zone 5.

'Gracilis' is slower growing to about 20-30 feet and has a more open habit.

'Globosa' is a dwarf cultivar, which slowly grows into a dense 2- to 3-foot dome of blue-green foliage, rusty-colored in winter.

CUNNINGHAMIA LANCEOLATA CHINA FIR *Taxodiaceae (Taxodium family)*

An important economic tree in its native China, where it is prized for its lumber and firewood, China fir is an attractive ornamental conifer with thick, spreading branches that cast their ends down gracefully. China fir is a lovely and unusual conifer, suitable for the home garden.

BEST CONDITIONS China fir responds well to the general conifer setting: full sun, slightly acid, evenly moist soil. They are usually recommended only for warm climates (Zone 7 and south) but specimens are thriving in a slightly sheltered site at The New York Botanical Garden and at Morris Arboretum.

PLANTING Plant in spring or fall and water and fertilize well for the first two years. In the cooler end of the plant's hardiness range, plant in spring.

ROUTINE CARE Water during dry spells. A mulch is beneficial.

PRUNING Prune minimally, cutting back branches to keep the tree within bounds. It can also be pruned as a hedge.

PESTS, DISEASES, OTHER PROBLEMS None serious, but this species sometimes sheds prickly branches, making it somewhat messy.

PROPAGATION Propagate by seeds or cuttings.

CUNNINGHAMIA LANCEOLATA 'GLAUCA' (BLUE CHINA FIR)
Evergreen. 10 years: 10 feet; 20 years: 20 feet; 50 years: 50-55 feet; maturity: to 90 feet. Pyramidal shape with drooping branches and pointed blue-green needles. Full sun or partial shade, well-drained, slightly acidic soil, warm climates. Zones 7-9, Zone 6 with protection.

CUPRESSUS GOVENIANA (GOWEN CYPRESS) Evergreen. 10 years: 8 feet; 20 years: 17 feet; 50 years: 40-45 feet; maturity: to 65 feet. Columnar to pyramidal habit, blue-green needles. Full sun, well-drained, slightly acidic soil, warm climates. Zones 7-9.

X CUPRESSOCYPARIS LEYLANDII (LEYLAND CYPRESS) Evergreen. 10 years: 15 feet; 20 years: 30 feet; 50 years: 60-65 feet; maturity: to 90 feet. Columnar to pyramidal habit, blue-green needles. Full sun, well-drained, slightly acidic soil, warm climates. Zones 6-9.

CYDONIA OBLONGA 'SMYRNA' (COMMON QUINCE) Deciduous. 10 years: 6 feet; 20 years: 12 feet; 50 years: 20-25 feet; maturity: to 30 feet. Compact small tree with pink or white flowers, attractive yellow fruit. Moist, deep fertile soil. Zones 5-10.

DAVIDIA INVOLUCRATA 'VILMORINIANA' (DOVE TREE) Deciduous. 10 years: 8 feet; 20 years: 16 feet; 50 years: 30-35 feet; maturity: to 40 feet. Broadly pyramidal, especially when young; flowers with very large creamy white bracts. Light shade, deep rich moist but well-drained soil. Zones 6-8.

DIOSPYROS VIRGINIANA 'JOHN RICK' (PERSIMMON) Deciduous. 10 years: 10 feet; 20 years: 20-25 feet; 50 years: 55-65 feet; maturity: to 75 feet. Glossy dark green foliage, 2- to 3-inch yellow fruits. Full sun, rich moist soil. Zones 5-10.

DISANTHUS CERCIDIFOLIUS (DISANTHUS) Deciduous. 10 years: 6 feet; 20 years: 10 feet; 50 years: 12-18 feet; maturity: to 20 feet. Small tree with dull green foliage that turns bright purple in autumn; small red to purple flowers appear in autumn as well. Sun or shade, moist well-drained soil. Zones 5-8.

ELAEAGNUS ANGUSTIFOLIA (RUSSIAN OLIVE) Deciduous. 10 years: 11 feet; 20 years: 18-20 feet; 50 years: 30-35 feet; maturity: to 35 feet. Small creamy flowers and yellow fruit, attractive gray-green foliage, open spreading habit. Full sun or light shade, any soil. Zones 3-8.

USE One of the palest-colored evergreen conifers, China fir is an interesting and exotic departure from more traditional background conifers.
SELECTIONS *C. l.* '**Glauca**', blue china fir, has blue-gray needles.

CUPRESSUS CYPRESS *Cupressaceae (Cypress family)*

The groves of cypress that occur in the forests of the southwestern United States are part of our national heritage. These conifers will only grow in warm climates, but impart a look of natural luxury when they are grown right.
BEST CONDITIONS Cypresses need warm climates, full sun, and when young, lots of water. They are more tolerant of drought once established. Moderately well-drained, slightly acid soil is best.
PLANTING Plant from containers in spring or fall; water well during establishment.
ROUTINE CARE Provide extra water for young plants; established plants do not need additional water. A mulch will help keep soil moist and fertile.
PRUNING Prune out branches that go out of bounds.
PESTS, DISEASES, OTHER PROBLEMS None serious.
PROPAGATION Propagate by seeds.
USE Cypresses are excellent background or screening trees, particularly when towering over a riverbank. They are suitable only for warm climates and for large sites.
SELECTIONS *C. arizonica* is hardier than most cypresses, and is used in Zones 6-9; it is also drought tolerant. The cultivar '**Blue Ice**' has striking blue foliage.
C. macrocarpa, Monterey cypress, has an interesting, irregular form. It is often grown as a windbreak on the Pacific coast. It grows to 75 feet and is hardy in Zones 8-10.
C. sempervirens, Italian cypress, grows to 75 feet and is hardy in Zone 8. Its wood is very strong and durable; it was used for the doors of St. Peter's Cathedral in Rome. The cultivar '**Stricta**' is a narrow, columnar form that is particularly appropriate for formal gardens.
x *Cupressocyparis leylandii,* Leyland cypress, is a hybrid of false cypress and cypress first found in the gardens of C. J. Leyland in England. It reaches 100 feet and has feathery, blue-green foliage. It is one of the fastest growing cypresses. '**Hagerstown Grey**' is an excellent cultivar, hardy in Zone 6 if protected when young.

CYDONIA QUINCE *Rosaceae (Rose family)*

This genus of small trees, as well as the shrub *Chaenomeles,* produces quinces, small fragrant fruits used for preserves and jellies. It is more often grown as an ornamental, for its lovely orchidlike flowers and foliage that turns bright red in fall.
BEST CONDITIONS Hardy to Zone 5, quinces need heavy, moist soil and full sun.
PLANTING Set out one- or two-year-old saplings. Protect the shallow roots by mulching during establishment.
ROUTINE CARE Provide generous water and fertilizer for the first few years and water during dry spells thereafter.
PRUNING Prune out dead wood to keep an open shape.
PROPAGATION Take hardwood cuttings in the fall.
PESTS, DISEASES, OTHER PROBLEMS Fireblight is the most serious problem, particularly in warm areas; monitor carefully and cut away affected parts. Borers can be a problem, and moth infestations sometimes require spraying.
USE Cydonia is a lovely specimen tree for a small area; its fruit is used in preserves.

Above: Cupressus macrocarpa, Monterey cypress.

Several cypresses, including Leyland cypress have been subject to attack by insects in recent years. Periodically, insects defoliate or do other damage to specific trees. Beech is another example of a tree that has recently been found suffered insect damage and some hemlocks have been destroyed by the woolly adelgid in the Northeast. Ethan Johnson recommends against panic. Most trees can survive even a serious attack with only temporary, cosmetic damage and wide-scale spraying or avoidance of susceptible trees does more harm than good. The best practice is to avoid planting one type of tree in close proximity in great numbers (monoculture) and to maintain sanitary and proper cultural conditions.

VIEWPOINT

BEST BACKYARD TREES

I would choose an *Amelanchier* x *gran-diflora* because it performs well in both sun and shade and its intermediate size makes it an option for most any landscape. The upright, vase-shaped habit allows traffic in and around it and its bark, flowers, fruit, and fall color make it a four-season plant.
GALEN GATES,
CHICAGO BOTANIC GARDEN

Fall color, flowers, and interesting winter effects are important in my choice of trees. For a home-garden-sized tree, I would consider *Cornus kousa* (maybe a cultivar like 'Milky Way') oxydendron or *Stewartia pseudocamellia*. Because flowers last so short a time, I would also consider *Acer griseum* or *Acer davidii*.
SUSAN THOMAS,
HOYT ARBORETUM, PORTLAND

Here, I would choose a mesquite. It is unrivaled for the combination of fast growth, delicate shade, and excellent performance in desert areas.
MARY IRISH, DESERT BOTANICAL GARDEN, PHOENIX

In the eastern U.S., I might plant a fast-growing Japanese maple like *Acer palmatum* 'Osakazuki': with excellent fall color, good summer foliage, no messy leaves or fruit, tolerant of sun and partial shade. For flowering, I lean toward plants that flower during seasons other than spring, so I would plant koelreutia, maakia, or hamemelis. For a larger, slower-growing tree I'd select *Nyssa sylvatica*.
RICK LEWANDOWSKI, MORRIS ARBORETUM , UNIVERSITY OF PENNSYLVANIA

If I could plant only one tree, I would plant a katsura in my garden where it would be in full view from my house so I could watch it yearround. Katsuras have red foliage in spring, beautiful fresh blue-green leaves all summer, yellow fall color and a nice branching pattern than is visible in winter.
DORTHE HVIID,
BERKSHIRE BOTANICAL GARDEN

SELECTIONS *C. oblonga* grows to about 20 feet tall and is hardy to Zone 5. *C. sinensis* is hardy to Zone 6, and turns brilliant red in autumn.

DAVIDIA INVOLUCRATA DOVE TREE *Nyssaceae (Sour-gum family)*

Considered by some to be the most beautiful of all flowering trees, dove tree is native to China. In cultivation it may reach 40 feet and when in bloom, usually for about two weeks in late spring, it is a spectacular sight. The "doves" are actually two large white bracts, of unequal size, which subtend the real flowers. Sometimes called the handkerchief tree. After the flowers are spent, solitary greenish fruits develop, which turn rusty color and speckled with red. The large leaves are reminiscent of linden. The dove tree was discovered by and named for Abbe Armand David (1826-1900). Subsequently it was introduced into Europe by plantsman Pere Paul Guillaume Farges and E. H. Wilson. Wilson collected a great quantity of seed which he sent to Veitch's Nursery in England in 1901. A year later thousands of seedlings had germinated and some flowered ten years later. Dove trees at The Arnold Arboretum are all descended from a scion received from Vilmorin Nursery in France.

BEST CONDITIONS Light shade is best, but if the soil remains moist full sun is tolerated. Well-drained soil, thoroughly amended with organic matter is ideal.

PLANTING Select balled-and-burlapped stock and plant in spring. Water well and mulch. Bear in mind that young plants may not flower until they are ten years old or more. The tree at Blithewold took 25 years to bloom which it did for the first time in 1995. At maturity dove trees will be as wide as tall and need space.

ROUTINE CARE Keep watered during dry weather.

PRUNING Prune out crossing branches and remove diseased or dead wood in winter.

PESTS, DISEASES, OTHER PROBLEMS None serious, but foliage has an unpleasant odor, so the tree should not be planted very near a home.

PROPAGATION Seeds are doubly dormant and difficult to germinate and grow on. Buy nursery-grown plants.

USE A spectacular specimen tree that must have space to show off. Since flowering may not occur for several years, one must exercise patience. Even after the first flowering individual specimens may not flower every year.

SELECTIONS The cultivar **'Vilmoriniana'** has yellow-green coloring on the underside of the leaves and is slightly more available than the species. Zones 6-8.

DIOSPYROS PERSIMMON *Ebenaceae (Ebony family)*

Native to eastern and southeastern United States, the common persimmon (*D. virginiana*) grows to 75 feet tall and has remarkably prominent black bark. It produces luscious orange-yellow fruits; harvesting fruit after a light frost makes them sweeter. Persimmons are dioecious trees, so male and female plants are needed if fruit is desired.

BEST CONDITIONS Persimmons thrive in full sun, in any moderately fertile soil. They are hardy to Zone 7.

PLANTING Persimmons have a long taproot and are therefore difficult to transplant. Planting very small, young trees is easiest.

ROUTINE CARE Once the plant is established, water only during dry spells and fertilize only if natural soil fertility is low.

PRUNING Prune out dead wood in fall, after fruiting.

PESTS, DISEASES, OTHER PROBLEMS This tree is often attacked by the persimmon borer; treat immediately. It is uncommon in the Middle Atlantic states.

PROPAGATION Propagate by seeds or cuttings.

USE The persimmon is not particularly ornamental, but is sometimes used as a specimen tree. It is usually grown for its edible fruit.

SELECTIONS *D. virginiana* is described above.

D. kaki, native to China and Korea, is popular in Japan, where many selections have been made for size and taste of fruit. If you are interested in growing this species for its fruit, check with your local extension service to see which varieties do best in your area.

DISANTHUS CERCIDIFOLIUS DISANTHUS *Hamamelidaceae (Witch-hazel family)*

A moderately difficult-to-grow shrub or small tree, growing to 25 feet tall, disanthus has simple, almost round blue-green leaves; in fall, they turn an exquisite dark red with glints of orange. The leaves begin changing color long before most other plants, progressing from green to dark purple, burgundy, red, and orange-red. Small blood-red flowers are insignificant and emit a foul odor.

BEST CONDITIONS Plant in full sun or, preferably, light shade in moderately fertile, acidic soil that is not very dry. In alkaline soils, the tree often becomes stunted or dies. Zone 6.

PLANTING In spring or fall.

ROUTINE CARE Requires little care.

PRUNING Prune in spring to shape or keep in bounds.

PROPAGATION By seeds or cuttings.

PESTS, DISEASES, OTHER PROBLEMS None serious.

USE Disanthus blends well in the garden, requiring no special care; in fall, when its leaves turn red and orange, it is dazzling.

ELAEAGNUS ANGUSTIFOLIA RUSSIAN OLIVE, OLEASTER

Elaeagnaceae (Oleaster family)

This deciduous large shrub or small tree was introduced from Europe during colonial times. Its somewhat craggy appearance results from the crooked trunk, covered with bark that appears to be shredded, and loose, wide-spreading crown. In the home landscape it is valued for its young silvery white foliage which matures to dull dark green, with silvery woolly undersides. The creamy white flowers that open in late spring are fragrant and attract insect pollinators. In late summer, silvery yellow fruits provide food for wildlife. Since they fix nitrogen in the soil, they can grow in the poorest of soil, but sometimes crowd out native species.

BEST CONDITIONS Grow elaeagnus in full sun where the soil is light and sandy. In heavy water-logged soil they are susceptible to root diseases. They tolerate the salt spray of seasides and pollution of urban conditions well. Good in windy positions, but not in hot southern gardens or in other humid regions.

ROUTINE CARE Water during dry spells, but avoid standing water. Fertilization is usually unnecessary unless the soil is very poor.

PLANTING Easy to transplant in spring or fall.

PRUNING For additional vigor and to accentuate the leaves, prune into a tighter canopy. If root suckers develop, they should be removed.

PESTS, DISEASES, OTHER PROBLEMS Russian olive is susceptible to a number of diseases, including canker, leaf spots, rusts and crown gall. The most important is

EUCOMMIA ULMOIDES (HARDY RUBBER TREE) Deciduous. 10 years: 13 feet; 20 years: 20-25 feet; 50 years: 40-50 feet; maturity: to 60 feet. Oval elmlike green leaves. Full sun, any soil. Zones 5-8.

EUONYMUS ALATUS (WINGED EUONYMUS) Deciduous. 10 years: 5 feet; 20 years: 8-10 feet; 50 years: 12-15 feet; maturity: to 20 feet. Can be trained to single trunk; bright green leaves turn brilliant red in fall. Tolerates heavy shade and any soil type; soil must be well drained. Zones 3-8.

EVODIA DANIELII (KOREAN EVODIA) Deciduous. 10 years: 15-20 feet; 20 years: 30 feet; 50 years: 35-45 feet; maturity: to 45 feet.Compound leaves; flat clusters of small white flowers in mid to late summer; red or black berries in fall; open habit. Full sun, any moist, well-drained fertile soil. Zones 5-9.

FAGUS GRANDIFOLIA (AMERICAN BEECH) Deciduous. 10 years: 10 feet; 20 years: 20 feet; 50 years: 50 feet; maturity: to 90 feet. Leaves open as gray-green, darken in summer and turn gold or brown in fall; broadly spreading crown. Full sun, rich moist (but not wet) soil. Zones 3-8.

verticillium wilt which can be devastating. To protect them from disease, avoid stressing the plants and keep them growing vigorously. Scale insects may infest the trees, and should be controlled. In its native areas, sometimes weedy.

PROPAGATION Sow seed in the fall for germination the following spring or cold stratify for two to three months prior to sowing.

USE Plant Russian olive as a shelter, screen, or windbreak, especially in seaside gardens which are frequently windswept. They are excellent plants for urban gardens; their silvery foliage shows off well in night or white gardens.

SELECTIONS 'Red King' is notable for its rusty red, rather than silvery yellow fruits. Zones 3-7.

EUCOMMIA ULMOIDES HARDY RUBBER TREE *Eucommiaceae (Eucommia family)*

This Chinese native is the only tree that yields rubber in temperate climates. Although this product is difficult to extract, the tree has many other virtues. It provides excellent shade in a variety of difficult locations, bears handsome shiny dark green leaves in summer, and has a neat oval to round outline.

BEST CONDITIONS Best in full sun, the hardy rubber tree tolerates just about any kind of soil, of high or low pH. It is also drought tolerant.

PLANTING This tree is very easy to transplant.

ROUTINE CARE None necessary.

PRUNING This tree does not grow out of its bounds and forms a pleasing shape naturally; pruning is rarely needed.

PROPAGATION Cuttings root easily in sand.

PEST, DISEASES, OTHER PROBLEMS Remarkably free of pests and diseases.

USE Hardy rubber tree is an excellent, undemanding shade tree for the Midwest. Although it provides little fall color, its summer foliage is attractive.

EUONYMUS SPINDLE TREE *Celastraceae (Staff-tree family)*

The most popular forms of this plant are shrubs that turn bright red in fall, but many species become treelike with age, providing dense, attractive foliage and colorful fall fruit. All remain small, seldom growing above 15 feet tall.

BEST CONDITIONS Spindle tree will do well in full sun to almost full shade and thrives in relatively moist, well-drained acid to alkaline soil. It is hardy to Zone 4 once established, but can be killed by unexpected early frost in its first few seasons.

PLANTING Plant in spring or fall; cover with a thin layer of organic mulch.

ROUTINE CARE Once established, watering is necessary only during dry spells. Fertilization is usually not necessary unless the soil is very poor.

PRUNING Pruning is not only unnecessary, but will destroy this tree's natural pleasing shape if not done properly.

PROPAGATION From seeds or cuttings.

PESTS, DISEASES, OTHER PROBLEMS Most species are susceptible to euonymus scale, which requires careful attention and spraying; if you are not willing to monitor and spray your plants, be sure that your area is free of this pest before planting euonymus.

USE These small trees make excellent hedges or backgrounds to flowerbeds; their fall color adds interest when the flowers begin to tire in the fall.

SELECTIONS *E. alatus,* winged euonymus, is usually grown as a low shrub, but can

TREE HUNTERS

Perhaps the most famous of the plant hunters was Scotsman Robert Fortune, who traveled to the Orient, discovering and introducing many of the best-known Chinese garden plants as well as many trees, including the golden larch (*Pseudolarix amabilis*), the Chinese fringe tree (*Chioanthus retusus*), cryptomeria (*Cryptomeria japonica*), and the lacebark pine (*Pinus bungeana*).

Englishman William Lobb (1809-63) was the first of 22 collectors sent by the Veitch firm to seek out "the new and the novel." During his first trip to South America, he noticed a tree that had been introduced to England by Archibald Menzies and was known as the Chile pine. It was then no more than a curiosity, but Lobb believed it was destined for greater success; he named the trees genus *Araucaria,* and it was the only conifer from south of the Equator to grow to timber size in Europe.

When the Veitch firm first sent Ernest Henry Wilson (1876-1930) to China, it was to find a single tree, *Davidia involucrata;* the directors told him not to "spend time and and money wandering about . . . [for] probably most every worthwhile plant in China has now been introduced in Europe." Wilson eventually found 1,000 new plants there and became known as "Chinese" Wilson. Known for his bad luck, he came close to drowning, starving, and being killed in an avalanche. He later became keeper of the Arnold Arboretum, and, having escaped perils in many foreign lands, died in 1930 in a car accident in Massachusetts.

FAGUS SYLVATICA 'TRICOLOR' (EUROPEAN BEECH) Deciduous. 10 years: 10 feet; 20 years: 20 feet; 50 years: 50 feet; maturity: to 90 feet. Pyramidal tree with dense glossy variegated leaves that are principally bronze in summer. Full sun, rich moist soil. Zones 4-8.

FAGUS SYLVATICA 'ATROPUNICEA' (PURPLE BEECH) Deciduous. 10 years: 10 feet; 20 years: 20 feet; 50 years: 50 feet; maturity: to 90 feet. Pyramidal tree with dense glossy coppery leaves that turn bronze in summer. Full sun, rich moist soil. Zones 4-8.

FAGUS SYLVATICA 'ROSEOMARGINATA' (ROSEPINK EUROPEAN BEECH) Deciduous. 10 years: 9 feet; 20 years: 18 feet; 50 years: 45 feet; maturity: to 80 feet. Pyramidal tree with dense glossy purplish leaves with lighter pink margins. Light shade, rich moist soil; difficult to grow. Zones 4-8.

FAGUS SYLVATICA 'PENDULA' (WEEPING EUROPEAN BEECH) Deciduous. 10 years: 10 feet; 20 years: 20 feet; 50 years: 50 feet; maturity: to 80 feet. Widespreading well-branched tree with long, hanging branches, small green leaves. Light shade, rich moist soil; slow to grow. Zones 4-8.

be pruned to tree form, up to 15 feet tall. Its fall color is an unbeatable fiery red. It can be grown in shade, but will not color nearly as well.

E. bungeanus, midwinter euonymus, is a vigorous grower (15-30 feet tall), hardy to Zone 4. Its growth habit varies from broad-spreading to upright. It leafs out early in spring and is of particular interest in mid to late fall when its leaves turn a brilliant red and pink fruits appear; the fruits last until November. The variety **E. b. 'Pendula'** is a weeping form.

E. europaeus, spindle tree, grows 12-30 feet tall and 10-25 feet wide. It produces leaves that are dull green in summer and turn purplish red in fall and pink or red fruit. The cultivar **'Red Cascade'** bears abundant fruit.

E. hamiltoniana, to 25 feet, is hardy in Zone 5 and has marvelous pink arils in autumn and spectacular purple and red fall color; fairly resistant to euonymus scale.

EVODIA DANIELLII KOREAN EVODIA *Rutaceae (Rue family)*

Korean evodia was introduced from Korea and northern China by E. H. Wilson in 1905. It has attractive shiny green, pinnately compound leaves that remain fresh-looking and large white clusters of flowers in summer, which are highly attractive to bees. By late summer the ornamental fruits develop, first red and then turning to black. Fall color is insignificant. Unfortunately this fast-growing tree is weak-wooded, and may not be very long-lived. Seldom planted in the U.S.

BEST CONDITIONS Plant in a sunny position in fertile, moist soil. It is not fussy about soil pH, but likes good drainage. Zones 5-8.

PLANTING Planting is best in spring or fall, usually about 25-35 feet apart. Select strong, vigorous plants that are well branched and have good bark. Keep well watered until established in about two years. Transplants easily. Plant male and female plants if fruit is desired.

ROUTINE CARE Keep mulched routinely; not affected by heat or drought.

PRUNING Little pruning is necessary.

PESTS, DISEASES, OTHER PROBLEMS No major pests or diseases. Although it has a reputation for weak wood, it is grown at Morris Arboretum without problem. At Berkshire, the specimen has been badly damaged by frost cracks; site carefully.

PROPAGATION Propagate by softwood cuttings. Seeds germinate easily without special treatment.

USE This an underused but useful small tree for planting in a lawn or anywhere else on a small property. Korean evodia deserves to be more widely planted. It is also very popular with beekeepers.

SELECTIONS E. hupehensis may grow to 40-50 feet in height.

FAGUS BEECH *Fagaceae (Beech family)*

A deservedly popular tree, beeches possess many virtues, including a tall, stately shape and interesting bark. The insignificant flowers are followed by small nuts in spring, but beeches put on their best show in fall, when their leaves turn every shade of red, brown, yellow, and orange.

BEST CONDITIONS Beeches are hardy in Zones 4-8, depending on the species and cultivar. They do best in moist soil that is rich in organic matter and well drained. Any amount of sun is tolerated, but full sun results in the best color and shape.

PLANTING Look for balled-and-burlapped specimens and plant in spring. Root pruning before planting is recommended. Plant them no deeper than they were

Above: Fagus sylvatica 'Asplenifolia' in autumn. Top: *Fagus sylvatica* 'Laciniata'.

Fagus sylvatica 'Atropunicea', *Fagus grandifolia.*

planted in the nursery. Beeches have shallow roots; take care not to compact the earth around them when planting. Leave them plenty of room to spread.

ROUTINE CARE Amend soil with leaf mold or other organic matter before planting and at regular intervals.

PRUNING Pruning is necessary only on young trees; prune lower and horizontal branches off young trees in summer to achieve a single, straight trunk. The trees also look beautiful when left unpruned, with their branches hanging to the ground all around them. Prune only in summer or early fall to avoid bleeding.

PROPAGATION Seed may be sown in fall; grafting may be done in late winter or early spring.

PESTS, DISEASES, OTHER PROBLEMS Beeches do not tolerate wet feet; otherwise, they rarely suffer from pests or diseases. However, some people fear beech bark disease, carried by beech scale, may become problematic. (See page 81.)

USE A grove of beech trees makes a wonderful shady spot for a picnic in a large site. It is also worthy of use as a specimen. These trees create dense shade and have shallow roots, so it is difficult to plant under them.

SELECTIONS *F. sylvatica*, European beech, grows to 100 feet and has a smooth gray bark. The cultivar **'Fastigiata'** is narrow and upright; **'Asplenifolia'** has narrow, fern-like leaves; and **'Purpurea'** has dark purple foliage. **'Roseomarginata'** has particularly attractive pink-edged leaves but is slow to grow because it does not have a full share of chlorophyll. A weeping version, **'Pendula',** takes several years to reach a graceful shape, but is worth the wait.

F. grandifolia, American beech, has a lighter gray bark and larger leaves; it is hardy to Zone 3. It is difficult to transplant and is therefore rarely available. Remove suckers that may form on the root.

FICUS FIG *Moraceae (Mulberry family)*

Ficus is a very large genus, encompassing excellent large shade trees for the South, small trees grown for their delicious fruit, and some popular houseplants. Some species, particularly the fascinating banyan tree, have hanging roots that twist and intertwine: some specimens take up half an acre.

BEST CONDITIONS Most fig trees are hardy only in Zones 9-10, though some small fig trees are grown for fruit with protection in the North. The trees need full sun, but will adapt to any soil, heavy to sandy.

PLANTING Plant in spring or fall; water well.

ROUTINE CARE Although fig trees adapt to dry soil, a generous watering during dry periods will keep them looking healthy. Fertilize lightly but regularly.

PRUNING Prune to maintain an open shape, cutting out crossed branches and dead wood.

PROPAGATION By seeds or cuttings.

PESTS, DISEASES, OTHER PROBLEMS None serious.

USE Ficus trees are an important source of shade in the South. They are grown along highways and as street trees in many parts of Florida. In the tropics, they grow extraordinarily large with age and are often covered with vines or with their own epiphytic roots.

SELECTIONS *F. benjamina,* grown as a houseplant in the North, reaches about 40 feet tall in Zones 9-10, where it is an important shade tree. It needs more light than most species and does not tolerate overwatering.

FICUS BENGHALENSIS (BANYAN TREE) Evergreen. 10 years: 15 feet; 20 years: 25 feet; 50 years: 30-40 feet; maturity: to 50 feet. Glossy, leathery leaves, very widespreading branches, hanging epiphytic roots; one tree can take up a block. Warm climates, rich soil, full sun. Zone 10.

FIRMIANA SIMPLEX (CHINESE PARASOL TREE) Deciduous. 10 years: 20 feet; 20 years: 40 feet; 50 years: 45-50 feet; maturity: to 50 feet. Upright habit, coarse leaves, greenish bark. Warm climates, well-drained, moist soil, full sun. Zones 7-9, Zone 6 with protection.

FRANKLINIA ALATAMAHA (FRANKLIN TREE) Deciduous. 10 years: 7 feet; 20 years: 13 feet; 50 years: 20-25 feet; maturity: to 30 feet. Upright tree with shiny green leaves and large white flowers with yellow stamens in early autumn. Partial shade or full sun with adequate moisture, alkaline soil is best but acid is tolerated. Zones 5-8.

FRAXINUS EXCELSIOR (EUROPEAN ASH) Deciduous. 10 years: 12 feet; 25 years: 20 feet; 50 years: 55-60 feet; maturity: to 80 feet. Dense, rounded canopy of compound foliage, fragrant white flowers in spring. Deep, evenly moist but well-drained soil; thrives in alkaline soils. Full sun. Zones 3-9.

Franklinia alatamaha in fall; the foliage often colors simultaneously with the appearance of flowers.

F. carica, common fig, can be grown with protection as far north as New York and Chicago (Zone 5), where dedicated gardeners regularly bring it to fruiting; it needs to be wrapped and covered for winter, or grown in a pot and brought indoors. In Zones 7-10, it is perfectly hardy and reaches 30 feet tall, providing shade as well as fruit. Excessive fertilizer will reduce fruiting but improve foliage. Root pruning and application of superphosphate aid in fruit production.

F. elastica, rubber plant, another popular houseplant, has long, almost black oval leaves and needs very little light and even less water. With protection, it can be grown outdoors in Zones 9-10.

F. macrophylla, Moreton Bay fig, has a spreading shape that makes it useful as a backyard shade tree. Zones 9-10.

F. religiosa, peepul, bo-tree, has an open habit that reveals its graceful structure. It is deciduous, but loses its pale green leaves for a only a few weeks in spring.

FIRMIANA SIMPLEX CHINESE PARASOL TREE *Sterculiaceae (Sterculia family)*

This native of eastern Asia grows quickly to 40 feet and has large, lush maplelike leaves. Its bark is smooth gray-green, and the yellow-green flowers hang in long racemes.

BEST CONDITIONS Firmiana needs full sun and well-drained, moist soil; it tolerates partial afternoon shade.

PLANTING Transplant balled-and-burlapped trees in spring or fall.

ROUTINE CARE Provide ample water throughout its life–it will not tolerate drought well. Do not fertilize. Protect from wind.

PRUNING Prune only as necessary

PESTS, DISEASES, OTHER PROBLEMS None serious.

PROPAGATION Propagate by fresh seed.

USE Although it has interesting flowers and fruits, it is generally used as a shade or street tree. Its rich appearance lends a tropical look to the garden.

FRANKLINIA ALATAMAHA FRANKLIN TREE *Theaceae (Tea family)*

This rare and precious find by Philadelphia plantsman John Bartram in the eighteenth century no longer grows in the wild. Bartram found the Franklin tree growing on the banks of the Altamaha River (the name of the river was misspelled in the first records) in Georgia and named it for Benjamin Franklin. It was last seen in its native habitat in 1803. Franklinia makes a very ornamental, upright small tree or large shrub, especially notable for its moderately fragrant, showy white 3-inch flowers in late summer until frost. This is a time period when few shrubs are in bloom. As the weather cools in fall, the leaves turn brilliant red. The gray, smooth bark is interesting in winter.

BEST CONDITIONS Full sun to partial shade is best for flowering. Soil must be acidic but otherwise most soil types will do. Not very well adapted to droughty or waterlogged sites. Amend with plenty of organic material.

PLANTING Select young, well-branched plants with thick basal stems. Plant balled-and-burlapped or container plants in spring or fall. In light soils plant on the level, but plant high where soils are heavy and may not drain well. Water well and mulch.

ROUTINE CARE Keep well watered for two years or so until well established. Mulch

FRAXINUS ORNUS (FLOWERING ASH) Deciduous. 10 years: 9 feet; 20 years: 18 feet; 50 years: 30-40 feet; maturity: to 50 feet. Abundant showy white flowers, borne in 5-inch panicles in spring. Full sun, deep, evenly moist but well-drained fertile soil. Zones 5-9.

FRAXINUS QUADRANGULATA (BLUE ASH) Deciduous. 10 years: 12 feet; 20 years: 25 feet; 50 years: 50-55 feet; maturity: to 75 feet. Dense compound dark green foliage turns pale yellow in autumn. Full sun, deep, fertile soil; tolerates dry soil. Zones 4-9.

GINKGO BILOBA (MAIDENHAIR TREE) Deciduous. 10 years: 12 feet; 20 years: 25 feet; 50 years: 55-60 feet; maturity: to 90 feet. Fan-shaped leaves on overlapping branches emerge yellow-green, turn darker green in summer and bright gold in autumn. Full sun, well-drained moist soil. Zones 4-9.

GLEDITSIA TRIACANTHOS (COMMON HONEY LOCUST) Deciduous. 10 years: 10-15 feet; 20 years: 20-30 feet; 50 years: 50-70 feet; maturity: to 100 feet. Broadly pyramidal tree with compound fine-textured leaves. Full sun, rich moist soil; tolerates sandy soil but not excessive dryness or humidity. Zones 4-9.

Fraxinus americana 'Autumn Purple'.

routinely.

PRUNING Prune in fall to remove crossing branches or to shape.

PESTS, DISEASES, OTHER PROBLEMS *Phytophthora* root rot is a serious disease, especially in the South. Control with fungicidal tree stakes placed in the ground.

PROPAGATION Collect seed in midfall and sow at once. Do not allow the seed to dry out prior to or after sowing. Take cuttings in early summer.

USE An excellent small tree to use as a specimen in a lawn or close to a patio. Franklinia is also appropriate in shrub borders and in mixed borders with perennials, although this aristocrat really deserves to be seen alone.

FRAXINUS ASH Oleaceae (Olive family)

There are many reasons for the popularity of the ash tree in American gardens: fragrant white flowers in the spring (on some species), dense foliage that provides excellent shade, dramatic warm yellow and purple foliage in the fall. Some species grow to 120 feet tall.

BEST CONDITIONS Ash trees do best in moderate climates, Zones 5-8. They prefer deep, evenly moist, and fertile soil, which must be well drained.

PLANTING Plant in spring and fall; during establishment period, mulch to retain moisture in soil.

ROUTINE CARE Provide extra water during dry periods, but do not fertilize unless soil is poor. Overfeeding results in the production of lush foliage, which promotes pests and disease.

ROUTINE CARE Special care after the establishment period is rarely needed, except for watering during dry spells.

PRUNING Prune dead wood in fall when necessary.

PROPAGATION Seed can be sown in fall; graft in spring.

PESTS, DISEASES, OTHER PROBLEMS Ash trees are prone to scale attacks, ash yellows, and ash decline; overfertilized trees are particularly susceptible.

USE Ash trees provide excellent shade and are often used to mark borders between properties. Avoid stressful sites, like parking lots.

SELECTIONS *F. americana,* white ash, grows quickly and can reach 120 feet tall. Its bark is gray and deeply furrowed. It is suffering from disease problems in the Northeast (see page 81).

F. excelsior, European ash, grows as tall as white ash, but has a more oval form.

F. ornus, flowering ash, rarely exceeds 40 feet, but has large flowers.

F. pennsylvanica, green ash, will grow rapidly in many difficult sites; it tolerates salt, wet soil, poor and alkaline soil, and drought. It has glossy medium to dark green leaves that yellow in fall. Avoid seedling-grown trees, which do not color and produce messy fruit. Grows 50-80 feet tall, at a rate of 2-3 feet per year. Zones 3-8.

GINKGO BILOBA GINKGO, MAIDENHAIR TREE Ginkgoaceae (Ginkgo family)

The only species in its family, ginkgo is one of the oldest living trees on earth, having survived the continental drift and the coming and going of dinosaurs and ice ages. Often considered native to China, it also existed in North America 200 million years ago. We owe its current availability to trees that survived in temple and palace gardens of China. Ginkgo is probably the first Asian tree to be widely cultivated as an ornamental in Europe and America. It grows slowly to 50-80 feet tall; its habit varies, but usually exhibits large, upright spreading branches and distinctive fan-shaped leaves.

BEST CONDITIONS Grow ginkgo in full sun, in reasonably moist, fertile soil. It tolerates acid or alkaline soil. Zone 3. Ginkgo is surprisingly tolerant of road salt and most air pollutants (except sulfur dioxide).

PLANTING Look for cultivars in apparent health and ascertain their habit before planting; some have a more upright habit and can be spaced closer than others. Ginkgo transplants without difficulty or special care. Keep moist until established. Ginkgos do not flower or fruit until they are 20 years old, so it is best to purchase grafted plants.

ROUTINE CARE Once established, additional water is not necessary unless conditions are severe. However, since it tends to grow a little more slowly than some less valuable trees, you may wish to provide some fertilizer.

PRUNING Prune to improve structural development so that the tree develops a good framework when young.

PESTS, DISEASES, OTHER PROBLEMS Exceptionally problem free.

PROPAGATION Propagation is difficult. Purchase cultivars.

USE A large tree, ginkgo is often considered only for the open expanses of parks, but it is extremely well adapted to city street conditions (upright forms are available) and, when placed properly, is a beautiful addition to a home garden. Ginkgos fit easily in a front or back yard. Its brilliant yellow color outside a window is a welcome sight in autumn.

SELECTIONS Cultivars are preferable to the species because of their uniform habit and the fact that female trees have a powerful and unpleasant fruit odor and can cause skin rashes.

'Lakeview' is a male tree (named for Cleveland's Lakeview Cemetery) with a tight, conical form, 45 feet tall and 25 feet wide. Overall shape is narrowly pyramidal.

'Maygar', another male tree, has a uniform upright branching habit, grows to 60 feet tall, and is extremely tolerant of city conditions.

'Princeton Sentry', male, has an upright form that makes it ideal for street use. Selected in 1967 from a seedling of **'Fastigiata',** it grows 65 feet tall, 30 feet wide.

Ginkgo biloba.

GLEDITSIA TRIACANTHOS COMMON HONEY LOCUST *Fabaceae*
(Pea family)

This lovely native tree from the Central states has become too popular and is overused as an ornamental. It has bright green, compound or doubly compound leaves which have little fall color, but are fine enough that they do not require raking when they fall. However, the long, reddish brown fruit pods, to 18 inches in length, may create a litter problem. The common name "honey locust" refers to the sweet gummy substance found in the pods, which also has a sweet edible flesh. At Holden Arboretum, three specimens line the entrance drive. They were planted in 1964 and are in fine condition, over 60 feet tall. The huge thorns on the trunk and branches contrast well with the surrounding sycamores and sweet gum trees.

BEST CONDITIONS Best in full sun where the soil is rich and moist. Honey locusts thrive under a wide range of conditions, excepting only swampy or desertlike places. Possible salt tolerance. Optimum pH range of 4.5-7.5.

PLANTING Easy to transplant. Select plants with healthy looking branches and foliage. Fall plantings at Holden have done well. Water until established.

ROUTINE CARE Avoid overwatering and fertilizing, which promotes overly vigorous, soft growth.

PRUNING Prune out dead branches in fall. Avoid pruning too late in the season, stimulating young growth which will be subject to cold damage. Destroy infected branches. If allowed to grow naturally, this tree has low sweeping branches, but these are often pruned out to allow people to walk underneath.

PESTS, DISEASES, OTHER PROBLEMS Honey locusts are susceptible to a host of pests and diseases. These have proliferated partly because so many honey locusts were planted to replace the American elms lost to Dutch elm disease in the 1950s and 60s. It is wise to plant a diversity of trees. Perhaps the worst problem is an aggressive canker, *Thysonectria austroamericana,* which causes wilt, cankers or both. Affected branches must be removed and burned. In the Midwest other serious problems include mimosa webworm, which can defoliate a tree, and honey locust borer, which tunnels beneath the bark, sometimes girdling the trunk. Roots can be shallow, and in some cases have been known to upheave sidewalks and paths.

PROPAGATION Scarify seeds in concentrated sulfuric acid for one to two hours, rinse, and sow. Cultivars are budded onto seedling stock in the nursery.

USE A beautiful if overused shade or street tree. The delicate nature of the leaves allows enough sun to filter through, allowing grass to flourish underneath. Healthy specimens may live for 125-175 years.

SELECTIONS The most commonly grown cultivars are of the thornless common honey locust, **G. t. var. inermis.** These have been used extensively as a substitute for American elms.

'Imperial' is somewhat resistant to webworm. The reddish brown bark separates into long vertical plates. Holden's specimen spreads widely, with a full, rounded crown at almost 40 years old; 35-50 feet tall.

'Moraine', selected in 1937, is both thornless and fruitless. The Holden specimen, planted in 1964, is now about 50 feet, but may reach 70-90 feet with a broad crown. One of the most resistant to webworm.

'Sunburst' is thornless, with beautiful golden yellow leaves that gradually turn dark green. Unfortunately it is very susceptible to webworm. Two specimens at Holden planted in 1954 and 1960 are upright and spreading, with good reddish brown bark. Interesting crooked branches in winter.

'Skyline' has a pyramidal habit with a strong central leader reaching 70-90 feet. At Holden three specimens were planted in 1968 in full sun, where the soil is moist. Their attractive shape provides winter as well as summer interest.

'Perfection' may reach 70-90 feet. It has a good branch structure and its crown is a little broader than 'Skyline'. A young tree (1987) at Holden has smooth bark with prominent lenticels. Its companions are *Juniperus chinensis* 'Saybrook Gold' and *Spiraea salicifolia;* together they provide an effective grouping.

GYMNOCLADUS DIOICUS KENTUCKY COFFEE TREE *Fabaceae (Pea family)*

The sturdy branches and compound bipinnate leaves of the Kentucky coffee tree make it light and airy, allowing sun to stream through; it is the perfect tree for the south side of a home or other structure for winter solar gain. Flowers in spring are small and only slightly fragrant. In fall, leaves turn lemon yellow and large

GYMNOCLADUS DIOICUS (KENTUCKY COFFEE TREE) Deciduous. 10 years: 10-12 feet; 20 years: 20-25 feet; 50 years: 50-60 feet; maturity: to 80 feet. Open habit with large branches and compound green leaves; thick pulpy pods appear in fall. Tolerates drought and pollution; full sun is best, light shade is acceptable. Zones 4-8.

HALESIA CAROLINA (CAROLINA SILVERBELL) Deciduous. 10 years: 10 feet; 20 years: 15-18 feet; 50 years: 30-35 feet; maturity: to 40 feet. Rounded habit with green foliage that turns yellow in fall and bell-shaped white flowers in May. Sun or partial shade, rich well-drained acidic or neutral soil; does not tolerate alkaline soil, salt, or compacted soils. Zones 5-8.

HAMAMELIS VIRGINIANA (COMMON WITCH-HAZEL) Deciduous. 10 years: 6 feet; 20 years: 12 feet; 50 years: 20-25 feet; maturity: to 30 feet. Irregularly spreading shrub or small tree with thin crooked branches that are covered in fragrant yellow blossoms in late autumn, at the same time green leaves turn yellow. Full sun or partial shade, moist soil. Zones 4-8.

HIPPOPHAE RHAMNOIDES (SEA BUCKTHORN) Deciduous. 10 years: 10 feet; 20 years: 18 feet; 50 years: 25-30 feet; maturity: to 30 feet. Loose and irregular shape, silvery leaves turn green in summer, bright orange berries in early fall through winter. Sun or partial shade, any soil; tolerates salt, seashore conditions. Zones 3-8.

There are trees that are all a-strain upward like a prayer; there are trees that rise only to flow eternally downward, drooping like death; there are trees that are all a-twist, an agony of contortion, writhing, serpenting now towards earth and now towards sky, inwards and outwards, upwards and downwards, tortured, uncertain lives, very dreadful and very beautiful: but in all trees there is beauty, and the birds of God rest and nest and sing in all.
STEPHEN MACKENNA,
JOURNAL AND LETTERS

thick pods that some people consider ornamental mature on female trees; the pods may persist through winter. The bark is attractive, acquiring an alligator-skin look as it matures. One of its best characteristics, its bold, picturesque winter silhouette, is often overlooked, partly because it does not develop at an early age. Kentucky coffee tree, naturally found on low bottom lands, is a slow-growing tree (1 foot per year), but it is consequently very strong. Although a coffee substitute was made from roasted seeds by early pioneers, recent research has shown seeds and leaves to be carcinogenic.

BEST CONDITIONS This tree needs full sun. It does very well in the heavy, clay soil of the Midwest if the soil is moist and fertile. Zones 3-8. It tolerates salt, high and low pH, and dry soil.

PLANTING Kentucky coffee tree is best planted in spring from balled-and-burlapped specimens. Keep the mature size in mind when planting. This tree has many stems rather than a central leader. It will have few branches before leafing out, but the large leaves make it appear larger during the growing season.

ROUTINE CARE Of easy culture. Water once a week until established and during dry spells. Addition of fertilizer can speed growth rate. Mulching is beneficial.

PRUNING Remove any dead or crossing branches that may appear. Do not cut branches back severely or limb up low branches; insect and disease problems may result and since the wood is strong there is no danger of falling branches.

PESTS, DISEASES, OTHER PROBLEMS None serious.

PROPAGATION Propagation is difficult; purchase plants.

USE This is an underused tree; recommended for its large compound leaves that turn yellow and drop in fall and its interesting bark and dramatic silhouette in winter. It is a tough plant, resistant to poor soil, infrequent flooding, heat, and drought. Although some people dislike litter caused by the pods, these are easily removed with a bag attachment on a mower. Try rubbing the seeds on concrete and then placing them on your forearms.

SELECTIONS 'Variegata' has variegated leaves. Researchers are working on finding a fruitless male clone.

HALESIA CAROLINA CAROLINA SILVERBELL *Styracaceae (Styrax family)*

An understory tree in its native southeastern U.S., Carolina snowbell may reach 50 feet in cultivation. The snowbells are valued for their attractive white flowers in late spring, which appear just as the leaves are emerging. These are followed in early fall by yellowish green winged fruits that become brown at maturity. The young bark of the Carolina snowbell is smooth but has an interesting striped quality that reaches up into the canopy on some older branches. It has been noted that multistemmed specimens retain this striping much longer than single-trunk plants. Older trees have a blocky bark. The genus is named for the English clergyman Stephen Hales.

BEST CONDITIONS Plant in full sun or partial shade for best results. Ideally the soil should be rich and well drained, acidic to neutral, with plenty of organic matter to retain moisture. In alkaline soils, Carolina snowbell displays chlorotic foliage. They are sensitive to compacted clay soil and have a low tolerance to salt.

PLANTING Plant young container-grown or balled-and-burlapped stock in spring. Avoid undue disturbance of the deep lateral roots. Water well and mulch.

ROUTINE CARE Water during periods of drought.

Halesia carolina.

PRUNING Prune to shape and to remove crossing branches only.

PESTS, DISEASES, OTHER PROBLEMS None serious; good pest resistance. However, the tree is weak wooded and sometimes loses many branches during storms.

PROPAGATION Seeds display double dormancy and must be cold and then warm stratified, or scarified to induce germination. Seed sown in fall will take 18 months to germinate. Cuttings taken in late spring and treated with rooting hormone are easily propagated.

USE This lovely small tree combines well in shrub and woodland borders and is especially compatible with rhododendrons, azaleas and redvein enkianthus, which enjoy similar conditions. In the autumn, the yellow fall color of the Carolina snowbell contrasts well with the red foliaged enkianthus. Carolina snowbell is good for up-close viewing especially from underneath, where one can look up into the bell-shaped flowers from a sitting area, perhaps on a patio or terrace. It trains easily into a single trunk as a shade tree or lawn specimen, or can be grown multi-stemmed in more informal places.

SELECTIONS *H. c.* '**Rosea**' has pink-tinged flowers. Hot weather tends to reduce color intensity.

H. monticola, mountain snowbell, is a larger plant to 60-80 feet tall, with bigger flowers. It has a conical treelike habit, with strong single or double leaders. *H. m.* '**Rosea**' has light pink flowers.

HAMAMELIS WITCH-HAZEL *Hamamelidaceae (Witch-hazel family)*

Witch-hazels are beloved of gardeners for their unusual period of bloom–autumn/winter, or winter, or early spring, depending on variety. The flower petals, which are usually bright yellow, curl into a ball under frost and then unfurl again when the temperature rises–a trick that allows them to survive temperatures that would kill other blossoms. The flowers of many cultivars have an appealing spicy fragrance, and the clear, bright green foliage sometimes turns yellow or bright orange in midautumn. Although most are considered shrubs, tree forms exist.

BEST CONDITIONS Witch-hazel does best when provided with at least partial shade and will grow in any slightly acid to slightly alkaline, ordinary soil, supplemented with well-composted organic matter.

PLANTING Plant in fall or early spring. In clay soils, plant high in a shallow hole.

Ilex opaca.

Take special care in choosing a site, for witch-hazels have deep root systems and are difficult to move. *H. virginiana* is easier to move, and other species are often grafted onto it.

ROUTINE CARE Water well during establishment, particularly during the first two summers. Fertilizing witch-hazel is not only unnecessary, but can be harmful.

PRUNING Prune weak V-crotches. For an early hint of spring, prune late-winter bloomers in winter and force flowers indoors (but be prepared for heavy fragrance).

PROPAGATION Witch-hazels are difficult to propagate from seed unless seed capsules are harvested in early autumn, before seeds are ejected, and placed in paper bags to open. The seeds, when planted fresh, will germinate the following spring. However, if the seeds are stored, they require a complex stratification process to restore them to viability.

PESTS, DISEASES, OTHER PROBLEMS Witch-hazels are very disease resistant, although gall-forming and leaf-folding insects are occasional problems, as are leafspot diseases. Grafted trees often sprout from below the graft and need to be removed.

USE Tree-form witch-hazels make effective screens, backdrops, or specimen plants. They blend well in woodland settings.

SELECTIONS *H. japonica,* Japanese witch-hazel, grows to 30 feet tall and wide. The foliage of *H. x intermedia* turns reddish in fall. Cultivars like **'Arnold's Promise'** (yellow flowers) and **'Copper Beauty'** (copper flowers) grow 15-20 feet tall and wide. *H. mollis,* Chinese witch-hazel, also reaches 30 feet tall and is one of the hardiest species. The cultivar **'Brevipetala'** has fragrant, larger, deep yellow flowers. **'Pallida'** has beautiful, fragrant pale yellow flowers.
H. virginiana can reach 15 feet in height; leaves turn bright yellow after flowering.

HIPPOPHAE RHAMNOIDES SEA BUCKTHORN *Elaeagnaceae (Oleaster family)*

The sea buckthorn is named for its ability to withstand seashore conditions, where its abundant, bright orange berries and willowy silver leaves add color to a sometimes bleak landscape; because the fruit is acidic, it is not devoured by birds. It rarely grows above 15 feet tall (though it can attain 30 feet in height), but often spreads to 8 feet wide. Both male and female plants are needed to produce fruit. This plant is used more in England than in North America.

BEST CONDITIONS Hardy in Zones 3-8, sea buckthorn will grow in almost any soil, in sun or partial shade. It is exceptionally tolerant of salt and sandy soil.

PLANTING Difficult to transplant; more successful from young plants.

ROUTINE CARE No additional water or fertilizer is needed once established.

PRUNING Little pruning is necessary; prune lightly in spring.

PROPAGATION Propagate from cuttings. Seeds can be sown in a cold frame in the fall or stored and then stratified for spring sowing.

PESTS, DISEASES, OTHER PROBLEMS None serious.

USE An excellent specimen or screen tree, sea buckthorn is useful inland as well as near the shore for its orange fruit and silver foliage.

ILEX HOLLY *Aquifoliaceae (Holly family)*

With their well-shaped leaves and showy, berrylike fruit, hollies are a major factor in the winter garden. Since ancient times, the word *holly* has been virtually synonymous with the holiday season. The ever-festive Romans decked their

ILEX AQUIFOLIUM 'GOLDEN QUEEN' (ENGLISH HOLLY) Evergreen. 10 years: 5-7 feet; 20 years: 10-15 feet; 50 years: 25-30 feet; maturity: to 40 feet. Pyramidal form with densely packed branches, handsome shiny dark green leaves, abundant bright red berries. Full sun to half shade, moist fertile acid soils. Zones 6-8.

ILEX ATTENUATA (HOLLY) Evergreen. 10 years: 4-5 feet; 20 years: 8-10 feet; 50 years: 20-25 feet; maturity: to 35 feet. Pyramidal form with densely packed branches, dull, dark green, spiny leaves, bright red or yellow berries. Full sun to half shade, moist fertile acid soils. Zones 5-8.

ILEX OPACA (AMERICAN HOLLY) Evergreen. 10 years: 5-7 feet; 20 years: 10-15 feet; 50 years: 25-30 feet; maturity: to 40 feet. Pyramidal form with densely packed branches, dull, dark green, spiny leaves, red berries. Full sun to half shade, moist fertile acid soils. Zones 5-9.

JUGLANS NIGRA 'ELMER MEYERS' (BLACK WALNUT) Deciduous. 10 years: 12 feet; 20 years: 25 feet; 55-65 years: 70-90 feet; maturity: to 90 feet. Straight trunk, open rounded or oval crown, compound leaves and large edible nuts. Best in full sun, deep, rich moist soil; tolerates dry soil. Zones 4-9.

SACRED TREES

It seems likely that sacred groves were among the first places of worship, and that woods were the oldest temples. Tree worship played an essential role in the religious history of our world; in some places it continued until abolished by Christian missionaries in the Middle Ages.

The Egyptians revered the wild fig tree, the Assyrians the date palm, an image of their Tree of Life. The ancient Romans worshiped the sacred fig tree of Romulus, jealously guarded in the Forum. The yew was considered holy to peoples in ancient Britain. In Ireland and elsewhere in northern Europe it was the rowan or European mountain ash (*Sorbus aucuparia*), believed to ward off evil influences and made Thor's helper in myth.

The most sacred tree of ancient Europe was the oak, associated with the highest gods of many religions, the gods of the sky, rain, and thunder. The oracle of Zeus was an oak grove at Dodona near Epirus, where the god's will was revealed by the rustling of the oak leaves, interpreted by priests.

Worship of trees, notably oak and holly, is most closely associated with the Druids, the learned and priestly class of ancient Celtic Britain, Ireland, and Gaul and probably of all ancient Celtic peoples. The Druids were the leaders of a highly ritualistic religion that probably included animal and human sacrifice. They believed in the immortality and transmigration of the soul. They handed down their learning orally, the education of a Druid requiring as much as 20 years. The Druids conducted their rites in oak groves; oak, holly, and the mistletoe that grows on oak were sacred to them—the use of mistletoe in Christmas decorations is a reminder of the Druid religion.

Saturnalia gifts with it, and the Druids considered it a "holy" plant—which may explain the derivation of its common name. There are both evergreen and deciduous hollies; evergreen varieties are slower growing. Although most hollies are used as shrubs, several species are tall, even towering, trees with single central trunks. Hollies bear male and female flowers on separate plants, and both should be present to obtain fruit. Plant one male for every five female plants.

BEST CONDITIONS Hollies do well in full sun to half shade in any moist, fertile, acid soil (pH can range from 5.0-6.0). Avoid windy, dry, or exposed sites. At Chicago Botanic Garden *I. opaca* can be grown with protection from winter wind and sun.

PLANTING Look for well-shaped, strong vigorous plants with healthy, dark green foliage. Spring planting is best, but fall is fine in warmer climates. Holly is easy to transplant because it has a shallow root system. Prepare the ground fully before planting; if the soil is high in clay content, dig a hole twice as big as the rootball and add well-composted organic matter plus a conditioner like coarse sand, brick, or rubble to improve aeration. Make sure the earth is firm before you plant. Mulch immediately and stake as needed.

ROUTINE CARE Water well the first two years; thereafter water only if the soil dries out. Fertilize generously, particularly evergreens, with a high-nitrogen (10-6-4) fertilizer or manure until well established; annual fertilization in spring is beneficial even after establishment.

PRUNING Pruning is not necessary, but if you wish to restrict size, prune once or twice a year, in winter.

PESTS, DISEASES, OTHER PROBLEMS Some hollies are susceptible to leaf miners, holly midges, aphids, scale, red spider mites, root nematodes, and leafspot, but most are generally free of serious pests. Good siting and culture are essential to maintaining health and vigor.

PROPAGATION Propagate by cuttings, layering, or grafting. It is possible to obtain results from seeds, but you'll need to stratify, and germination can take up to 18 months.

USE Eminently useful at the back of the shrub border, hollies—especially those with a pyramidal habit—make fine specimen plants as well.

SELECTIONS *I. x altaclarensis* **'James G. Esson'** has spiny leaves and fruits that persist through winter. It grows 15-25 feet tall and can be propagated by cuttings taken in late fall. It is the only female cultivar with a male name.

I. aquifolium, English holly, has the form and berries most closely associated with hollies. It will grow to 70 feet in the right situation, and is cultivated commercially. Its leaves and berries are larger and shinier than *I. opaca,* but it is hardy only to Zone 6.

I. attenuata grows 50-60 feet tall and has a pyramidal form and bright red or yellow berries.

I. opaca, American holly, has dull dark green leaves. American holly is native to the eastern seaboard and the southern states, in sandy soil, but is more tolerant of clay soils than many other species. It will grow to a 20- to 40-foot tree. Among the best selections are **'Old Heavy Berry'**, **'Jersey Knight'**, **'Wyetta'**, and **'Jersey Princess'**. **'Wyetta'**, which has luminous dark green leaves and showy fruit, grows 15-20 feet tall and 7-10 feet wide. It is faster growing than the species and attains a pyramidal form. **'Canary'** bears yellow fruit and grows 20-30 feet tall and wide; it is tolerant of air pollution but susceptible to many pests and diseases, the most serious of which are leaf miner and scale. Zones 5-9.

I. pedunculosa, longstalk holly, grows 15-30 feet tall in cultivation, is hardy in Zones 5-8, and is more tolerant of poor soil and adverse conditions than most species. It has beautiful shiny green foliage and lovely red fruit that attracts birds in October and November. This graceful tree has a dense habit but is loose enough to display its berries. Dorthe Hviid of Berkshire Botanical Gardens considers it the best holly for cold climates.

JUGLANS NIGRA BLACK WALNUT *Juglandaceae (Walnut family)*

The word *juglans* is derived from *Jovis glans*–Jupiter's acorn, and the name dates to Roman times. Walnuts are considered invaluable for gunstocks because of their light weight, elasticity, lack of warpage, and smoothness. They have been used for their nuts, medicinal properties, dyes, confections, and candies. Because its beautiful wood is in such great demand for fine furniture, the majority of naturally occurring black walnuts have been harvested. The trees, which are native to North America from Massachusetts to Florida and west to South Dakota and Texas, occur in mixed hardwood forests and grow to 30-150 feet (the most common are about 100 feet tall). As ornamentals, they are valued for their occasional fall color and longevity.

BEST CONDITIONS Walnuts grow best in full sun on moist, rich land. They are hardy in Zones 4-9.

PLANTING Walnuts have deep taproots; containerized plants are the best choices. Plan placement carefully because taprooted walnuts are difficult to move.

ROUTINE CARE Water until established and during dry times thereafter. Addition of fertilizer will speed growth. Mulch is beneficial during establishment.

PRUNING Prune when young for a well-formed tree structure.

PESTS, DISEASES, OTHER PROBLEMS Walnut caterpillar and fall webworms can be problems. Many trees are free of these maladies, but if affected, check with your local botanic garden, arboreta, university, or extension agent for proper controls. Once clean, they may not need further treatment. Walnuts also cause problems for other plants; see sidebar at right.

PROPAGATION Purchase plants.

USE Walnuts are most often planted for fruit production, but can also be planted long term for harvesting its valuable lumber; individuals with land who wish to leave a legacy could plant walnuts for future generations. Due to the allelopathic (growth-inhibiting effect) properties of this tree, it should be sited carefully.

SELECTIONS *J. n.* 'Emma K.' was selected for size, quality, and quantity of tasty fruits. Ornamentally, it often displays attractive yellow fall color.

J. n. 'Laciniata' has a very attractive form with deeply dissected leaves that give the plant an open and airy appearance.

J. cinerea, butternut, is a round-topped tree producing sweet nuts; it has a mature height of 40-60 feet. The tree lives 80-90 years and grows 40-60 feet tall.

J. regia, English walnut, has an open crown reaching 40-60 feet tall. It produces tasty thin-walled nuts sold in stores. 'Hansen' performs particularly well at Chicago Botanic Garden; its nuts are of high quality. English walnut prefers moderately moist to dry, but not wet soil. It differs from black walnut in that it has an odd number of leaflets.

ALLELOPATHY

Walnut trees exude a toxic chemical called juglone into soil from fallen bark, leaves, and fruits. This chemical has allelopathic, or growth-inhibiting, properties that can cause plants within root range of walnut trees to fail and die. For this reason, walnuts are usually planted as single specimens. However, some plants are tolerant of juglone and will do well under walnut trees. Galen Gates has compiled the following list of plants that have shown resistance under mature trees for a minimum of 10 years and up to 25 years.

Aquilegia canadensis (wild columbine)
Arisaema triphyllum (Jack-in-the-pulpit)
Asarum canadense (wild ginger)
Cerastium tomentosum (snow-in-summer)
Cercis canadensis (redbud)
Convallaria majalis (lily-of-the-valley)
Cydonia oblonga (quince)
Daucus carota (queen Anne's lace)
Echinacea purpurea (purple coneflower)
Euonymus europaea (European spindle tree)
Forsythia x intermedia (forsythia)
Galium odoratum (sweet woodruff)
Hedera helix (English ivy)
Hesperis matronalis (dame's rocket)
Hosta (hosta)
Iris x *germanica* (bearded iris)
Juniperus virginiana (eastern redcedar)
Ligustrum vulgare (privet)
Lonicera tatarica (Tatarian honeysuckle)
Lunaria annua (money plant)
Lychnis coronaria (rose campion)
Lysimachia nummularia (moneywort)
Phaseolus vulgaris (beans)
Poa pratensis (Kentucky bluegrass)
Phlox divaricata (blue phlox)
Phlox paniculata (garden phlox)
Polygonatum commutatum (Solomon's seal)
Ranunculus (buttercup)
Rubus occidentalis (black raspberry)
Sanguinaria canadensis (bloodroot)
Senecio aureus (golden ragwort)
Taraxacum officinale (dandelions)
Viburnum lantana (wayfaring tree)
Viola (violet)
Zea mays (corn)
Zinnia elegans (zinnia)

Juniperus communis.

JUNIPERUS JUNIPER *Cupressaceae (Cypress family)*

Junipers have vastly varied habits. Some, like *J. virginiana*, are the exclamation points of the tree world; tall and narrow, they fit into places where few other significant trees would have a chance. At the opposite end of the range are prostrate forms that serve as groundcovers. Juniper cones look like small blueberries; they are edible and are used as a flavoring for gin.

BEST CONDITIONS Less fussy than many other conifers, junipers tolerate city pollution and dry conditions and will accept dry or heavy clay soils. They do, however, prefer full sun (they become straggly in shade), and moderately moist soils.

PLANTING Plant in spring or fall. They are somewhat difficult to transplant, but are usually fine if planted from containerized or balled-and-burlapped plants.

ROUTINE CARE No special treatment is required.

PRUNING Most types naturally form a rigid column. Some types can be left unpruned for a less formal effect.

PROPAGATION Junipers can be propagated by seeds sown in fall (stratification is necessary), cuttings taken in winter, and grafts made in late winter and early spring.

PESTS, DISEASES, OTHER PROBLEMS When planted near trees in the rose family (like hawthorns and crabapples) junipers are susceptible to cedar apple rust; they also host this rust and can spread it to members of the rose family. Twig blight, mites, and bagworms can often be controlled with mild spraying if caught early.

USE Junipers make excellent anchors to flowerbeds or shrub borders. Planted in rows, they provide a neat, formal effect. They are often used in rock gardens.

SELECTIONS *J. chinensis,* Chinese juniper, cultivars include **'Columnaris'** and **'Hetzi'** (upright varieties that grow to about 15 feet); **'Mint Julep'**, a dwarf with mint green needles; **'Obelisk'**, which has steel blue needles; and **'Pfitzerana'**, a spreading variety.

J. communis, common juniper, tolerates just about any abuse that is heaped on it. It usually grows 5-10 feet tall in most home landscapes and spreads as wide; it is a useful groundcover for areas where little else will grow.

J. rigida, needle juniper, is an upright tree with a more open, picturesque habit than most junipers. It has sharp, bright green needles on pendulous branchlets and a slightly exfoliating bark. 40-45 feet tall.

J. scopulorum, Rocky Mountain juniper, Colorado redcedar, forms a narrow pyramid 30-40 feet tall and 3-15 feet wide; many cultivars have attractive blue-green or gray-green foliage. This species is the most drought-tolerant of the tree-form junipers. It performs best in the West, where air is drier.

J. virginiana, Eastern redcedar, grows 40-50 feet tall and spreads 8-12 feet. It transplants easily (especially if planted from container stock and root pruned) and tolerates rocky and alkaline soils. ***J. v. var. creba*** has a conical habit.

KALOPANAX PICTUS CASTOR ARALIA *Araliaceae (Aralia family)*

Not commonly available but worth seeking for its impressive rounded outline, castor aralia is an unusual tree that usually grows 40-50 feet tall (sometimes 80 feet). It is an imposing specimen with large, 5- to 7-lobed tropical leaves up to 12 inches across. The leaves are maplelike and afford good shade; in fall they turn warm yellow. The tree is somewhat sparse when young, fills out with age.

BEST CONDITIONS Full sun is best. Castor aralia tolerates well-drained and heavy

JUNIPERUS CHINENSIS 'HETZI GLAUCA' (CHINESE JUNIPER)
Evergreen. 10 years: 4 feet; 20 years: 8 feet; 50 years: 10 feet; maturity: to 12 feet. Upright, spreading form, light blue-green awl-shaped leaves, bluish berries. Full sun or partial shade, slightly alkaline soil. Zone 4.

JUNIPERUS SCOPULORUM 'CUPRESSIFOLIA ERECTA' (ROCKY MOUNTAIN JUNIPER) Evergreen. 10 years: 8 feet; 20 years: 15 feet; 50 years: 30-35 feet; maturity: to 45 feet. Narrow pyramidal form. Flat-pressed leaves in light green, gray-green, blue-green, or dark green. Full sun, slightly acid to alkaline well-drained soil; tolerates adverse conditons. Zones 5-8.

JUNIPERUS VIRGINIANA 'CANAERTII' (EASTERN REDCEDAR)
Evergreen. 10 years: 8-12 feet; 20 years: 17-25 feet; 50 years: 45 feet; maturity: to 60 feet. Picturesque form with dense branches covered in scalelike needles, small purplish berries. Full sun, slightly acid to alkaline well-drained soil; tolerates adverse conditions. Zones 2-8.

KALOPANAX PICTUS (CASTOR ARALIA) Deciduous. 10 years: 12-15feet; 20 years: 25-30 feet; 50 years: 50-60 feet; maturity: to 70 feet. Round clusters of small flowers in large umbels (flowers in summer); large lobed leaves turn yellow in fall; small black seedlike fruits. Deep rich moist soil, full sun. Zones 4-8.

Juniperus virginiana 'Caneartii'.

soils, acid and alkaline. It has survived occasional flooding at Chicago Botanic Garden. Zones 4-7.

PLANTING Purchase young plants. Plant in spring or fall.

ROUTINE CARE After establishment, water only during dry spells. Mulch to preserve moisture.

PRUNING Prune to develop a well-rounded tree outline.

PESTS, DISEASES, OTHER PROBLEMS None serious. Thorns are not problematic because trees are usually limbed up.

PROPAGATION Seeds can be sown directly into the ground.

USE Castor aralia is a welcome sight in the heat of summer when huge (12- to 24-inch) white flower clusters cover the tree. This is a pest-free tree with large leaves and a good branching habit; it deserves greater attention and use for summer shade and winter sun in the North.

SELECTIONS The variety **K. p. var. *maximowiczii*** has deeply lobed leaves.

KOELREUTERIA GOLDEN-RAIN TREE *Sapindaceae (Soapberry family)*

This beautiful shade tree, also known as "varnish tree," is originally native to China, Korea, and Japan, and bears multitudes of fragrant yellow blossoms in 12- to 15-inch clusters in the early summer–it is one of the few yellow-flowering trees. It derives its common name from the "golden rain" of spent blossoms that carpet the ground. The flowers are followed by 2-inch brown and papery seed pods shaped like balloons; they turn from green to pink to brown. The golden rain tree grows 30-40 feet tall with a spread of 25 feet.

BEST CONDITIONS Golden-rain tree needs full sun, but can be grown in any well-drained soil, including alkaline types. It is hardy in Zones 5-8. It tolerates heat, wind, and air pollution.

PLANTING Look for small trees that are strong and vigorous and have good branching patterns. Trees up to 12 feet tall can be planted bare-rooted; they need room for their deep root systems. Trees over 12 feet tall should be planted with their roots balled-and-burlapped.

ROUTINE CARE Mature trees can withstand drought, but water generously for the first two years and then during dry periods. Fertilize only if soil is poor.

PRUNING While older trees seldom need pruning, stake and prune young golden-rain trees to promote high branching and prune weaker branches. The wood of the golden rain tree is somewhat weak.

PROPAGATION Propagate golden rain by root cuttings taken in December; seeds must be scarified and stratified.

PESTS, DISEASES, OTHER PROBLEMS Although usually disease- and pest-free, golden-rain tree can be susceptible to root rot, wilt, leaf spot, canker and coral-spot fungus.

USE Golden rain tree makes a beautiful lawn decoration, both for the beauty of its blooms and the interest of its foliage; its leaflets unfold in red, turn purplish in spring, and yellow in the autumn. Try it in a spot where its flowers can be viewed from below. Because it tolerates air pollution, it is also a good candidate for planting on an urban or suburban street. Because it is deep rooted, golden rain tree can be planted on a lawn with annuals and perennials beneath it. It is also fast growing: an 8-foot tree will more than double its height in five years.

SELECTIONS *K. paniculata* is described above. A cultivar of golden-rain tree, *K. p.* 'September', flowers in late summer, extending the blooming period. Another cultivar, **'Fastigata'**, is narrow and columnar in habit. *K. bipinnata* (Chinese flame-gold tree) grows 30-40 feet tall, bears yellow blossoms in quantity, and bright pinkish seed pods shaped like Chinese lanterns. It does best in Zones 8-10. *K. elegans* (Flamegood) is best grown in Zone 9 and is not as hardy as either of the other two species.

NOTE This tree is considered a weed in the South and is not recommended there.

LABURNUM GOLDEN-CHAIN TREE, BEANTREE *Fabaceae (Pea family)*

For a two-week period in midspring, laburnum are covered with long, hanging clusters of pealike flowers; although they produce no ornamental fruit, have foliage that is too open to provide shade, are poisonous, and drop their leaves before autumn, this display of flowers is showy enough to keep them popular. In the Pacific Northwest, many consider them to be the best ornamental tree.

BEST CONDITIONS Most laburnums are hardy to Zone 6; *L. x watereri* is hardy to Zone 4. It prefers fertile soil and full sun, but will tolerate some shade and most soils that are at least somewhat fertile and very well drained.

PLANTING Plant in spring or fall; amend soil before planting and water generously.

ROUTINE CARE Keep soil evenly moist and somewhat fertile for the first few years after planting.

KOELREUTERIA PANICULATA (GOLDEN-RAIN TREE) Deciduous. 10 years: 8 feet; 20 years: 15 feet; 50 years: to 30 feet; maturity: 40 feet. Open, rounded tree with upright pyramidal clusters of yellow flowers in early summer. Full sun, any well-drained soil (acid to alkaline). Zones 5-9.

LABURNUM X WATERERI 'VOSSII' (GOLDEN CHAIN TREE, BEAN TREE) Deciduous. 10 years: 10 feet; 20 years: 20 feet. Short-lived tree. Long, drooping racemes of golden flowers in spring; Fertile soil and full sun, but will tolerate some shade and most soils that are at least somewhat fertile and very well drained. Zones 6-8.

LARIX DECIDUA (EUROPEAN LARCH) Deciduous. 10 years: 18 feet; 20 years: 30 feet; 50 years: 60-65 feet; maturity: to 80 feet. Open pyramidal forms becomes irregular with age. Needlelike foliage turns yellow in fall. Full sun or light shade, most soils; tolerates wet soils. Zones 3-7.

LARIX LARICINA (EASTERN LARCH, TAMARACK) Deciduous. 10 years: 18 feet; 20 years: 30 feet; 50 years: 60-65 feet; maturity: to 80 feet. Very open pyramidal form with horizontal branches covered in needles that turn yellow in fall. Full sun or light shade, any soil; tolerates wet soils. Zones 2-6.

PRUNING Remove sucker shoots.

PROPAGATION Propagate by seeds sown in spring.

PESTS, DISEASES, OTHER PROBLEMS Aphids and twig blight can be problematic.

USE Laburnums are used as part of tree borders, as backgrounds to beds, or near buildings; they steal the show for a few weeks and then blend in quietly.

SELECTIONS *L. alpinum* is the hardiest variety, to Zone 5.

L. x watereri produces larger flowers, in longer chains, than most, and they are of a deeper yellow color. Hardy to Zone 6.

LARIX LARCH *Pinaceae (Pine family)*

Introduced to the United States by the early colonists, the larch is a graceful deciduous tree with drooping branchlets. Twenty years after planting, it bears cones that remain on the tree for years, adding to its ornamental beauty. Native to the colder parts of the northern hemisphere, European larch can grow to a height of 100 feet, spreading 40 feet wide. It grows in a pyramidal shape, with loose, open foliage and most selections provide excellent golden yellow color in fall.

BEST CONDITIONS Larch thrives in full sun and well-drained, moist, acid soil; it does not appreciate shade or polluted air. It does best in Zones 2-6.

PLANTING Look for strong, vigorous, well-shaped plants and transplant in late fall. Larch transplants easily when dormant.

ROUTINE CARE Keep larch moist, mulching in dry spells; an organic mulch provides fertility.

PRUNING Prune in midsummer to shape.

PROPAGATION Propagate by seeds that are cold stratified.

PESTS, DISEASES, OTHER PROBLEMS Unfortunately, larches are prey to a number of pests, the most common and serious being larch case bearer, woolly larch aphid, rust, and canker.

USE Its handsome shape and foliage make it a fine tree for background planting; it can also be used successfully as a screen. Most larches are very large, and are most suitable for large yards or public spaces.

SELECTIONS *L. decidua,* European larch is native to mid and northern Europe. It grows to 100 feet tall and 40 feet wide. *L. d.* **'Pendula',** a cultivar, has horizontal, pendulous branchlets, and is extremely graceful; the soft droop of the tree is even more emphatic in another cultivar, **'Polinica',** whose branches and branchlets hang down. Zones 3-7.

L. laricina (Eastern larch or tamarack) is native to the northern United States and Canada, and has red scaly bark and very small cones. A hardy tree, it needs plenty of moisture and grows best in Zones 2-6 (Zone 8 in Pacific Northwest). It turns bright yellow in the fall.

L. kaempferi (Japanese larch) needs to be grown in moist acid soil and full sun, and thrives in Zones 5-6. Its beautiful needles form star patterns, that are bright green in spring and turn a lovely yellow in fall.

LIQUIDAMBAR STYRACIFLUA SWEET GUM *Hamamelidaceae (Witch-hazel family)*

Sweet gum is attractive in the summer and smashing in the fall, when its large green maplelike leaves turn bright red, purple, and orange. The tree grows to 75

MYTHOLOGY

Trees often appear in the myths of the ancient Greeks. Aside from the oak sacred to Zeus, there was the olive tree of Athena, the cypress of Artemis, the myrtle of Aphrodite, and the laurel of Apollo. A mythical connection was made between each god and his or her tree: Athena, for example, was said to have created the olive; Apollo took the laurel as his tree after the beautiful but chaste huntress Daphne–pursued and almost caught by Apollo–had her prayers answered when she turned into a laurel tree.

When Phaeton, son of Helios, perished trying to drive his father's golden chariot, his three sisters were so overcome with grief that the gods turned them into poplars. And the Thracian princess Phyllis, who killed herself out of love for Demophon, son of Theseus, was changed by the gods into an almond tree.

Trees also appear in Norse mythology. In fact, having just created the earth, sun, and moon, Odin and his brothers walked by the side of the sea and were pleased with what they had done but sensed that something was lacking. So they took an ash tree and made a man out of it and of an alder they made the first woman--the progenitors of the human race. The most important tree in Norse mythology, however, was the Yggdrasill, the Ash of the World, which supported the whole universe, its branches and roots extending into the heavens, the earth, and the underworld. At its top sat an eagle, at its bottom twined a serpent, and between them ran a squirrel breeding discord. It was prophesied that the tree would eventually be destroyed, bringing with it the doom of the gods.

Liriodendron tulipifera.

feet tall and 50 feet wide. The tree has a stong pyramidal shape when young, and later becomes slightly irregularly rounded and upright. The common name sweet gum is derived from the tree's sweet, gummy sap.

BEST CONDITIONS Sweet gums do best in moist, well-drained slightly acid soil and full sun to light shade. They do not tolerate intense city pollution. Zones 6-8.

PLANTING Plant containerized or balled-and-burlapped trees in spring. Sweet gums have fleshy root systems that take some time to establish, so feed and water generously after planting.

ROUTINE CARE Once established, fertilize and water to maintain evenly moist, rich soil.

PRUNING Prune lightly in winter to shape and to remove dead wood.

PROPAGATION Propagate by seeds, which germinate better if cold stratified, or leafy cuttings taken with heels and kept under mist.

PESTS, DISEASES, OTHER PROBLEMS None serious, though sometimes susceptible to webworms and scale. In highly alkaline soils, chlorosis is sometimes a problem. The fruit does not disintegrate and can be messy.

USE Sweet gum is an excellent specimen tree for a medium- or large-sized yard; it does not do well in a small space. It blends well in a natural setting.

SELECTIONS Several cultivars selected for the South; in the North, they produce little fall color and can be damaged by unexpected frost in spring or autumn.

'Moraine' has particularly good fall color as well as a more uniform oval habit; it grows somewhat faster than the species. Coldhardier than most.

'Variegata' has yellow-marked leaves.

'Festival' has a more columnar habit than the species.

'Gumball' is a dwarf form, up to 15 feet tall, good for small gardens.

'Rotundiloba' has rounded leaves, and does not produce fruit—a real plus.

LIRIODENDRON TULIPIFERA TULIP TREE *Magnoliaceae (Magnolia family)*
This handsome native tree is found in the wild from Massachusetts to Wisconsin, and south to Florida and Mississippi. The fossil record shows that in preglacial times it grew in parts of Alaska, Greenland, and Europe. It is one of our tallest natives and may reach 190 feet tall. The unusually-shaped leaves are bright green and turn brilliant yellow in fall. In late spring, greenish yellow and orange, goblet-shaped flowers open, blotched at the base in orange. Regrettably these are often borne too high for close inspection. The wood, sometimes known as yellow poplar or whitewood, was used extensively for furniture and for flooring in colonial times.

BEST CONDITIONS Although tulip trees are often found growing in the wild in woodland conditions, under cultivation they should have full sun. They prefer deep, well-drained, acid soil that is moisture retentive and very organic.

PLANTING Tulip trees do not transplant easily. Best to buy young container-grown stock and plant only in spring. Larger specimens that will be balled and burlapped should be root pruned at least a year in advance. Keep well watered until established.

ROUTINE CARE These trees are somewhat messy and often drop leaves from midsummer on, even when kept moist.

PRUNING Prune to shape or to remove damaged branches in winter. They are susceptible to branch breakage in ice and wind storms.

PESTS, DISEASES, OTHER PROBLEMS Aphids may be a real problem as their secretions

LIQUIDAMBAR STYRACIFLUA (SWEET GUM) Deciduous. 10 years: 15-18 feet; 20 years: 25-30 feet; 50 years: 60 feet; maturity: to 85 feet. Symmetrical pyramidal form, with horizontal branches bearing star-shaped green leaves; excellent fall color. Full sun, moist, well-drained or rocky soil that is not too rich. Zones5-9.

LIRIODENDRON TULIPIFERA (TULIP TREE) Deciduous. 10 years: 20 feet; 20 years: 40 feet; 50 years: 75-80 feet; maturity: to 110 feet. Tall upright irregular oval form with very large horizontal branches and dense, attractively shaped leaves that turn yellow in autumn. Full sun, deep rich moist soil; does not tolerate pollution. Zones 5-9.

MAACKIA AMURENSIS (AMUR MAACKIA) Deciduous. 10 years: 8 feet; 20 years: 15 feet; 50 years: 30-35 feet; maturity: to 55 feet. Small tree with a round head, small compound oval leaflets, interesting exfoliating bark, and a neat outline. Full sun, well-drained soil (acid or alkaline). Zones 4-8.

MACLURA POMIFERA (OSAGE ORANGE) Deciduous. 10 years: 15-18 feet; 20 years: 30-35 feet; 50 years: 40-50 feet; maturity: to 50 feet. 2- to 5-inch-long simple chartreuse green leaves, open oval crown. Tolerates drought, poor soil, wetness, acid and alkaline soils, wind, and pollution. Zones 4-9.

encourage the growth of sooty mold fungus, which is not only unsightly but blocks the pores of the leaves. Cankers and leaf spots may sometimes become serious. Sometimes affected by tulip tree mildew and tulip tree scale. This is a weak-wooded tree and sometimes drops branches after storms.

PROPAGATION Seeds germinate readily after three months of stratification.

USE Although too big for small residential gardens, where there is space in parks and larger landscapes tulip trees are handsome as specimens or grouped in groves.

SELECTIONS 'Aureo-marginatam' has striking variegated leaves rimmed with yellow or greenish yellow. It was introduced into cultivation in the mid 1700s.

'Aureo-pictum' ['Medio-pictum'] has green leaves blotched in the center with yellow. Both names are used.

'Compactum' is a dwarf form with smaller leaves.

'Fastigiatum' is an upright growing form, with branches almost parallel to the main trunk. It grows 50-60 feet tall. Arnold Arboretum has some good specimens.

MAACKIA AMURENSIS AMUR MAACKIA *Fabaceae (Pea family)*

This Asian native from China and Korea is little known in American gardens. It resembles and is closely related to yellowwood. It makes a clean-looking, round-headed tree, which is grown for its shiny, bronze, curled bark which exfoliates in older specimens. The compound dark green leaves have an almost iridescent quality as they emerge in spring. In midsummer, stiff erect racemes of white flowers open, scenting the air with the fragrance of new mown hay.

BEST CONDITIONS Plant in full sun in porous, fertile soil, which can be acid or alkaline. Very tolerant of heat and drought.

PLANTING Not easy to find in the trade but worth looking for. Transplanting is not easy; buy container-grown stock. Mulch.

ROUTINE CARE Keep soil evenly moist and fertile.

PRUNING Prune only to shape young plants and to remove crossing branches.

PESTS, DISEASES, OTHER PROBLEMS None serious.

PROPAGATION Seeds germinate easily after soaking in hot water for several hours. Root cuttings are also successful.

USE This very hardy tree should be sited to show off its interesting bark and midsummer flowers. Possibly good in containers. Rick Lewandowski considers it a possible replacement for sophora, which has developed disease problems.

MACLURA POMIFERA OSAGE ORANGE *Moraceae (Mulberry family)*

The Osage Indians used the bright orange wood of this tree to make bows; others have used the wood for long-lived fence posts, firewood, rustic furniture, and yellow dye. A deciduous tree with glossy green leaves that sometimes turn yellow in fall, Osage orange is a vigorous grower quickly reaching 30-40 or even 60 feet. It is readily identified by the bark's orange cast, 1-inch spines on the branches, and 5-inch yellow-green orangelike fruit.

BEST CONDITIONS Though native to rich bottom lands, this tree is extremely tolerant of difficult growing conditions, such as poor soil, drought, pollution, and harsh climates. It thrives in rich or poor, moist or dry soil of high or low pH in full sun in Zones 4-9.

PLANTING Seek male or thornless varieties. Plant in spring or fall.

ROUTINE CARE Once established, Osage orange will need no additional water or fertilizer. Mulching is beneficial during establishment.

PRUNING Pruning the young tree helps it develop a good form.

PESTS, DISEASES, OTHER PROBLEMS None serious. Fruit and thorns can be problematic but can be avoided by using named cultivars. Robert Bowden of Leu Gardens considers this too large and messy a tree for use.

PROPAGATION By softwood cuttings; seeds need a 30-day cold treatment.

USE This tree should be considered for its incredible durability and endurance.

SELECTIONS 'Wichita' is a male clone that does not produce fruit and has few thorns. It was selected by Dr. John Pair of Kansas State University after 25 years of maclura evaluation.

MAGNOLIA MAGNOLIA *Magnoliaceae (Magnolia family)*

Magnolia trees have many charms in addition to their showstopping flowers. Many species have picturesque habits, smooth gray bark, fragrant flowers, large foliage, or glossy evergreen foliage. The bright orange seeds of magnolias are also attractive and are relished by songbirds and small mammals.

BEST CONDITIONS This agreeable tree will thrive in full sun or partial shade in moist, peaty, and loamy soil with a pH of 5.5-6.5; even very acid soil is ok, so long as it is deep enough to accommodate the long roots. It does, however, require careful siting—strong winds can shatter the flowers, and south-facing buds can open too soon, leaving them susceptible to frost damage and discoloration, particularly in cold climates.

PLANTING Balled-and-burlapped or containerized saplings work best; fleshy roots are often damaged on bare root trees; handle carefully to avoid snapping roots off. Look for plants with well developed branching habits. Plant in a fairly shallow hole—just deep enough to cover the roots—but give them enough space to develop horizontally and leave enough space for the tree in its mature size. Plant in spring before buds break or early enough in fall to allow establishment before frost.

ROUTINE CARE Provide generous water and adequate fertilizer until established, then taper off to watering only during dry spells. If the soil is not naturally rich, provide an annual application of organic matter.

PRUNING Remove dead wood. Prune out crossing and inward growing branching while the tree is young; little pruning will be needed later on.

PROPAGATION Magnolias can be propagated from seeds, layers, or grafts but the most common method is softwood cuttings taken in late spring to early summer.

PESTS, DISEASES, OTHER PROBLEMS Some species are attacked by scale. If not controlled carefully, it can cover the plant and black mildew may appear on the foliage. Powdery mildew, leafspot, leaf scab, and leaf blight are rare but possible. The tree is usually able to repel disease if properly sited. Older trees under stress often succumb to verticillium wilt. The wood of magnolia can be brittle.

USE This tree looks lovely as a specimen, set off from others, particularly evergreens. *M. soulangiana* is a good specimen tree for a small area, or can be planted in groups as a border. *M. grandiflora* is an attractive evergreen shade tree.

SELECTIONS M. acuminata, cucumber tree, remains compact and pyramidal until it is about 20-30 years old; then it becomes broadly rounded, with large, spreading branches, sometimes growing to 70 feet tall and wide. Flowers are not showy; the tree is grown for its attractive habit. Avoid overly wet or dry soils. Zones 4-9.

M. campbellii blooms after only six or seven years, compared with up to 12 for

Magnolia x *soulangiana*.

BREEDING MAGNOLIAS

Magnolias have been the subject of some of the most extensive breeding programs of any plant; the result has been a large group of excellent cultivars extending range, providing sizes useful in every garden, and introducing new colors. Some of the best magnolia cultivars: 'Elizabeth', (Brooklyn Botanic Gardens, 1987) a precocious light yellow. Vigorous and large, to 50 feet tall and wide. Zones 5-8. The "Eight Little Girls" ('Ann', 'Betty', 'Jane', 'Judy', 'Pinkie', 'Randy', 'Ricki', and 'Susan'; U. S. National Arboretum, 1968). Precocious flowers marked red-purple or pinkish purple. 15 foot plants with equal or greater spread. Zones 5-8. 'Butterflies' (Phil Savage, Michigan, 1991) A precocious deep yellow with red stamens. Upright tree, potentially to 50 feet tall. Zones 5-8. 'Vulcan' (Mark Jury Nursery, New Zealand, 1990). Brilliant large ruby-red precocious flowers, to 25 feet tall. Zones 5-9. 'Legacy' (David Leach, Ohio, 1985). A precocious bloomer with bicolored flowers, giving the effect of a clear, soft pink. To 45 feet. Zones 5-8. 'Yellow Lantern' (Phil Savage, Michigan, 1985) Upright single-trunked tree to about 60 feet. Precocious lemon yellow flowers. Zones 4-8. 'Golden Sun' (David Leach, Ohio, 1993). Spectacular large butter yellow flowers of heavy substance. Precocious. To 30 feet. Zone 5-8. Available 1997. 'Galaxy' (U.S. National Arbor-etum) Upright, almost columnar tree, to 30 feet in 25 years. Flowers precocious and profuse, light purplish pink. Zones 5-9. *M. grandiflora* cultivars recommended for the South include 'Bracken's Brown Beauty' and 'Little Gem'. Another recommended cultivar for the South is *Magnolia sprengeri* 'Diva', a precocious pink.

other species. It is hardy only in Zones 8-9, but flourishes in the Pacific Northwest. It produces fragrant, light pink flowers, up to 10 inches in diameter. *M. denudata [M. heptapeta],* Yulan magnolia, native to central China, bears fragrant white flowers, 5-6 inches across; its flowers appear earlier than most species and are sometimes damaged by early frost. 30-40 feet tall; Zone 5. **'Purpurascens'**s flowers are reddish outside, pink inside. *M. grandiflora,* the southern or bull magnolia, can grow to 60-80 feet tall; it is hardy to Zone 8, as far north as Pennsylvania. A healthy tree is a treasure, but needs lots of room. This is one of the few magnolias that grows on a single trunk. Its flowers are up to 12 inches across, both delicate and striking as well as heavily fragrant; they have been accepted as a symbol of the South. *M. x kewensis* **'Wada's memory',** is a prolific bearer of large white flowers. Zone 6. *M. kobus,* kobus magnolia, is more tolerant of different soil types; it can even be grown in alkaline soils. It grows to 30-40 feet tall and after 20-30 years produces slightly fragrant white flower, up to 4 inches across, in early spring. Zone 5. *M. x loebneri* **'Merrill',** Loebner magnolia, grows at about twice the rate of *M. stellata,* and reaches 25-30 feet. In midspring, it is covered with 3- to 3½-inch white flowers; it flowers when it is about five years old. It is easily propagated. and is hardy from Zones 5-9. **'Ballerina'** and **'Spring Snow'** produce excellent flowers that remain pure white. *M. macrophylla,* bigleaf magnolia, is valued for its attractive, rounded habit, creamy white flowers (8-10 and up to 14 inches across) and large (12-30 inches long) leaves. The leaves, though attractive themseles, give the tree a coarse appearance. To 30 feet tall; Zone 5. *M. f. var. ashei* is a smaller, shrubbier plant. *M. sieboldii,* Oyama magnolia, from Japan bears particularly beautiful and fragrant cup-shaped white flowers with red stamens, to 5 inches across. Its habit and foliage are less attractive. To 30 feet tall; Zones 6-9. *M. x soulangiana,* the saucer magnolia, is a many-branched small tree, to 25 feet tall and hardy to Zone 5. Its large flowers–2-6 inches in diameter–open slowly from buds to floppy, cup-shaped blooms, as large as saucers. The blossoms cover several shades of pink, purple, white, or yellow and several colors often appear on te same tree, even in the same flowers. This tree will flower even when it is 2-3 feet tall and a few years old. The saucer magnolia's leaves appear after the flowers; once the stunning floral display is over, the tree can be enjoyed for its attractive shape, smooth gray bark, and small green leaves. The tree can be trained to grow on a single trunk. It was introduced around 1820 by one of Napoleon's retired soldiers. **'Alba',** a compact cultivar, has purple-tinged white flowers. **'Alexandrina'** bears rosy flowers with pure white interiors; flowers are earlier and larger than others. **'Brozzoni',** one of the best of the white-flowering cultivars, bears flowers up to 10 inches across. Late-flowering **'Lennei'** has dark purple petals, **'Verbanica'** blooms later than most, producing clear rose-pink flowers with white interiors. *M. stellata,* star magnolia, has pure white flowers, 3 or more inches in diameter, each sporting 5-20 narrow petals; it blooms in late April and is sometimes damaged by sudden frost. Hardy to Zone 5, it usually does not exceed 20 feet in height and grows on a multistemmed trunk with much branching. **'Centennial'** is a particularly attractive upright cultivar with pure white flowers; **'Rosea'** is pink. *M. x thompsoniana* **'Urbana',** a medium-sized cross between *M. virginiana* and *M. tripetala,* has fragrant creamy white flowers. Zone 6.

MAGNOLIA CAMPBELLII (CAMPBELL MAGNOLIA) Deciduous. 10 years: 10 feet; 20 years: 20 feet; 50 years: 40-50 feet; maturity: to 60 feet. Open habit, coarse 6- to 10-inch-long leaves, fragrant cup-shaped flowers, usually shell pink, up to 10 inches in diameter. Full sun or partial shade, moist, slightly acid soil. Zones 8-9.

MAGNOLIA GRANDIFLORA (SOUTHERN MAGNOLIA) Evergreen. 10 years: 12 feet; 20 years: 25 feet; 50 years: 50-55 feet; maturity: to 85 feet. Stately tree with dense glossy foliage and very large flowers. Full sun or partial shade, moist, slightly acid soil. Zones 7-9.

MAGNOLIA x LOEBNERI 'LEONARD MESSEL' (MESSEL MAGNOLIA) Deciduous. 10 years: 8-10 feet; 20 years: 15-20 feet; 50 years: 30 feet; maturity: to 35 feet. Dense, mounding shrub or small tree with long dark green leaves and fragrant, large purplish pink flowers, up to 6 inches across. Full sun or partial shade, moist slightly acid soil. Zones 5-9.

MAGNOLIA x SOULANGIANA (SAUCER MAGNOLIA) Deciduous. 10 years: 10 feet; 20 years: 15-20 feet; 50 years: 30 feet; maturity: to 35 feet. Can be shrubby, with many stems, or can be trained to tree form with a single trunk. Coarse dull green leaves, large showy flowers, 5-10 inches in diameter in mid spring. Tolerates heat and cold; full sun or partial shade, moist, slightly acid soil. Zones 5-9.

MAGNOLIA STELLATA 'WATERLILY' (STAR MAGNOLIA) 10 years: 5-7 feet; 20 years: 10-15 feet; 50 years: 15-20 feet; maturity: to 20 feet. Dense, mounding shrub or small tree with fine-textured dark green leaves and fragrant, double flowers, up to 3 inches across. Full sun or partial shade, moist, slightly acid soil. Zones 5-9.

MAGNOLIA VIRGINIANA (SWEETBAY) Deciduous or evergreen. 10 years: 10-15 feet; 20 years: 20-30 feet; 50 years: 25-55 feet; maturity: to 60 feet. A tall evergreen in South, usually remains a shrub in North; long, shiny oval leaves, very fragrant white flowers in late May. Tolerates heat and cold. Full sun or partial shade, moist, slightly acid soil. Zones 6-10.

MALUS 'LISET' (CRABAPPLE) Deciduous. 10 years: 7 feet; 20 years: 10 feet; 50 years: 15-20 feet; maturity: to 20 feet. Dense, columnar habit, dark red buds open to light red flowers; dark red fruit. Full sun; any good soil; prefers dry areas with low humidity. Zones 4-8.

MALUS 'BOB WHITE' (CRABAPPLE) Deciduous. 10 years: 7 feet; 20 years: 10 feet; 50 years: 15-20 feet; maturity: to 20 feet. Rounded dense crown, fine-textured foliage, cherry-colored buds fading to white, yellow fruit. Full sun; any good soil, acid to alkaline. Zones 4-8.

M. virginiana, sweetbay magnolia, has creamy white flowers that are not as large or showy as other species but do have a strong lemon fragrance in midsummer. It grows to 60 feet in the South and stays almost shrublike in the North. It is grown not for its flowers, but for its glossy green foliage (undersides are white) and intense fragrance. It likes wet soils and tolerates shade and acid soils but is not drought tolerant. It is cold hardy in Zones 6-10 and native from Massachusetts to Florida. It is evergreen in the South.

MALUS ORNAMENTAL CRABAPPLE *Rosaceae (Rose family)*

This large diverse group of medium-sized trees consists mainly of hybrids or plants of garden origin. They display a wide range of habits, flower color, fruit display, and fall color. There are almost 1,000 cultivars on the market, some superior but others only second rate, so beware when making selections; some cultivars that are dazzling in one region are lackluster in other areas. Those listed here show good disease resistance throughout most of the country. Most are of Asian parentage. (See pages 206-209 for information on growing apples for fruit.)

BEST CONDITIONS Plant in full sun. Ornamental crabapples tolerate many types of soil conditions from heavy to well-drained, as well as a range of soil pH. They usually tolerate dry conditions well once established. Where humidity is high, poor-quality selections are prone to disease.

PLANTING Spring planting of balled-and-burlapped or containerized stock is best. Water well and mulch. Give sufficient space for mature size.

ROUTINE CARE Keep mulched. Fertilizer is seldom necessary; avoid high-nitrogen fertilizers which encourage soft leafy growth over flowers.

PRUNING Prune every three to four years to shape and remove crossing branches. If water sprouts appear (usually after hard pruning) remove them to the trunk. Remove any root suckers. Keep mulched.

PESTS, DISEASES, OTHER PROBLEMS In the past, crabapple trees were often overlooked because of disease problems and, in some cases, messy fruit. Today, excellent trees exist, many with highly ornamental fruits that do not cause problems. Crabapples may suffer from three primary diseases: apple scab, cedar apple rust, and fireblight. While some infection may occur, it rarely hinders the ornamental qualities of the selections listed below.

PROPAGATION Crabapples can be grown from seed but the results are highly variable, and are often diseased with virus. Best to buy nursery-grown stock.

USE Crabapples are an excellent choice for landscapes in most of the country. The beautiful flowers are fragrant and the persistent fruit is extremely ornamental for many months. They vary in size from shrubs to medium-sized trees and can be used in small as well as large landscapes; in containers on terraces, in the mixed border with perennials, in wildlife gardens, even in large rock gardens as well as in collections of shrubs or as specimens.

SELECTIONS "If variety is the spice of life–crabapples are the spice of the tree landscape"–Tom Green.

Pɪɴᴋ ꜰʟᴏᴡᴇʀs ᴡɪᴛʜ ʀᴇᴅ ꜰʀᴜɪᴛ

'Adams' makes a globe-shaped tree 20 feet tall and wide. The ⅜-inch fruit persists into winter but is not as brightly colored as some. Excellent disease resistance. Zones 3-8.

'Indian Summer' is also globe-shaped but only 18 feet tall and wide. Flowers are almost red, ¾-inch bright red fruits persist, and it has good fall color. Zones 3-8.

Fruit of *Malus* 'Callaway', a selection well-suited to southern climates.

Malus sieboldii has spreading branches that create a perfect picnic spot.

'**Prairifire**', developed at the University of Illinois, is a more upright grower but overall globe-shaped. Flowers are deeper red-pink, against early spring red-purple foliage which matures to dark green, veined with purple. Small red-purple fruit is not as bright as others but persists partway through the winter. Zones 3-8.

WHITE FLOWERS WITH RED FRUIT

Red Jewel ('Jewelcole') is vase-shaped, 18 by 15 feet. Its white flowers are followed by bright red fruit that remains attractive through rugged midwestern winters. More uniform than Sugar Tyme. Zones 3-9.

Sugar Tyme ('Sutyzam') is a vigorous grower 20 by 18 feet, most suitable for a relaxed, naturalistic site. Its bright red ½-inch fruits remain through the winter in the upper Midwest. Further south they may not color as well due to temperature fluctuations. Tremendous ornamental value in winter. Zones 5-8.

'**Donald Wyman**', named for the Arnold Arboretum plantsman, has 1½-inch flowers and its disease-resistant leaves turn golden yellow in fall. The dark red ½-inch fruit persists until the birds consume them in spring. Zones 4-8.

M. x zumi '**Calocarpa**'. This older variety has remained the benchmark over time for white-flowered/red-fruited forms. At the Chicago Botanic Garden, evaluations have shown this to have greater salt and pollution tolerance than the other stalwart, *M. floribunda*. In time it spreads to 20 by 24 feet with glistening red ½-inch fruit that persists for the songbirds in spring. Zones 4-8.

WHITE FLOWERS WITH GOLD OR ORANGE FRUIT (All gold and orange fruited forms evaluated by Galen Gates at the Chicago Botanic Garden lose their fruit color consistently at 12-15° F in winter.)

'**Bob White**' grows broader than tall, 20 by 25 feet. It forms a well-branched, fine-textured tree with golden fruit. Zones 4-8. Developed by Arnold Arboretum.

M. floribunda (Japanese crabapple). This is an older species that remains one of the best. It is wider than tall at maturity, 18 by 25 feet, with an irregular branching habit that develops a graceful character over time. The single 1½-inch flowers are profuse; the ⅜-inch fruits are yellow-red. Zones 4-9.

'**Professor Sprenger**' A fast-growing, upright to spreading tree, 20 by 20 feet, with excellent disease resistance. Its 1¼-inch white flowers followed by persistent orange ⅜-inch fruit make it a unique and showy specimen from a distance. Zones 4-8.

WEEPING FORMS

'**Red Jade**' grows to 15 feet but can be kept smaller. It has a broad pendulous habit, white flowers, and glossy red fruit. In areas with deer populations, use this sparingly; at Morton Arboretum this plant is heavily browsed. Zones 4-8.

'**White Cascade**' grows 10-15 feet tall and produces a solid display of white flowers followed by yellow/gold fruit. This was used successfully at Chicago Botanic Garden's Japanese garden as a replacement for flowering cherries which do not do well there. Zones 4-8.

UPRIGHT GROWTH HABIT (currently all will broaden with time—"middle-age spread")

'**Red Baron**' is well-suited to narrow spaces and parkway plantings. Excellent red-orange fall color. Its deep red flowers produce persistent oxblood red ⅜₆-inch fruit.

'**Sentinel**' remains upright with minimal pruning. Excellent disease resistance. The 1-inch flowers which open pink fading to white are followed by crimson ¾-inch fruits which persist.

DWARF FORMS (under 15 feet tall)

M. sargentii, Sargent crab. This disease-resistant dwarf form (6-10 feet tall and 10-

Malus hupehensis has a particularly attractive vase-shaped habit.

14 feet wide) tends to be an alternate bearer: it flowers profusely one year, less so the next. The single, white flowers are fragrant and produce ⅓-inch red fruits. At the Chicago Botanic Garden these remain on the tree until the birds consume them in October and November. Excellent choice for a small property. Zones 4-9.

M. s. **'Tina'** is an improved fine-textured dwarf, only 3 by 5-6 feet, when grown from cuttings. It has excellent disease resistance. White flowers and red fruits.

M. s. **Pink Princess ['Parsii']** is a disease-resistant dwarf with pink flowers. Matures to 8-10 by 12-15 feet. The foliage is red-bronze, but it has all the desirable attributes of the Sargent crab. Zones 5 (4)-9.

M. **'Amberina'** was bred by Father Fiala who felt it was the best of his 130 crabapple introductions. This semi-dwarf spreading tree has white flowers followed by small, firm fruits of "amberina" red, the color created when gold is diffused into molten glass. Zones 4-8.

MAYTENUS MAYTEN *Celastraceae (Staff-tree family)*

Although usually grown only in very warm climates, maytenus is hardy all the way to northern California, where it is often used as a street tree. It is an evergreen, with particularly lush bright green foliage; although the tree is upright, it oftens resembles a willow because its foliage tends to be pendulous. It grows to 30 feet tall.

BEST CONDITIONS Average soil is sufficient for this tree, as long as it is well drained. Full sun is best. Maytenus is hardy in Zones 9-10.

PLANTING Plant in spring or fall.

ROUTINE CARE Established trees are quite drought tolerant, but lushest appearance will be produced when the tree is given plenty of moisture. Fertilizer is not necessary unless soil is very poor.

PESTS, DISEASES, OTHER PROBLEMS None serious, except that this tree can only be grown in warm climates.

PRUNING Maytenus can be grown as a spreading, multitrunked tree or pruned to a central leader. Digging around roots can stimulate suckering. If spreading is desired, allow suckers to develop; otherwise, remove them. Staking also helps establish a single trunk. Once shape is developed, prune only to remove dead wood.

PROPAGATION Maytenus is easily propagated from cuttings or suckers.

USE This is an excellent specimen for a large yard where it can spread out. It also tolerates seashore conditions.

SELECTIONS *M. boaria* is the only species commonly found. Its cultivar **'Green Showers'** has a particularly nice shape.

METASEQUOIA GLYPTOSTROBOIDES DAWN REDWOOD
Cupressaceae (Cypress family)

This extremely old tree from China was first described by paleontologists from fossil remains. It was introduced into cultivation in the U.S. by Arnold Arboretum in 1947 and is sometimes called a "living fossil." Dawn redwood is a tall-growing deciduous conifer, with a narrow crown. Its trunk is straight and if the lower branches are retained, becomes buttressed at the base. The light green foliage is soft and fine-textured. In late fall it turns a rusty brown.

BEST CONDITIONS Best growth occurs in full sun where the soil is moist or even wet,

MALUS SARGENTII 'TINA' (SARGENT CRABAPPLE) Deciduous. Dwarf form. 10 years: 3-4 feet; 20 years: 4-5 feet; 50 years: 5-6 feet; maturity: to 6 feet. White flowers, red fruit. Full sun; any good soil, acid to alkaline. Zones 4-8.

MALUS 'RED JADE' (CRABAPPLE) Deciduous. 10 years: 4-5 feet; 20 years: 8-10 feet; 50 years: 12-15 feet; maturity: to 15 feet. Broad crown, pendulous branches; white flowers, glossy red fruit. Full sun; any good soil, acid to alkaline. Zones 4-8.

MALUS 'ORMISTON ROY' (CRABAPPLE) Deciduous. 10 years: 7 feet; 20 years: 10-12 feet; 50 years: 18-20 feet; maturity: to 20 feet. Buds open rose red, turn lighter pink and open to single white flowers. Full sun; any good soil, acid to alkaline. Zones 4-8.

MALUS 'RED BARON' (CRABAPPLE) Deciduous. 10 years: 7 feet; 20 years: 10-12 feet; 50 years: 18-20 feet; maturity: to 20 feet. Narrow, upright habit, deep red flowers, red fall color. Full sun; any good soil, acid to alkaline. Zones 4-8.

Metasequoia, above, was not introduced in North America until 1947, but this fast-growing tree is now popular. It is among the fastest growing of conifers and can grow over 3 feet per year when young.

with an acid to neutral pH. Dawn redwoods do not care for dry soil or low humidity. Good throughout the eastern U.S., in the Pacific Northwest, and other regions of high humidity. It is native to areas in China where winters are mild, but summers are hot and humid.

PLANTING Select plants with intact branches and leader. Even the large sizes transplant readily in spring or fall. Plant so that the root collar is level with the surrounding soil. Keep well watered until established and mulch.

ROUTINE CARE Mulch routinely. Otherwise little routine care is required.

PRUNING Do not prune the lower limbs or buttressing will not develop.

PESTS, DISEASES, OTHER PROBLEMS Not prone to pests and diseases.

PROPAGATION Take cuttings in early summer or start from seed. Use a porous potting mix as the seedlings are susceptible to damping off, as are most conifers.

USE Dawn redwood makes a striking specimen tree, and is spectacular massed or in groups of 3-5, especially near watercourses.

SELECTIONS 'National' was selected by the U.S. National Arboretum. **'Sheridan Spire'** is a Canadian selection. Both have an even narrower branching habit than the typical species.

MORUS MULBERRY *Moraceae (Mulberry family)*

A great tree for dry areas, mulberries flower in early spring and grow quickly to 30-50 feet tall. Their fruit is often used for jams, but is more often a treat for birds; in fact, many people plant mulberries to lure birds away from more valuable crops like cherries, apples, and peaches. At least two types—fruitless male and fruiting female—need to be planted in order to obtain fruit.

BEST CONDITIONS Full sun or light shade is acceptable to all the mulberries. Although any soil, acid or alkaline, will suffice, a deep moist soil is best because the trees have long, complex roots. Zones 5-9.

PLANTING Plant in spring or fall; water generously.

ROUTINE CARE Keep evenly moist for the first year; once established, mulberries withstand drought quite well. Addition of fertilizer is almost never necessary.

PRUNING Removal of lower branches or pruning to limit size is sometimes necessary; prune in winter.

PESTS, DISEASES, OTHER PROBLEMS Monitor for bacterial blight and remove affected branches immediately.

PROPAGATION Propagate by leafy summer cuttings or by hardwood cuttings.

USE Male varieties produce the best shade trees and are often planted for that purpose. Fruiting female trees are usually kept away from seating areas or paths because their fruits stain everything they fall upon.

SELECTIONS *M. alba,* white mulberry, has overly sweet fruit that is rarely used, but it is the most cold-resistant of the mulberries and among the tallest, reaching 50 feet.

M. nigra, black mulberry, rarely exceeds 30 feet, but its fruit is tasty enough to be eaten fresh or used in jams.

M. rubra, red mulberry, also reaches 50 feet and produces excellent berries.

NYSSA SYLVATICA SOUR GUM, TUPELO *Nyssaceae (Sour-gum family)*

Sour gum wood is tough enough to be used in docks and wharves, but its flowers and fruits feed bees, robins, ducks, woodpeckers, and turkeys. The tree is grown

MALUS SUGAR TYME (CRABAPPLE) Deciduous. 10 years: 7 feet; 20 years: 10-12 feet; 50 years: 18-20 feet; maturity: to 20 feet. Bright red ½-inch fruit through winter. Full sun; any good soil, acid to alkaline. Zones 4-8.

MALUS 'INDIAN MAGIC' (CRABAPPLE) Deciduous. 10 years: 6 feet; 20 years: 9-12 feet; 50 years: 15-20 feet; maturity: to 20 feet. Single, deep pink flowers, small shiny red fruit turns orange and persists to winter. Full sun; any good soil, acid to alkaline. Zones 4-8.

MAYTENUS BOARIA (MAYTEN TREE) Evergreen. 10 years: 15 feet; 20 years: 25-35 feet; 50 years: 40-75 feet; maturity: to 75 feet. Upright tree with sprawling pendulous branches covered in dense, light green foliage. Full sun, average, well-drained soil. Zone 9-10.

METASEQUOIA GLYPTOSTROBOIDES (DAWN REDWOOD) Deciduous. 10 years: 15-20 feet; 20 years: 30-40 feet; 50 years: 60-80 feet; maturity: to 110 feet. Tall, straight trunk, fine-textured light green leaves turn rusty brown in fall. Full sun, moist or wet soil, acid to neutral pH. Zones 5-9.

MORUS ALBA (WHITE MULBERRY) Deciduous. 10 years: 12-15 feet; 20 years: 20-25 feet; 50 years: 40-50 feet; maturity: to 50 feet. Dense, round-topped tree with lobed bright green leaves, small berrylike fruit. Sun or light shade, deep moist soil, acid or alkaline. Zones 4-8.

NYSSA SYLVATICA (SOUR GUM) Deciduous. 10 years: 10 feet; 20 years: 20 feet; 50 years: 50 feet; maturity: to 75 feet. Pyramidal habit, dense leathery green leaves turn brilliant red and orange in fall. Full sun, moist, rich soil; does well in marginally alkaline soil. Zones 4-9.

OSTRYA VIRGINIANA (HOP HORNBEAM, IRONWOOD) Deciduous. 10 years: 10 feet; 20 years: 18 feet; 50 years: 35-40 feet; maturity: to 45 feet. Pyramidal shape, dense green leaves turn yellow in fall, hoplike fruit pods. Full sun or partial shade; tolerates dryness, thrives in alkaline conditions. Zone 3-9.

OXYDENDRUM ARBOREUM (SOURWOOD, SORREL TREE) Deciduous. 10 years: 7-10 feet; 20 years: 15-20 feet; 50 years: 30-40 feet; maturity: to 50 feet. Long pointed oval compound leaves turn brilliant red in fall; racemes of white flowers complement the red foliage. Full sun or partial shade (flowering best in sun); well-drained acidic soil. Zones 5-8.

as an ornamental for its attractive form, glossy leaves, brilliant fall color—reds and oranges that vary from year to year but are always spectacular—and affinity for moist conditions.

BEST CONDITIONS A highly adaptable tree. According to many listings, sour gum does not tolerate high pH soils, but Galen Gates has found that it thrives in soils with a pH up to 7.5. It loves moisture and fertile soil helps speed up its slow growth. This species is found naturally on slopes well above streams with good drainage and is usually an understory tree, but it is quite tolerant of seasonally dry soils and has proven to be excellent in low-fertility soils, though it grows more slowly. It is best in full sun, but tolerates some shade.

PLANTING It is easiest to establish from container-grown stock. Spring planting is best; mulch and water regularly during establishment. Transplants best when young; older trees sometimes stop significant growth for years after transplanting.

ROUTINE CARE Once established, water during dry spells. This tree needs more fertilizer than most, and benefits from an annual application.

PRUNING Rarely needed.

PESTS, DISEASES, OTHER PROBLEMS None serious; sometimes cankers and leaf spots.

PROPAGATION Propagate by seeds, cuttings, or tissue culture.

USE Due to its natural tolerance of low-oxygen soils and adverse conditions, sour gum is an excellent street or seaside tree. It is best used as a specimen where its habit, glossy leaves, and remarkable autumn colors can be appreciated.

SELECTIONS *N. aquatica*, water tupelo, is a narrow tree up to 100 feet tall. Like many trees that inhabit periodically flooded lands or swamps, it has a broadly flared trunk at the base that narrows and straightens. Leaves and fruits are larger than black gum. It inhabits the southeast and southern parts of the U.S. and extends to southern Illinois. Hardiness is listed as Zones 6-9, but evaluations are underway for a hardier strain at Chicago Botanic Garden.

Morus alba 'Pendula' makes an interesting display in the garden and a living arbor providing shade over a walkway.

OSTRYA VIRGINIANA HOP HORNBEAM, IRONWOOD *Betulaceae* (Birch family)

Ironwood is found in over half the U.S. and is adapted to many conditions. It is a tough, resilient tree whose wood has been used for tool handles; woodsmen tell of axes in the hands of unsuspecting novices simply bouncing off the trunks of these tough trees. Another common name, hop hornbeam, refers to the inflated, hop-like fruits borne in hanging clusters 2-3 inches long. The foliage resembles that of birches or elms, deep green and finely toothed. Ironwood is a fine-textured, graceful tree, pyramidal when young and developing a rounded crown when older.

BEST CONDITIONS Ostrya is one of the best medium-sized trees that tolerates shade. It also adapts beautifully to a variety of soils, moist and dry, acid and alkaline, and to humid or dry conditons. Zones 3-9.

PLANTING Because they are grown from seed, ironwoods are variable. You may be able to select from multistemmed and single-trunked types. Select for your particular situation. Containerized or balled-and-burlapped plants are best planted in spring.

ROUTINE CARE Mulch and water to establish. Once established, water during dry spells. Fertilization is not necessary.

PRUNING Prune to shape young trees. Otherwise, prune only to occasionally clean out the center.

PESTS, DISEASES, OTHER PROBLEMS None serious, but intolerant to salt.

Nyssa sylvatica with *Salix alba* 'Tristis' (weeping willow)–two trees that perform well in moist conditions.

PROPAGATION Propagate by seeds.

USE Although it lends itself to a naturalistic landscape, ironwood can also be used as a traditional shade tree. An underused plant, ironwood has attractive dangling flower catkins in spring, clean green foliage in summer, yellow fall color, and vertically striated bark strips that are effective in winter. It is fast growing (15-18 inches per year), medium sized, and casts enough dense shade for relaxing but not so dense as to kill the vegetation beneath it.

OXYDENDRUM ARBOREUM SOURWOOD, SORREL TREE *Ericaceae* (Heath family)

One of our most beautiful natives, sourwood grows in the wild as an understory tree in the eastern and southeastern U.S. In the home landscape it is ideal as a small specimen tree or may be used singly or grouped in more informal settings. It has an irregular branching habit forming a somewhat triangular canopy with slick, leathery foliage. In midsummer, when few other trees are in bloom, long curving racemes of flowers extend from the ends of each branch. The fragrant curving racemes of flowers extend from the ends of each branch. The fragrant white flowers hang like a lacy gown along the outline of the tree, set off by the lustrous green leaves beneath. The flowers resemble those of their relative, Japanese pieris (*Pieris japonica*). In early fall, the same racemes bear the fruiting capsules which stand upright rather than hanging. These persist for some time even after the leaves have turned a dazzling range of reds, scarlet, and purples, and dropped in mid October. In the southern Appalachians, sourwood honey is a delicacy. The wood was used to make wagon sled runners in mountainous regions, and is still used for tool handles.

BEST CONDITIONS Sun or partial shade. The best flowering and fall color is on specimens in sun. Moisture-retentive but well-drained, acid soil is a must; sourwoods do not tolerate lime, although neutral soils are satisfactory. They are very sensitive to clay and compacted soils.

PLANTING Select young balled-and-burlapped or container-grown plants; be careful not to disturb the roots unnecessarily. Due to their deep lateral roots, sourwoods may go into root shock when transplanting large specimens. Both spring and fall planting are successful. Water well until established and mulch with an acidic mulch such as pine bark.

ROUTINE CARE Water during periods of drought and mulch with pine bark, compost, or other acidic mulch.

PRUNING No routine pruning necessary.

PESTS, DISEASES, OTHER PROBLEMS Sometimes leaf spot or twig blight attacks sourwoods, but there are no major pests.

PROPAGATION Softwood cuttings taken with a heel in late July can be rooted, but propagation by seed is more reliable. Sow the tiny seed on the surface of the medium and keep under mist until germination.

USE Sourwood makes a good specimen or container plant. It can also be used in shrub borders, especially with rhododendrons, leucothoe, pieris, and other shrubs requiring similar conditions. It is not used as much as it should be, possibly because it grows slowly.

SELECTIONS 'Chameleon' is a Polly Hill selection. It is notable for its range of fall colors from yellows to deep reds.

PARROTIA PERSICA PERSIAN PARROTIA *Hamamelidaceae (Witch-hazel family)*

Named for the German naturalist F. W. Parrot, Persian parrotia is, as one would expect, a native of Persia, now Iran. It makes a small tree eventually some 30-40 feet tall, or may grow as a multistemmed shrub. Its oval-shaped crown may spread to 30 feet and often specimens are wider than tall. It blooms in spring (or even late winter) before the foliage leafs out, in the manner of its close relatives witch-hazel and fothergilla, but the flowers are conspicuous only for their red stamens. Reddish at first, the leaves mature to dark green but put on an exquisite fall display of yellows, orange, and reds. (Fall color is inconsistent in some areas.) Mature specimens develop exfoliating bark, which flakes off to reveal a mosaic of gray, green, brown, and white underneath, a very attractive feature in the winter garden. The horizontal branching habit and low branching facilitate close inspection.

BEST CONDITIONS Plant in full sun or light shade, where the soil drains freely; poor

---

VIEWPOINT
WEEPING TREES

Giant sequoias and European beeches, both humongous trees, can be used in small gardens when their weeping cultivars are planted. Consider the beautiful weeping forms of smaller trees such as styrax, *Salix caprea,* cercidiphyllum, and others as well.
SUSAN THOMAS,
HOYT ARBORETUM, PORTLAND

Palo blanco (*Acacia willardiana*) is exquisite, with graceful weeping foliage and white peeling bark.
MARY IRISH, DESERT BOTANICAL GARDEN, PHOENIX

Outstanding trees, these weepers! *Cornus kousa* 'Lustgarten Weeping' from the famous Baer Lustgarten of Long Island is a real horticultural and architectural jewel. I never thought I would recommend a mulberry, but I have seen striking specimens of a pendulous sterile form in the South. *Prunus serrulata* 'Pendula' also works well in the mid South.
ROBERT BOWDEN, HARRY P. LEU GARDENS, ORLANDO

Among the best: *Carpinus betulis* 'Pendula', *Cercidiphyllum japonicum* 'Pendulum', *Prunus subhirtella* 'Pendula', *Cornus kousa* 'Elizabeth Lustgarten', *and Tsuga canadensis* 'Pendula'.
RICK LEWANDOWSKI, MORRIS ARBORETUM , UNIV. OF PA

I like *Betula pendula* 'Youngii', *Malus* 'Red Jade' and *Caragena arborescens* 'Pendula'
DORTHE HVIID,
BERKSHIRE BOTANICAL GARDEN

Malus 'Red Jade' provides several seasons of interest; *Cercidiphyllum japonicum* 'Pendula' is one of the loveliest of all weeping forms; *Morus alba* 'Chaparral' is a non-fruiting mulberry, that, when properly pruned provides a hiding place for kids.
JULIE MORRIS, BLITHEWOLD

There aren't many small-scale weeping forms beyond *Malus* 'Red Jade', *Malus* 'White Cascade', and *Salix caprea* 'Pendula'. But some trees, such as *Cercidiphyllum* 'Pendula' and *Fagus* 'Pendula' can be limbed up so you can walk under them.
GALEN GATES, CHICAGO BOTANIC GARDEN

PARROTIA PERSICA (PERSIAN PARROTIA) Deciduous. 10 years: 8-10 feet; 20 years: 15-20 feet; 50 years: 30-40 feet; maturity: to 50 feet. Oval crown, sometimes multistemmed, shiny oval leaves begin reddish, become green in summer and exquisite yellow, orange, and red in fall. Full sun or light shade. Slightly acid to alkaline, loamy soil. Zones 5-8.

PAULOWNIA TOMENTOSA (EMPRESS TREE, PRINCESS TREE) Deciduous. 10 years: 20-25 feet; 20 years: 35-40 feet; 50 years: 50-60 feet; maturity: to 60 feet. Tall stately habit, branching on top, clusters of lavender flowers in spring, dense foliage. Light shade; will adjust to many soil types. Zones 5-9.

PHELLODENDRON LAVALLEI (LAVELLE CORKTREE) Deciduous. 10 years: 15 feet; 20 years: 25 feet; 50 years: 45-60 feet; maturity: to 60 feet. Spreading branches, glossy green compound leaves turn gold in fall, shiny black fruit, corky bark. Full sun, any soil so long as it is not soggy. Zones 3-8.

PICEA ABIES 'PENDULA' (NORWAY SPRUCE) Evergreen. 10 years: 3-6 feet tall; 20 years: 5-12 feet tall; 50 years: 10-30 feet tall; maturity: to 40 feet tall. Pyramidal form with long, pendulous branches; form is somewhat stiff but matures gracefully; long, dark, shiny needles, 4- to 7-inch brown cones. Full sun, moist rich soil, cool climates. Zone 2.

drainage is not acceptable. A slightly acid, loamy soil is good, with a pH of 6.0-6.5 or even a little on the alkaline side.

PLANTING A little tough to transplant; best results are from balled-and-burlapped stock in the early spring. Keep well watered until established for the first two years or so. Rick Lewandowski has transplanted 3- to 3½-inch-caliper trees in spring without loss.

ROUTINE CARE A very tolerant tree once established, parrotia needs water or fertilizer only in extreme conditons.

PRUNING Prune to shape or to remove damaged or dead wood in spring.

PESTS, DISEASES, OTHER PROBLEMS Pest and disease free.

PROPAGATION Take softwood cuttings in early to midsummer, and allow to over-winter dormant before potting them up. Seeds must be stratified warm and then cold to break dormancy.

USE One of the most beautiful ornamental shrubs or small trees. Excellent as a specimen in a lawn or close to the house where its four-season interest can be appreciated. Also used as a street tree.

SELECTIONS There is a weeping form, **'Pendula'**.

PAULOWNIA EMPRESS TREE, PRINCESS TREE *Bignoniaceae* (*Bignonia family*)

The empress tree combines incredibly beautiful blossoms that last for just a few weeks in spring with a regal bearing that extends through all four seasons. The flowers are clusters (sometimes 15 inches long) of vanilla-scented blue bells. The tree rapidly reaches a height of 35-40 feet and produces dense shade, sometimes making it impossible to grow anything underneath it.

BEST CONDITIONS The empress tree withstands cold weather, but sometimes does not bloom after a particularly cold winter; it has died back to the ground in Zone 5, even in normal winters. Light shade and moist, well-drained, soil is best, but the tree will adapt to almost any kind of soil.

PLANTING Establishment is sometimes difficult; buy healthy 3- to 5-foot saplings (balled-and-burlapped are best) and plant in early spring. Water and fertilize well until the tree begins to put on new growth.

ROUTINE CARE Water and fertilizer are usually needed for only the first few years.

PRUNING Prune to shape and remove dead wood in winter, before flowering begins.

PESTS, DISEASES, OTHER PROBLEMS No serious pests or diseases, but the empress tree can become weedy. A single seed capsule can produce tens of thousands of seedlings and this tree has invaded some woodlands in the eastern U.S. This fast-growing tree is weak-wooded and sometimes breaks after storms.

PROPAGATION Propagate by seeds.

USE Empress trees cast too dense a shade to be used as a backdrop to most other plants; but they make a stately addition along a pathway or driveway where their shade and their lovely flowers are appreciated.

SELECTIONS *P. tomentosa* is the commonly cultivated species.

PHELLODENDRON AMURENSE AMUR CORKTREE *Rutaceae (Rue family)*

Ranging in size from 30-45 feet tall and wide, corktrees have spreading branches with large, glossy green compound leaves that turn gold in autumn. Flowers,

Paulownia glabrata.

Picea abies 'Acrocona'.

which smell slightly of turpentine, are small and insignificant, but masses of shiny black fruit are ornamental in the fall. The bark is deeply fissured, like cork.

BEST CONDITIONS Grow corktree in full sun, in moist but not wet soil of high or low pH. Zones 3-7.

PLANTING Look for balled-and-burlapped or containerized plants and a good branching pattern and healthy bark free of injury. Plant in spring or fall. The root system is shallow and spreading and should be given a reasonable amount of room to grow.

ROUTINE CARE Water and fertilizer are usually not needed after establishment. Mulch during establishment.

PRUNING Pruning is rarely necessary.

PESTS, DISEASES, OTHER PROBLEMS None serious, but in some areas it has become invasive at the expense of native trees.

PROPAGATION Seeds germinate readily; in fact, in some areas this tree is weedy.

USE Corktrees have an open canopy that provides light shade, warm yellow fall color, and corklike bark. It is an excellent choice for rural or suburban areas, but because it needs room for its roots, is not as tolerant of urban conditions as some literature suggests. Choose male clones for areas near walkways or patios, as females drop fruit that is sometimes messy.

SELECTIONS *P. a.* 'Macho' was the first named male; it has thick leathery leaves and a moderately spreading habit. It was introduced in 1985 by Bill Wandell of Illinois. **'Shademaster'**, another male, is a strong-growing selection.

P. lavallei, Lavalle corktree, is considered by some to be more upright in form, though corktree species are difficult to separate.

P. sachalinense, Sakhalin corktree, is a more regularly formed, vase-shaped tree that is faster growing and, according to horticulturists at The University of Minnesota, hardier than *P. amurense.* Its bark is thin and gray.

PICEA SPRUCE *Pinaceae (Pine family)*

Symmetrical, conical spruce trees are a staple in northern gardens. Unfortunately, they have been used indiscrimately in foundation plantings so that their commanding presence has been reduced to a cliche. Spruces are among the most dependable of conifers, holding their needles densely even in extreme conditions and developing evenly and uniformly into tall trees. Most species (*P. abies, P. glauca, P. pungens*) are not damaged by deer as often as other conifers.

BEST CONDITIONS Like most conifers, spruce trees like cool climates, moist, rich, slightly acidic soil, and full sun. They do not appreciate heat or pollution, but will accept heavy soils.

PLANTING Spruces have shallow but spreading roots; look for balled-and-burlapped or container plants. Spring planting is best.

ROUTINE CARE Mulching with organic matter helps keep soil moist and rich.

PRUNING Pruning is rarely needed, except to cut away dying lower branches. If healthy branches need pruning, midsummer to fall is best (to avoid excessive bleeding of pitch).

PESTS, DISEASES, OTHER PROBLEMS A spruce grown under proper conditions will resist pests and diseases. Heat, drought, and city pollution will cause stress that leaves the tree open to attack. Mites, spruce gall aphids, and bagworms are the most frequent pests, but a host of others is possible; *Cytospora* canker sometimes kills the lower branches of Colorado blue spruce.

PROPAGATION Spruces can be propagated easily by seeds sown in fall, cuttings taken in winter, and grafts made in late winter and early spring.

USE Tall spruces are usually used as screens or specimens. Placement alongside doorways at the front of houses has been overdone, though. Dwarf varieties have their place in the shrub or perennial border.

SELECTIONS *P. abies,* Norway spruce, is a fast-grower for northern gardens (to 30 feet in 20 years). **'Acrocona'** grows at half the rate of the species and bears purplish red spring cones on branch tips. **'Cupressina'** is narrow with ascending branches. Zones 2-6(7).

P. breweriana, Brewer spruce, is recommended for humid climates only. Native to the Siskiyou mountains of California and Oregon, it bears decurved branches and long pendulous branchlets. It reaches 30 feet tall, 15 feet wide. Zones 5-8.

P. engelmannii, Engelmann spruce, is similar to Colorado spruce, but with softer needles. It requires acid soil. **'Glauca'** has blue foliage. Zones 2-7.

P. glauca, white spruce, is a popular Christmas tree in the North and Midwest, with aromatic foliage; it grows to 25 feet in 20 years, eventually reaching 50 feet tall and 20 feet wide. **'Conica'** (dwarf Alberta spruce) requires a cool, moist spot; it reaches 7 feet at 20 years and eventually grows to 15 feet and 5 feet wide with a perfect conical shape. Zones 2-(6)7.

P. likiangensis, Likiang spruce, from China, has bright purplish red young cones and is no stranger to heat and drought. 20 feet in 20 years and eventually 50 feet tall and 25 feet wide. *P. l. var. purpurea* has violet purple cones. Zones 5-7.

P. omorika, Serbian spruce, has beautiful arching branches and cascading bicolor foliage. Pyramidal when young, it becomes spirelike with maturity. To 20 feet in 20 years, eventually to 60 feet tall, 15 feet wide. Zones 4-7.

P. orientalis, Oriental spruce, is elegantly clothed in tiny, deep green needles and bears small bright red cones in spring. It grows to 18 feet in 20 years and eventually to 80 feet tall and 20 feet wide. **'Skylands'** has golden yellow foliage and requires shade when young. Zones 5-7.

P. pungens, Colorado spruce, is a supreme landscape tree with prickly needles; to 20 feet in 20 years. **'Hoopsii'** has powder blue foliage, to 80 feet tall, 25 feet wide. **'Hunnewelliana'** has blue foliage. 25 feet tall and 8 feet wide in 50 years. Zones 3-7.

PINUS PINE *Pinaceae (Pine family)*

There are 100 species of pines, ranging from the tropics to the taiga, from the mountains to the sea. From dwarf shrubs used in foundation plantings to towering ponderosa pines that form magnificent forests, pine trees are a staple of the tree world. Their economic usefulness is parallelled by their ornamental value.

BEST CONDITIONS Pines thrive in a great variety of climates. Moist, fertile, well-drained soil and full sun are best. Most will not grow in poorly drained soil.

PLANTING Plant balled-and-burlapped plants in the spring or fall. Some pines are taprooted and difficult to transplant in large sizes. Buy bare-root plants only if they are very small, and then make sure roots are kept moist.

Colorado spruces form a backdrop for the perennial border at The New York Botanical Garden.

PICEA OMORIKA (SERBIAN SPRUCE) Evergreen. 10 years: 7 feet; 20 years: 15-20 feet; 50 years: 40-50 feet; maturity: to 60 feet. Pyramidal form with short upward-reaching branches covered densely with dark green needles (whitish on underside). Full sun, moist, rich soil, cool climates. Zones 4-8.

PICEA PUNGENS 'GLAUCA' (COLORADO SPRUCE) Evergreen. 10 years: 7 feet; 20 years: 18 feet; 50 years: 40-50 feet; maturity: to 75 feet. Stiff, pyramidal shape, dense blue-green needles. Full sun, moist, rich soil, cool climates. Zones 2-7.

PICEA ORIENTALIS (ORIENTAL SPRUCE) Evergreen. 10 years: 7 feet; 20 years: 18 feet; 50 years: 40-50 feet; maturity: to 75 feet. Pyramidal shape, glossy dark green needles (smaller than most other spruces), brown cones in fall through winter. Full sun, moist, rich soil, cool climates. Zones 4-8.

PINUS BUNGEANA (LACEBARK PINE) Evergreen. 10 years: 6 feet; 20 years: 14 feet; 50 years: 35-45 feet; maturity: to 50 feet. Pyramidal shape, often single trunked, interesting blotched gray bark; dense bright green needles, 5 per bunch, 2- to 3-inch cones in winter. Full sun, moist, rich soil, cool climates. Zones 4-7.

ROUTINE CARE Apply a 2- to 3-inch layer of organic mulch around the roots.
PRUNING Pruning back new shoots in the spring will keep the plants compact. Otherwise, prune only to remove dead wood or to shape. In pruning to hedge shape, keep the base wider than the top. Prune live wood during summer dormancy to avoid excessive pitch flow.
PROPAGATION Pines can be propagated by seeds sown in fall and grafts made in mid to late winter.
PESTS, DISEASES, OTHER PROBLEMS Grown under proper conditions, pine trees can resist attacks by pests and diseases to which they often fall prey in poor, dry soil or hot climates. Keep five-needle pines away from the *Ribes* family to avoid pine blister rust; Asian species are less susceptible. Tip blight, blister rust, sawflies, weevils, borers, scale, and various other maladies are occasional problems.
USE Windbreaks, screening, background plantings, or specimens. Pines make a fine border and Scotch pine is a popular Christmas tree.
SELECTIONS *P. aristata*, bristlecone pine, of the Rocky Mountains grows to 6-7 feet tall in 20 years, 15 feet at 20 years. Usually multistemmed and asymetrical, its needles are marked with resin dots. Trees at Holden are 62 years old and still bear no cones. Zones 4-7.

P. bungeana, lacebark pine, from China, is open-branched and often multitrunked; attractive mottled bark.

P. contorta, shore pine, of the Pacific Northwest, is round-topped with dense, deep green foliage. It grows only 15-25 feet tall and is excellent for gardens on the West Coast. *P. halepensis* and *P. eldarica*, are excellent for dry climates.

P. coulteri, Coulter pine, a large, striking tree with open branching, occurs in the foothills and coast ranges of Southern California and northern Mexico and has

Above: Pinus bungeana.
Below: Pinus nigra.

PINUS CEMBRA (SWISS-STONE PINE) Evergreen. 10 years: 5 feet; 20 years: 12-15 feet; 50 years: 30-45 feet; maturity: to 50 feet. Often an open habit, becomes round-topped when mature. Soft, dark green needles 2-4 inches long, 3 per bunch. Interesting mottled bark. Full sun, moist, rich soil, cool climates. Zones 2-7.

PINUS DENSIFLORA (JAPANESE RED PINE) Evergreen. 10 years: 7 feet; 20 years: 18 feet; 50 years: 40-50 feet; maturity: to 60 feet. Horizontal branches covered in blue-green needles, 3-5 inches long. Full sun, moist, rich soil, cool climates. Zones 4-8.

PINUS DENSIFLORA 'OCULUS DRACONIS' (DRAGON'S EYE PINE) Evergreen. 10 years: 5 feet; 20 years: 11 feet; 50 years: 25-30 feet; maturity: to 35 feet. Dark green needles marked with two yellow lines. Full sun, moist, rich soil, cool climates. Zones 4-8.

PINUS NIGRA (AUSTRIAN PINE) Evergreen. 10 years: 12 feet; 20 years: 25 feet; 50 years: 35-60 feet; maturity: to 75 feet. Dense, pyramidal shape with dark green 3- to 6-inch-long needles, 2 per bunch. Full sun, moist, rich soil, cool climates. Zones 4-8.

cones weighing 1½-5 pounds. 30 feet in 20 years, 70 feet in 50 years. Zones 8-9.

P. densiflora, Japanese red pine, has reddish flaking bark on branches and young trunks. **'Umbraculifera'** reaches 14 feet in 20 years, 35 feet in 50 years has yellow and green variegated needles. Zones 5-7.

P. elliottii, slash pine, of the deep South, thrives especially in wetlands; needles are 9-12 inches long. To 25 feet in 20 years, 90 feet in 50 years. Zones 8-10.

P. flexilis, limber pine, is native to the Rockies. **'Vanderwolf's Pyramid'** has upright branches that spread with age; 17 feet in 20 years, 40 feet in 50 years, Zones 4-7. Adapts to heat, drought, and high pH.

P. glabra, Walters pine, of the deep South, grows in moist soil and tolerates shade when young. 30 feet in 20 years, 60 feet in 50 years. Zones 7-10.

P. koraiensis, Korean pine, is a very handsome tree with flaky bark and shimmering foliage; its pine nuts are a gourmet feast for squirrels. 20 feet in 20 years, 50 feet in 50 years. Zones 4-7.

P. leucodermis, Bosnian pine, has purplish cones borne at an early age and upswept branches with thick, glossy green needles. It prefers rich soil with a neutral pH and is salt tolerant. 17 feet in 20 years, 40 feet in 50 years. Zones 5-7.

P. monophylla, single-leaf pinyon, native to southeast Utah, requires perfect drainage; its 2-inch needles have a light blue cast. It grows to 7 feet in 20 years, 17 feet in 50 years. Zones 6-7.

P. monticola, western white pine, the most popular pine in the Northwest, responds well to shearing. Aromatic. 30 feet in 20 years, 70 feet in 50 years, Zones 4-8.

P. nigra, Austrian pine, is picturesque and widely planted but susceptible to a twig blight. 20 feet in 20 years, 50 feet in 50 years. Zones 4-7.

P. palustris, longleaf pine, the premier southern pine, develops deep roots in the first few years. 25 feet in 20 years, 90 feet in 50 years. Zones 8-10.

P. parviflora, Japanese white pine. Strong horizontal branches, red male "flowers" in spring, attractive mature cones. 12 feet in 20 years, 40 feet in 50 years. Zones 5-8.

P. ponderosa, Ponderosa pine, is an imposing tree in its native habitat but usually not suited for the eastern U.S. In the West, it commonly reaches 150 feet in majestic open stands. The bark is fissured into reddish plates. Grows to 30 feet in 20 years. Zones 3-8.

P. radiata, Monterey pine, is a flat-topped tree with a massive trunk and persistent cones; salt tolerant. 30 feet in 20 years, 80 feet in 50 years. Zones 8-9.

P. sylvestris, Scotch pine, has bright orange-tan flaking bark on branches and young trunks. **'Argentea'** has silvery blue-green needles. To 55 feet in 50 years. Zones 3-8.

P. taeda, loblolly pine, is a southern species of easy culture, open-branched and rounded at maturity. To 80 feet in 50 years. Zones 6-9.

P. thunbergii, Japanese black pine, forms a contorted picturesque trunk; salt tolerant. To 25 feet in 20 years, 35 feet in 50 years. Zones 6-8.

PLATANUS PLANETREE, SYCAMORE *Platanaceae (Planetree family)*

Planetrees are large, deciduous trees mostly with a broad irregular outline. They are used extensively as street trees, and have been for centuries. In Europe they are frequently pollarded, a training method that involves extremely severe pruning;large specimens thus treated can be seen lining the banks of the Seine in Paris.

BEST CONDITIONS Plant in full sun for best results. Planetrees prefer a rich, moist soil, but are very adaptable. They are not fussy about soil pH and will even stand

Pinus strobus, eastern white pine, is the most majestic conifer in the northeastern and Great Lakes regions. It grows to 24 feet in 20 years, and is aromatic. 'Fastigiata', with ascending branches, grows to 60 feet in 50 years. *Above: Pinus strobus* 'Pendula', to 20 feet in 50 years. Zones 3-7.

Top: Pinus wallichiana, Himalayan white pine, has pendant needles that give it a graceful appearance and ornamental 6- to 10-inch cones. Zones 5-8.

London planetree leaf and fruit.

seasonal flooding, drought, and compacted soil conditions. Tolerant of city heat but not of high humidity, which may result in foliage problems.

PLANTING Best to transplant either bare root or as balled-and-burlapped stock. Select healthy plants with no visible foliage problems. In the past, Holden Arboretum has planted in the fall with good success but spring planting is also satisfactory. Water well until established.

ROUTINE CARE In a suitable site, addition of water and fertilizer is not necessary after establishment.

PRUNING Generally pruning should be done in the winter. Planetrees tolerate severe pruning, but this should be done only where space is a problem or for some other good reason. Routinely remove dead or damaged branches.

PESTS, DISEASES, OTHER PROBLEMS The most serious problem is anthracnose which affects the stems and leaves as they develop. Some species are more resistant than others. Cankers may also become serious.

PROPAGATION Mostly by seed.

USE Some of these large trees may reach 150 feet or more over a lifetime of 150-200 years. It is therefore essential that initial siting be done carefully, with thought to the long-term growth. Can be used as a shade tree, street tree, or specimen depending upon the species. As street trees, it is important to consider the location of powerlines and subsequent pruning.

SELECTIONS *Platanus* x *acerifolia,* London planetree. This widely-grown tree is probably a hybrid between *P. occidentalis* and *P. orientalis*. It grows 70-100 feet tall or more and has a broad, rounded head, with slightly sagging lower branches. It was planted widely in London in the early 1800s and is extremely tolerant of urban conditions. Today it is found in major urban centers around the world. In most respects it is intermediate between its parents, and tolerates minimal care, drastic pruning, and inhospitable conditions better than almost any other tree. Full sun or light shade is best where the soil is deep, rich, moisture-retentive, and well-drained. However, almost any soil will do. Tolerant of high pH and pollutants. Generally shows good resistance to anthracnose, but *Botryospaeria* canker can become serious, as can cankerstain. Cracking bark is usually a sign of frost damage; this is seen especially in the Midwest. Softwood or hardwood cuttings root readily when treated with rooting hormone. Seeds should be stratified for seven to eight weeks. Too large for use as a street tree, this fine hybrid is superb in large landscapes such as parks, golf courses, and other open areas. An excellent specimen where there is room. **'Bloodgood'** has greater resistance to anthracnose than some cultivars, but is more susceptible to cankerstain. It tolerates soil compaction, heat, and drought well. At Holden Arboretum several specimens thrive. They were planted in 1979 and after 16 years have developed a clean pyramidal shape. Their exfoliating bark reveals a yellowish to orange-salmon underlayer and a large number of fruits are retained through the winter. **'Columbia'** is resistant to anthracnose and mildew. The specimens at Holden, planted in 1968, are in full sun, with little or no competition. They display little bark exfoliation or color variation. **'Liberty'** is slower growing than 'Bloodgood'. It is resistant to anthracnose and powdery mildew. The Holden specimen has a beautiful pyramidal shape and holds its fruits well through the winter. Little bark exfoliation or color variation. *Platanus occidentalis,* American planetree, sycamore, buttonwood. This long-lived, eastern North American species was introduced into cultivation in 1640, and may

PINUS SYLVESTRIS 'FASTIGIATA' (SCOTCH PINE) Evergreen. 10 years: 12 feet; 20 years: 25 feet; 50 years: 55-60 feet; maturity: to 75 feet. Upright habit with dark green needles, 2 per bunch. Full sun, moist, rich soil, cool climates; does not tolerate pollution. Zones 3-8.

PLATANUS x ACERIFOLIA (LONDON PLANETREE) Deciduous. 10 years: 20 feet; 20 years: 35 feet; 50 years: 65-75 feet; maturity: to 100 feet. Broad, rounded head, sagging lower branches, lobed leaves. Full sun or light shade, deep, rich, moist soil. Zones 4-8.

PLATANUS OCCIDENTALIS (SYCAMORE) Deciduous. 10 years: 20 feet; 20 years: 35 feet; 50 years: 65-75 feet; maturity: to 100 feet. Wide-spreading, irregular crown, massive trunk, exfoliating bark, lobed leaves. Full sun or light shade, deep, rich, moist soil. Zones 4-8.

PLATYCLADUS ORIENTALIS 'ELEGANTISSIMA' (ORIENTAL ARBORVITAE) Evergreen. 10 years: 6 feet; 20 years: 14 feet; 50 years: 30-35 feet; maturity: to 40 feet. Narrow, upright tree with reddish bark and fernlike bright green foliage. Tolerates heat and humidity; slightly acid and alkaline, moist, well-drained soil; sun or light shade. Zones 6-10.

live for 350 years reaching over 100 feet tall. Its wide-spreading irregular crown is supported by a trunk which becomes massive with age. The reddish to gray-brown bark is notable in that it exfoliates in large plates, exposing the creamy white layer beneath; this is perhaps its best characteristic. American planetree tolerates some light shade, and does best where the soil is average to wet. It does well where there is a reliable supply of ground water, in pH 6.6-8.0. It is extremely tolerant of urban conditions. Anthracnose is a severe problem with this species. Avoid areas with high rainfall amounts and regions with cool moist weather, both of which encourage the spread of the disease. Seed sown in spring benefits from stratification at 41° F for two months. Widely used as a specimen and street tree, but considered too messy for some situations because of its leaf, twig, bark, and fruit litter.

P. orientalis, Oriental planetree, native from southeastern Europe to India, may reach 80-100 feet and has a more spreading, horizontal habit than other species, with creamy colored bark. It is extremely long lived and along the old silk road there are ancient giants under whose shade travelers have rested for centuries. This species is less hardy than some others, from the warmer areas of Zones 6-9. The fruit balls can be messy, but should be cleaned up to avoid disease. Though not widely planted in the U.S., this species is valuable for its resistance to anthracnose. At Holden there are two specimens growing side by side in the Specimen Tree Collection. They are multistemmed trees, planted in 1965 and growing in full sun. They do not hold their fruits through the winter.

P. racemosa (often sold as ***P. californica*** and ***P. wrightii***) is appropriate for California and the Southwest.

PLATYCLADUS ORIENTALIS ORIENTAL ARBORVITAE *Cupressaceae* (Cypress family)

Platycladus orientalis (also known as *Thuja orientalis* and in previous years as *Biota orientalis*) is a narrow, upright evergreen tree with reddish bark and ferny bright green foliage. Although it is similar to arborvitaes in habit, it is much more tolerant of hot and humid conditions; this is one the few conifers that is tolerant of tropical conditions as well as colder climates.

BEST CONDITIONS Like most conifers, Oriental arborvitae prefers slightly acid and alkaline, moist, well-drained soil; it grows best in sun or light shade. Unlike most conifers, it also thrives in hot, humid climates. Zones 6-10.

PLANTING Transplants easily in any season.

ROUTINE CARE An organic mulch is beneficial. Water deeply during drought.

PRUNING Prune out dead branches. Oriental arborvitae has a naturally pleasing shape, but can also be sheared to a more formal shape.

PESTS, DISEASES, OTHER PROBLEMS Though healthy plants will repel disease, a stressed plant will fall prey to any of several problems. Keeping the soil well-mulched will avoid problems.

PROPAGATION Seeds germinate well, especially if stratified. Small softwood cuttings will root if treated with rooting hormones and misted.

USE Oriental arborvitaes are invaluable in the South when conifer effects are desired. Their elegant shape is appreciated in northern climates as well.

SELECTIONS '**Elegantissima**' is a particularly well-shaped cultivar. '**Aurea nana**' has light yellow-green foliage and does not exceed 15 feet in height.

PONCIRUS TRIFOLIATA TRIFOLIATE ORANGE, HARDY ORANGE

Rutaceae (Rue family)

Grown only as a novelty tree in many parts of the country, trifoliate orange is most valuable in the fall for its decorative fuzzy, fragrant yellow fruits and in the winter when its bright green stems and thorns are displayed. It bears white, very fragrant 1- to 2-inch flowers in spring. Native to Korea and China, it is sometimes used as an understock for grafting oranges.

BEST CONDITIONS Plant in full sun in moist acid soil. It does not thrive in sandy, alkaline soils.

PLANTING Transplant in the spring and keep well watered. Transplanting is usually easy. Mulch.

ROUTINE CARE Water during dry spells.

PRUNING Prune just after flowering or at any time. This plant responds well to shearing and can be clipped into a dense hedge. The tangled growth of free-standing specimen plants may be cut back if it becomes overgrown. Extensive pruning is discouraged by the formidable spines; may be grown as a multi-stemmed shrub.

PESTS, DISEASES, OTHER PROBLEMS None serious.

PROPAGATION Seed germinates readily if somewhat slowly. Stratify at $41°$ F for 90 days. Use fresh seed as soon as it is ripe. Softwood cuttings taken in summer and treated with rooting hormone root readily.

USE Makes a good specimen tree in lawns, and combines well with shrubs and trees in collections. It is used extensively as hedge material, clipped or not, especially in the South. Suitable for container plantings but not near sitting areas.

Poncirus trifoliata in spring (above) and late summer (below).

PONCIRUS TRIFOLIATA (TRIFOLIATE ORANGE) Deciduous. 10 years: 6 feet; 20 years: 10 feet; 50 years: 20-25 feet; maturity: to 25 feet. Open, rounded head, fragrant white flowers in spring, fuzzy yellow fruit in summer, good fall color. Full sun, moist, acidic soil. Zones 5-9.

POPULUS NIGRA 'ITALICA' (LOMBARDY POPLAR) Deciduous. 10 years: 25 feet; 20 years: 50 feet; 50 years: 80-90 feet; maturity: to 120 feet. Tall, narrow habit, dark green leaves on oval crown. Full sun or part shade, any soil; tolerates dryness, but prefers moist soil. Often short lived. Zones 7-9.

POPULUS TREMULOIDES (QUAKING ASPEN) Deciduous. 10 years: 18 feet; 20 years: 30-35 feet; 50 years: 40-50 feet; maturity: to 50 feet. Loose open habit, small leaves attached by weak stems turn yellow in fall. Full sun or light shade, any soil (tolerates dryness). Zones 1-9.

PRUNUS X BLIREIANA (BLIREIANA PLUM) Deciduous. 10 years: 12 feet; 20 years: 20 feet; maturity: to 20 feet (40-year lifespan). Compact tree with rounded head, double, light pink flowers, reddish purple foliage. Full sun to partial shade, well-drained soil with neutral pH. Zones 5-8.

Take care to site where the thorns will not be dangerous to children or pets. The rather dry, seedy "oranges" are sometimes used for making marmalade; the skin can be candied.

POPULUS POPLAR, ASPEN *Salicaceae (Willow family)*

The chief value of the poplar–besides its beauty–is its ability to grow quickly; poplars can grow up to 5 feet in a single year. The tree has its drawbacks as well: it is very short-lived, and often has to be replaced after 20 years; its roots are notorious for causing mischief–in some areas, *P. canadensis* has been outlawed for this reason; and its fluffy white seeds are very hard to clean up. The well-shaped trees grow to 90 feet tall; leaves, which turn a clear yellow in the fall are dark green, and, in some species, silvery green underneath. One forgets the disadvantages of the poplar tree when its two-tone leaves shimmer in the breeze.

BEST CONDITIONS Although poplars will grow in light shade and any soil (even very dry soil), full sun and moist, deep, well-drained soil are best. They are very cold-hardy, surviving in Zones 2-7.

PLANTING Plant in spring or fall.

ROUTINE CARE An organic mulch will help to keep soil moist and fertile.

PRUNING Prune in summer and fall to avoid bleeding.

PROPAGATION Take cuttings in spring or fall; sow seed in summer.

PESTS, DISEASES, OTHER PROBLEMS Although healthy trees resist diseases and infestations, the wood of this tree is usually weak and the tree is usually short-lived. Before you plant a poplar, ask about the type of roots your selected species and cultivar may produce and make sure they won't affect structures or plumbing.

USE Poplars are often used to create a quick screen or mass planting.

SELECTIONS *P. alba*, white poplar, grows 50-60 feet tall and wide. This species is popular for its foliage, green on top, white underneath; it shows its white side in any breeze and the effect is mesmerizing. In the fall, the leaves turn yellow and red. However, it suckers profusely and is host to many diseases. *P. a.* **'Pyramidalis'** is a narrower form that spreads 15-20 feet.

P. deltoides, eastern poplar or cottonwood, grows 75-100 feet tall and spreads 50-75 feet across. It has a vaselike shape and and a balsamy fragrance. The cultivar **'Siouxland'** is disease resistant and has dark green leaves. **'Noreaster'** is seedless, avoiding the mess spread by many poplars.

P. nigra **'Italica'**, Lombardy poplar, is probably the most popular poplar, forming a narrow column that is very useful in garden design. The tree turns golden in the fall. Don't expect it to live more than 30 years except in the Pacific Northwest; it usually succumbs to canker.

P. tremuloides, quaking aspen, is hardy down to Zone 1; it grows in just about every part of North America, and is usually the first tree to appear after a fire in a conifer forest. It has a loose, open form that often does not fit into a garden, but in nature, groves of quaking aspens are magnificent, particularly in the autumn.

PRUNUS CHERRY, PEACH, PLUM, ETC. *Rosaceae (Rose family)*

A very large genus, *Prunus* includes stone fruits like almond, apricot, cherry, nectarine, peach, and plum, as well as ornamentals like choke cherry, blackthorn, and cherry laurel. Most trees in the genus are alternate-leaved and deciduous. Flowers can be pink, white, red, or greenish, and are usually borne

At Butchart Gardens in Victoria, British Columbia, a row of Lombardy poplars serves as a backdrop for a purple beech and a garden of annuals.

Above: Prunus laurocerasus.
Top: Prunus serrulata 'Kwanzan'.

in clusters. Although some of these trees have attractive foliage, some of the best bark available, and color and fruit well into autumn, they are best known for their incredibly lush display of flowers in spring. The most ornamental species do not bear edible fruit; if you want fruit, special selection, pruning, and insect control measures should be taken; see pages 208-211.

BEST CONDITIONS Deciduous species need full sun (though cherry laurel requires shade); evergreens will tolerate some shade. Soil should be well drained, with a neutral pH; mix in lime if the soil is too acid.

PLANTING Plant in early spring or fall.

ROUTINE CARE Trees in this genus require fertilizer, but too much will leave them increasingly susceptible to disease. Try to strike a balance. Keep evenly moist, particularly during dry spells.

PRUNING In the early years, prune to remove crossing and other problem branches. Some varieties need regular pruning to avoid overcrowding; removing large branches will help to discourage rot. Prune carefully, avoiding unnecessary cuts and leaving branch collars intact.

PESTS, DISEASES, OTHER PROBLEMS Watch for aphids, beetles, fruit worms, borers, and scale, as well as twig blight, powdery mildew, and fungus leaf spots. Foliage is favored by many insects, to the point where spraying sometimes becomes necessary even if you are not growing the trees for fruit. Keeping the tree healthy and clean helps prevent infestation and disease.

PROPAGATION Sow seeds outdoors or in a cold frame, or take cuttings.

USE Ornamentals generally have dramatic blooms as well and are often grown as specimens or in eye-catching groups. Some varieties can be espaliered on a wall or other support. When choosing a *Prunus* species for winter, spring, and summer interest as well as for fall flowers, choose types with good fall color, attractive bark, and lush foliage.

SELECTIONS *P. amygdalus*, almond, blooms earlier than other *Prunus* species, usually in February or March. It is hardy to Zone 6.

P. armeniaca, apricot, is another early bloomer. Its flowers are sometimes killed by late frost so it is most suitable to warmer climates. **'Charles Abraham'** has deep red flowers and blooms longer than most other varieties.

P. cerasus, sour cherry, is one of the few fruit trees for shady areas. It is also very hardy (to Zone 3) and has a double-flowering form (**'Rhexii'**) that is ornamental.

P. laurocerasus **'Otto Luyken'**, cherry laurel, is an evergreen tree with dense foliage and creamy white flowers. Growing to 25 feet, it is often used in southern gardens as a formal hedge or screen. Susceptible to scale and fungal leaf spot. Hardy to Zone 6. **'Schipkaensis'**, a compact cherry laurel, is hardy to New York City and Boston.

P. persica, peach tree, grows to 24 feet tall and is hardy to Zone 5 but will fruit well only in climates with very long growing seasons. It is grown more for peaches than for flowers, but flowers are attractive as well. The cultivar **'Helen Borchers'** has especially attractive clear pink flowers. **'Peppermint Stick'** has very double white flowers. **'Late Double Red'** is among the best red-flowering trees.

P. sargentii, Sargent cherry, among the hardiest, most adaptable, and most attractive of the cherry trees. It grows to 75 feet tall and is hardy to Zone 4. It grows on a single trunk, and is covered by single pink flowers in early spring. The foliage

PRUNUS x CISTENA (PURPLE-LEAF SAND CHERRY) Deciduous. 10 years: 8 feet; 20 years: 10 feet; maturity: to 10 feet (40-year lifespan). Single pink flowers, intense purple foliage, shrubby, multistemmed habit. Any average, well-drained soil, full sun or partial shade. Zones 2-8.

PRUNUS GRAYANA Deciduous. 10 years: 15 feet; 20 years: 25 feet; maturity: to 25 feet (40-year lifespan). Serrated green leaves, racemes of white flowers, small black fruit. Any average, well-drained soil, full sun or partial shade. Zones 5-8.

PRUNUS LUSITANICA (PORTUGUESE LAUREL) Deciduous. 10 years: 8 feet; 20 years: 16 feet; 50 years: 25-30 feet; maturity: to 30 feet. Dense rounded head, 5- to 8-inch-long glossy dark green leaves, racemes of small creamy white flowers, red fruit turns purple or black in late summer. Full sun, well-drained soil with neutral pH. Zones 7-9.

PRUNUS NIPPONICA (NIPPONESE CHERRY) Deciduous. 10 years: 10 feet; 20 years: 20 feet; maturity: to 25 feet (40-year lifespan). Dense, bushy habit, single white or pale pink flowers in summer, excellent fall color. Partial shade, well-drained soil with neutral pH. Sometimes reblooms in late fall, as seen here. Zones 5-8.

plant selector

starts out bronze following the flowers, turning green in summer and dark red in autumn. Its bark is one of its best features.

P. serrulata, Oriental cherry, grows 20-25 feet tall and is the variety most often seen. It grows 20-25 feet tall and is hardy in Zones 5-6. Its flowers range from single to very double and come in every shade of pink or white; some varieties impart an exquisite fragrance. **'Kwanzan'** has double pink flowers and is hardy to Zone 5; it is one of the best in the genus for fall color. At The New York Botanical Garden, it flowers at the same time as the tulips, to spectacular effect. **'Gyoiko'** has semidouble yellowish flowers, which contrast nicely in a collection of cherry trees. **'Shogetsu'** grows to about 15 feet tall and has single pale pink flowers about 2 inches in diameter.

P. subhirtella, higan cherry, has an interesting rounded form and grows to 30 feet tall. Its leaves are smaller than many other cherries, but its flowers last longer; they usually bloom earlier as well. It is hardy to Zone 5. **'Autumnalis'** sometimes blooms again in fall (unless the weather is cold). **'Pendula'** is a choice weeping form. This species was one of the first brought to North America from Japan.

P. yedoensis, Japanese flowering cherry or Yoshino cherry, is the species famous for its annual appearance in Washington, D.C.; almost 1,000 trees were planted along the Tidal Basin there in 1912, a gift from the mayor of Tokyo. This tree needs more space than most cherries, and should be planted 30-40 feet apart. They grow to almost 50 feet tall and are hardy to Zone 5. It is one of the longest-lived cherries, even in hot, humid areas where cherries often succumb to disease.

P. x **'Hally Jolivette',** a cross between *P. subhirtella* and *P. yedoensis,* is a lovely small shade tree for a small property, growing to about 15 feet tall. Its pinks buds open to double white flowers over several weeks in the spring.

Prunus subhirtella 'Pendula'.

PRUNUS PERSICA 'LATE DOUBLE RED' (PEACH) Deciduous. 10 years: 12 feet; 20 years: 20 feet; maturity: to 25 feet (30-year lifespan). Rounded head, dense foliage, red or yellow fruit, double red flowers in midspring. Full sun, well-drained soil with neutral pH. Zones 5-9.

PRUNUS SERRULATA 'KWANZAN' (ORIENTAL CHERRY) Deciduous. 10 years: 12 feet; 20 years: 25 feet; maturity: to 35 feet (40-year lifespan). Upright tree with long, oval toothed leaves that turn bronze in fall, very showy, very double pink flowers, 2-2½ inches in diameter. Full sun, well-drained soil with neutral pH. Zones 5-9.

PRUNUS YEDOENSIS (JAPANESE FLOWERING CHERRY) Deciduous. 10 years: 10 feet; 20 years: 20 feet; maturity: to 55 feet (40-year lifespan). Flat-topped, bushy habit with oval leaves and racemelike clusters of white or pink flowers, insignificant black fruit. Full sun, rich soil with neutral pH. Zones 5-9.

PSEUDOLARIX KAEMPFERI (JAPANESE GOLDEN LARCH)
Deciduous. 10 years: 8 feet; 20 years: 18-20 feet; 50 years: 40-50 feet; maturity: to 60 feet. Branches horizontally, in tiers, resulting in an open habit. Feathery needles 1½-2½ inches long turn golden in fall. Full sun; any well-drained soil except limey soil; tolerates heat better than larches. Zones 5-8.

PSEUDOTSUGA MENZIESII (DOUGLAS FIR) Evergreen. 10 years: 12 feet; 20 years: 25 feet; 50 years: 55-65 feet; maturity: to 100 feet. Flattened needlelike foliage on spreading, slightly pendulous branches; conspicuous cones. Full sun, slightly acidic well-drained soil. Zones 4-8.

PTEROCARYA STENOPTERA (CHINESE WINGNUT) Deciduous. 10 years: 15-20 feet; 20 years: 30-40 feet; 50 years: 70-80 feet; maturity: to 90 feet. Wide-spreading, open habit, dark green compound leaves, light green winged nuts in fall on female plants. Full sun, moist, deep soil; tolerates dry conditions. Zones 5-8.

PTEROSTYRAX HISPIDA (WISTERIA TREE) Deciduous. 10 years: 12 feet; 20 years: 20 feet; 50 years: 35-45 feet; maturity: to 45 feet. Slender spreading branches, covered in creamy white flowers in drooping wisterialike panicles in early summer. Full sun, well-drained, moist soil. Zones 5-9.

PYRUS CALLERYANA 'BRADFORD' (CALLERY PEAR) Deciduous. 10 years: 15 feet; 20 years: 30 feet; 50 years: 35-45 feet; maturity: to 45 feet. Pyramidal form, abundant white flowers, small reddish brown fruit, excellent autumn color. Full sun, slightly acid to alkaline soil. Zones 4-8.

PSEUDOLARIX KAEMPFERI [P. AMABILIS] JAPANESE GOLDEN LARCH *Pinaceae (Pine family)*

The golden larch adds a note of grace and elegance, growing quickly to great height (sometimes to over 100 feet tall) and branching horizontally in tiers. Its color is remarkable as well–fresh bright green in the spring, turning golden in fall.

BEST CONDITIONS The golden larch will grow in almost any soil except limestone, so long as it is well drained; moderately moist and fertile soil is best. It produces its best color in full sun. Golden larch is hardy to Zone 5.

PLANTING Follow general procedures for planting conifers.

ROUTINE CARE Although they will tolerate somewhat dry and poor soil, addition of fertilizer and water to keep soil moist and rich improves them.

PRUNING Do not prune this tree; you will only harm it.

PROPAGATION Propagate from seeds or cuttings.

PESTS, DISEASES, OTHER PROBLEMS None serious.

USE Because of its size and branching habit, the golden larch is not appropriate for small gardens. But on a large lawn or in a public area, it commands respect and admiration. It is also an appropriate subject for bonsai treatment.

PSEUDOTSUGA MENZIESII DOUGLAS FIR *Pinaceae (Pine family)*

The quintessential Christmas tree, Douglas firs are also valuable for timber and as ornamental trees.

BEST CONDITIONS Moderately well-drained, slightly acid soil is best for Douglas firs, as for most conifers. They need full sun to develop properly. Keep away from drying winds or very dry areas. This tree is reliably hardy only to Zone 4, and is often killed when young by unusual frost.

PLANTING Follow general planting procedures for conifers.

ROUTINE CARE Provide extra water for young plants; established plants do not need extra water. A mulch will help keep soil moist and fertile.

PRUNING Prune out branches that go out of bounds.

PROPAGATION Propagate by seeds or cuttings.

PESTS, DISEASES, OTHER PROBLEMS None serious.

USE Douglas firs can be used as screens, windbreaks, or specimen trees.

SELECTIONS *P. menziesii* can grow to 200 feet in the wild, but usually is no taller than 80 feet in cultivation. *P. m. var. glauca* is a blue-green form.

PTEROCARYA WINGNUT *Juglandaceae (Walnut family)*

Wingnuts are grown for long catkins, attractive, dark green leaves, and pendulous racemes of winged nuts that appear in the midsummer when other trees are beginning to lose interest. It is a large, fast-growing tree, reaching up to 50 feet in height.

BEST CONDITIONS Wingnuts prefer moist, deep soil and full sun, but will accept dry conditions. They are hardy in Zones 5-9.

PLANTING Plant balled-and-burlapped plants in the spring.

ROUTINE CARE Although they will tolerate poor, dry soil, addition of fertilizer and water will keep the trees at their best.

PRUNING Unless lower branches are pruned, the tree will develop horizontally. Prune in summer; trees pruned in fall or spring tend to bleed.

PROPAGATION Propagate by seeds, layers, or suckers.

MEMORIAL TREES

The first recorded instance of the planting of a memorial tree in the United States dates to 1647 and Peter Stuyvesant, who planted a pear tree in front of his "country" house on Manhattan island (the tree had been brought from Holland in a tub). The pear stood at what eventually became the corner of Third Avenue and Thirteenth Street for more than 200 years and was considered a city landmark. Just a year later, in 1648, Peregrine White, the first English person born in New England, planted an apple tree in Marshfield, Massachusetts; it was still bearing fruit in 1848. In 1787, Alexander Hamilton celebrated the success of the Constitutional Convention by planting 13 sweet gum trees, one for each of the new states, on the grounds of his New York City home, known as the Grange. The trees stood on the site, today the south side of West 143 Street between Amsterdam and Convent Avenues, until 1911, when they were removed to make way for a building.

PESTS, DISEASES, OTHER PROBLEMS None serious.

USE Although they are usually too large for home gardens because of their size and aggressive roots, wingnuts make excellent street trees and are particularly suitable for areas along the shores of a pond or stream.

SELECTIONS *P. fraxinifolia,* Caucasian wingnut, has light green fruit and compound leaves up to 24 inches long.

P. stenoptera, Chinese wingnut, is a smaller tree, with smaller leaves.

PTEROSTYRAX HISPIDA WISTERIA TREE *Styracaceae (Storax family)*

Also called fragrant epaulette tree because it produces sprays of tiny, fragrant flowers that cover its branches like epaulettes, this tree is best viewed from below. It flowers in midsummer, somewhat later than most other flowering trees.

BEST CONDITIONS The wisteria tree prefers moist, well-drained soil and full sun.

PLANTING Plant balled-and-burlapped plants in the spring. Allow enough space for the tree to spread its branches.

ROUTINE CARE Keep soil evenly moist and moderately fertile with the addition of water during dry spells and an annual application of fertilizer if soil is poor.

PRUNING Remove lower branches during winter to keep them from dragging on the ground.

PROPAGATION Propagate by seeds, layering, and cuttings of semi-hardwood.

PESTS, DISEASES, OTHER PROBLEMS None serious.

USE The top of a road, a raised bed, or a high patio or balcony—where it can be viewed from below—are excellent sites for a wisteria tree.

PYRUS PEAR *Rosaceae (Rose family)*

Pyrus, or pears, a group of deciduous or semi-evergreen trees native to Eurasia and North Africa, includes those grown for fruit and those cultivated as ornamentals. Pear trees have a rounded shape, edible fruit, and attractive flowers.

BEST CONDITIONS The pear tree thrives in full sun or part shade. It tolerates many types of soil, from clay to loam (pH 6.0-7.4). It grows best in Zones 5-9 and is somewhat drought tolerant.

PLANTING Look for healthy, vigorous plants with good branching patterns. Plant container-grown or balled-and-burlapped trees in late winter (when the ground can be dug). Pear trees have shallow root systems and are easy to transplant.

ROUTINE CARE Keep well watered (at least 1 inch per week) for the first two years, then keep evenly moist. Fertilize only if planted in poor, infertile soil.

PRUNING Prune in late winter or early spring to remove damaged or crowded branches.

PROPAGATION Start from seed stratified for three months at 40° F.

PESTS, DISEASES, OTHER PROBLEMS Fireblight is possible but infrequent.

USE Because it withstands pollution, pears can be planted on streets; they are highly ornamental, and have a pleasing symmetry that will enhance almost every property.

SELECTIONS *P. calleryana,* Callery pear, is descibed above. While the original Callery pear had thorns, the first selection introduced here, *P. c. 'Bradford',* was thornless and is a handsome ornamental. A pyramid-shaped tree, it can grow 30-40 feet tall, with a 15-20 foot spread; it has broad, ovate green leaves that turn a glossy red or scarlet in fall and stay that way until very late in the season. Adding to its

PYRUS SALICIFOLIA 'SILVER FROST' (WILLOWLEAF PEAR) Deciduous. 10 years: 10 feet; 20 years: 15 feet; maturity: to 15 feet (30-year lifespan). Slender, slightly drooping branches with silvery willowlike leaves, white flowers in May; fruit is inedible. Full sun, well-drained slightly acid to alkaline soil; does not tolerate wet or dry soils. Zones 4-9.

QUERCUS ACUTISSIMA (SAWTOOTH OAK) Deciduous. 10 years: 12 feet; 20 years: 25 feet; 50 years: 50-60 feet; maturity: to 70 feet. Broad, rounded head, dense serrated leaves that turn a color resembling chestnuts and remain on the tree through winter. Full sun or light shade; organic soil; tolerant of acid and slightly alkaline soils. Zones 5-8.

QUERCUS ALBA (WHITE OAK) Deciduous. 10 years: 10 feet; 20 years: 20 feet; 50 years: 50 feet; maturity: to 90 feet. Broad, rounded head with spreading branches, dense lobed leaves may turn orange to purple in autumn. Full sun or light shade; organic soil; not tolerant of highly alkaline pH soil. Zones 4-8.

QUERCUS BICOLOR (SWAMP WHITE OAK) Deciduous. 10 years: 10 feet; 20 years: 20 feet; 50 years: 50 feet; maturity: to 90 feet. Narrow, rounded head with open habit, dense lobed leaves that turn yellow, brown, and red in autumn. Full sun or light shade; acid or slightly alkaline organic soil. Zones 4-8.

Quercus coccinea.

beauty, it has showy white flowers, 1 inch in diameter in May, and bears russet-colored fruit. Bradford pears have branches that are inferior in the crotch angle compared to newer selections; they can break in winds and ice storms. *P. c.* **'Aristocrat'** has dark foliage and more intense fall color; its branches are strong and have crotch angles superior to 'Bradford'. *P. c.* **'Chanticleer'** (also known as 'Select' or 'Cleveland Select') is narrower and requires less space than 'Bradford' and is hardy to Zone 4. Its leaves turn yellow in autumn. *P. c.* **'Capital'** is narrow and columnar, and its glossy leaves turn red-purple in autumn. *P. c.* **'Autumn' Blaze'** is the best selection on the market for the upper Midwest, with strong branches and consistent fall color.

P. salicifolia, willowleaf pear, is perhaps the most beautiful of the pears because it has both silver-white foliage and slender, slightly pendulous branches; it is, however, very susceptible to fireblight. A cultivar **'Pendula'** has a weeping form, and is known as weeping willowleaf pear.

The hardiest of the pears resistant to fireblight and grows in Zones 4-6 is the Ussurian or Chinese pear (*P. ussuriensis*). It can grow to 50 feet tall, has shiny green leaves that turn an orange-red in fall, and bears ornamental yellow-green fruit. Its beautiful white blossoms are tinged with pink. It is often used for grafting.

QUERCUS OAK *Fagaceae (Beech family)*

A vast genus, oaks are available in many different plant and leaf sizes, growth rates, and levels of cold tolerance; both evergreen and deciduous types exist. Most are rounded, very long-lived and tough, and turn vivid red, yellow, or brown in the fall. Contrary to popular belief, they are not particularly slow growers; with adequate moisture throughout the growing season, they can grow 1 foot per year.

BEST CONDITIONS The best conditions for most oaks are full sun and moist, rich, well drained soil that is high in organic matter. The tree will tolerate light shade and soil that is only moderately rich, but will not grow as quickly or as well. Evergreen oaks (*Q. agrifolia* and *Q. virginiana,* the live oak) are considerably less coldhardy than the deciduous types, and are more tolerant of shade.

PLANTING Oaks have long taproots and resist transplanting; transplant young balled-and-burlapped trees in early spring or early fall.

ROUTINE CARE An established oak in an appropriate site will not need additional water and fertilizer.

PRUNING Prune young trees in winter; older trees rarely need pruning.

PROPAGATION Sow seed in fall.

PESTS, DISEASES, OTHER PROBLEMS Some species become chlorotic in alkaline soil. Gypsy moths can attack in the East (they prefer red, white, and black oaks); burlap bands placed around the tree will attract and catch larvae, which can then be discarded. Oak wilt can kill trees; pruning only in winter helps avoid this.

USE Although they are usually too large for many backyards, oak trees are wonderful in larger yards. Their shade is excellent, though filtered enough for grass and shade-loving plants to grow beneath them. And they convey an instant stamp of history and nobility wherever they are planted.

SELECTIONS *Q. acutissima,* sawtooth oak, grows 45 feet tall and has chestnutlike leaves that turn brown-red and remain on the tree through winter. Zones 5-9.

Q. agrifolia, coast live oak, has large glossy leaves and adapts well to dry soil. It is hardy in Zones 7-9.

QUERCUS ELLIPSOIDALIS (NORTHERN PIN OAK) Deciduous.10 years: 10 feet; 20 years: 20 feet; 50 years: 50 feet; maturity: to 90 feet. Broad, rounded head with spreading branches, narrowly lobed leaves. Far more tolerant of alkaline soils than pin oak. Full sun or light shade; organic soil. Zones 3-7.

QUERCUS MUEHLENBERGII (YELLOW CHESTNUT OAK) Deciduous. 10 years: 10 feet; 20 years: 20 feet; 50 years: 50 feet; maturity: to 90 feet. Long, toothed leaves turn yellow in autumn. Full sun or light shade; deep, rich, organic soil. Tolerant of alkaline soils. Zones 5-8.

QUERCUS PHELLOS (WILLOW OAK) Deciduous. 10 years: 17 feet; 20 years: 35 feet; 50 years: 65-75 feet; maturity: to 90 feet. Rounded or conical habit, spreading branches, dense slender, lance-shaped leaves that turn yellowish in autumn. Full sun or light shade; organic soil. Zones 5-8.

QUERCUS RUBRA (RED OAK) Deciduous. 10 years: 17 feet; 20 years: 35 feet; 50 years: 65-75 feet; maturity: to 90 feet. Pyramidal tree becomes broad and rounded when mature; shiny leaves turn dark red in autumn. Full sun or light shade; organic soil. Zones 3-8.

QUERCUS ROBUR (ENGLISH OAK) Evergreen. 10 years: 10 feet; 20 years: 20 feet; 50 years: 50 feet; maturity: to 90 feet. Dark green lobed leaves with pale green undersides; little fall color. Massive tree with broadly rounded crown. Full sun, rich, well-drained acid or alkaline soil. Zones 5-9.

RHODODENDRON ARBOREUM SSP. ARBOREUM (TREE RHODODEN-DRON) Evergreen. 10 years: 7 feet; 14 years: 20 feet; 50 years: 20-25 feet; maturity: to 25 feet. Pyramidal habit, often irregular. Long (5-10 inches), oval shiny green leaves; large dark red flowers in late spring or early summer. Full sun or part shade, acid soil. Zones 7-8.

ROBINIA PSEUDOACACIA 'FRISIA' (BLACK LOCUST) Deciduous. 10 years: 13 feet; 20 years: 20-25 feet; 50 years: 35-55 feet; maturity: to 80 feet. Upright tree with open head, few branches; ferny foliage turns gold in fall; long white pea-shaped flowers. Full sun, well-drained soil; tolerates alkalinity, salt, drought, heat. Zones 3-8.

SALIX x BLANDA (NIOBE WEEPING WILLOW) Deciduous. 10 years: 18 feet; 20 years: 35 feet; 50 years: 75-80 feet; maturity: to 90 feet. Wide head, strong weeping shape, narrow silvery gray foliage. Full sun, moist or wet soil of average fertility. Zones 4-9.

Q. alba, white oak, establishes with difficulty and grows slowly, but eventually reaches 50-80 feet tall and wide. It has strong horizontal branches and leaves that turn bronze to red in late fall or winter. Hardy in Zones 4-8. Contrary to some sources, which list it as very slow-growing, it will grow at an average rate if healthy, well-grown plants are obtained from the nursery.

Q. bicolor, swamp white oak, tolerates drought, soil compaction, and poor soil. It transplants more easily than many other oaks and does well in urban conditions. Hardy in Zones 4-7, it grows 50-80 feet tall and wide.

Q. coccinea, scarlet oak, is faster, growing to 75 feet tall, 50 feet across. It provides good shade and withstands pollution. It is somewhat difficult to transplant and establish (easiest from a small tree), but is very drought-tolerant once established. Leaves turn deep red in fall. Zones 5-8.

Q. imbricaria, shingle oak, has unlobed leaves that appear bright red in spring, bright green in summer, tan in fall. It can be used as a hedge. Zones 5-8.

Q. nigra, water oak, is a fast grower, hardy in Zones 5-8. It reaches 60-75 feet tall, 40-50 feet across. Its leaves do not have the typical oak leaf shape.

Q. palustris, pin oak, displays an interesting branching pattern: the middle branches extend horizontally, the upper ones are upright. It is usually pruned on the bottom. It transplants easily but turns chlorotic in alkaline soil. Leaves turn a nice red in fall in some areas (not in New York). Zones 5-9.

Q. phellos, willow oak, has willow-shaped leaves that turn light yellow in the fall. It tolerates wet soil, transplants easily, and has a finer texture than other oaks. It is used as a street tree in the South and in Philadelphia. It grows 40-60 feet tall, 30-40 feet across. Zones 6-9.

Q. prinus, chestnut oak, is a good choice for rocky, well-drained soil and difficult sites. Its leaves are similar to chestnut tree leaves and provide good fall color.

Q. robur, English oak, grows quickly, but provides little or no autumn color and is prone to mildew. It is hardy in Zones 5-9. The cultivar **'Fastigiata'** becomes a slen-

He who plants an oak looks forward to future ages, and plants for posterity. Nothing can be less selfish than this. He cannot expect to sit in its shade nor enjoy its shelter, but he exults in the idea that the acorn which he has buried in the earth shall grow up into a lofty pile, and shall keep on flourishing long after he has ceased to tread his paternal fields.

WASHINGTON IRVING

White oaks *(Quercus alba)* and tulip trees *(Liriodendron tulipifera)* with rhododendrons.

OAK LORE

Throughout the world are old trees, often oaks, famous for being in some way related to a historical event or tale from folklore. There was, for example, the De Soto Oak in Tampa Bay, Florida, under which that Spanish explorer was said to have rested. Until it was blown down by a storm in 1856, Hartford, Connecticut, had the Charter Oak, in the hollow of which the colony's charter was hidden when demanded by Sir Edmund Andros, governor general of New England. (Andros's name is also connected to an oak that he himself had planted at Schagticoke, New York, in 1676 and that was still standing in the 1920s.) England is spread with venerable oaks. There was, for example, Owen Glendower's Oak, said to be the very tree from which that Welsh national hero watched the battle of Shrewsbury (1403); and just as there really is a Sherwood Forest, there was once an oak known as Robin Hood's Larder, so-called because the merry outlaw was said to have stashed the deer he poached in its hollow. Unfortunately, much of the tree was lost to fire when schoolgirls boiled a kettle for tea inside the famous hollow.

der column, similar to the Lombardy poplar but much more long-lived.

Q. rubra, red oak, also called *Q. borealis,* has dark silver bark and grows 60-90 feet across, 75 feet wide. This sturdy tree is a good choice for parks and large lawns.

Q. virginiana, live oak, is a magnificent tree for the South; its architecture is stunning, with massive, arching branches, often covered with Spanish moss. It grows 40-80 feet tall, 60-100 feet across and is hardy in Zones 8-10.

RHODODENDRON MAXIMUM ROSEBAY RHODODENDRON
Ericaceae (Heath family)

A native understory plant from Nova Scotia and Ontario south to Georgia, Alabama and Ohio, rosebay rhododendron is the only one considered a tree in a genus of shrubs (except in the Pacific Northwest, where several Asian species reach tree height). In the North it may reach 15 feet; further south 30 feet is not unusual. Its clean-looking evergreen 4- to 8-inch-long leaves are dark green; in late spring or early summer, rosy pink to white flowers open, spotted at the throat with olive and orange. This is an excellent tree, but only in woodland settings where conditions are favorable.

BEST CONDITIONS Rosebay rhododendron prefers a sheltered position with some shade but tolerates medium shade well. Soil must be acid (pH 4.5-5.5), moist and

Above: Quercus virginiana with Cornus florida.

high in organic matter; poorly drained soil is not acceptable. Protect from winter sun as winter injury can be severe. Avoid sites that may become contaminated with salt, along roads or by the seashore.

PLANTING Plant balled-and-burlapped stock, taken with a large rootball, in spring. Make the hole twice as wide as deep and set root collar no deeper than it was growing in the field. Water well and mulch. Select stocky plants with many stems and thick healthy foliage that covers the plant from the ground up. Avoid leggy or yellowed plants. The plant must be firmly attached at the root line, not wobbly. Be sure to leave enough space for subsequent growth.

ROUTINE CARE Mulch with pine needles or some other acid organic material, or, better yet, plant a woodland groundcover plant to protect the surface roots, and enhance the woodland atmosphere.

PRUNING Prune out dead or diseased wood. Remove spent flowers where possible to increase bud set for next year.

PESTS, DISEASES, OTHER PROBLEMS To avoid the myriad of pests and diseases that affect this plant, site carefully and observe good cultural practices to maximize healthy growth. Be alert for *botryospaeria* canker, crown rot, leaf spot and scorch, powdery mildew, shoot blight and wilt. Insect pests include aphids, weevils, Japanese beetles, lace bugs and borers, scales, thrips, whitefly and nematodes, and the list is not complete.

PROPAGATION Take cuttings in August or grow from seed.

USE Excellent for woodland gardens as an understory tree and most other shade gardens.

ROBINIA PSEUDOACACIA BLACK LOCUST *Fabaceae (Pea family)*

Locusts are in the legume family, with pendulous clusters of small, white, fragrant, pealike flowers in 8- to 12-inch-long wisterialike chains. Black locust has an upright, somewhat open habit, growing 50-75 feet tall with displays of extremely sweet-scented, showy white flowers in early June. The bark is deeply furrowed and black, another picturesque attribute of this tree.

BEST CONDITIONS Robinia grows best in full sun. It tolerates a wide range of soil types, but does not like heavy clay or wet sites. It tolerates soil pH from 5.1-7.7 and is somewhat tolerant of salt. It is hardy in Zones 4-9.

PLANTING Plant balled-and-burlapped specimens in spring. This tree is susceptible to borers and stress should be avoided at all costs. Mulch plant immediately after planting and water regularly to avoid stress.

ROUTINE CARE Provide water regularly (1 inch per week) to establish and guard against stress during dry spells, but avoid excessive amounts. Once established, it tolerates drought but be sure to water it if the drought becomes severe–that's when borers attack. A member of the legume family, robinia produces its own nitrogren, so is reasonably self-sufficient without the addition of fertilizer even in infertile soils. Mulching helps reduce stress.

PRUNING Heavy pruning is not necessary.

PESTS, DISEASES, OTHER PROBLEMS Locust borer can be a serious problem, but it can be avoided if care is taken to avoid placing the tree under stress caused by dryness. Its stems are spiney but spines are not a problem on the parts of the trunk that passersby encounter.

PROPAGATION Propagate by seeds and root suckers; for cultivars, by cuttings.

WASHINGTON OAK

George Washington never cut down a cherry tree (even in the fictionalized tale, which first appeared in a life of Washington by Mason Locke Weems, Washington doesn't cut the tree down, but merely "barks" it). In fact, Washington was quite fond of trees, overseeing the planting of various kinds at Mount Vernon and evidently looking out for their welfare when on the road. While traveling through the South during the summer of 1791, he was entertained one morning at breakfast in a home in the suburbs of Charleston, South Carolina. He chanced to overhear the lady of the house giving instructions to her gardener to cut down a particular oak because it obstructed the view from the portico. Washington immediately interceded on behalf of the tree, which was spared and long after bore his name in memory of the event.

Salix alba 'Tristis'.

USE This fast-growing tree is well-suited for natural and naturalistic plantings. It has extremely fragrant flowers and a narrow upright habit ideal for smaller areas. Once established, it has a great tolerance for heat and drought.

SELECTIONS 'Frisia' is a beautiful yellow-leaved selection that retains its color throughout the season in the Pacific Northwest, fading only slightly; in the East, it is only yellow in spring. Interestingly, the fall color becomes a more intense shade of gold. Flowers are not as prominent as on the species. **'Umbraculifera'** is a dense, umbrellalike form that grows to 20 feet tall and wide. It is not as floriferous or as spiny as the species and is subject to borers when stressed.

SALIX WILLOW, OSIER *Salicaceae (Willow family)*

Some people complain about the willow's shortcomings: it needs copious water, is subject to insect and storm damage, and has weak wood that usually causes it to be short-lived. But a well-grown willow—in its magnificent weeping form or covered with its fuzzy flowers on one of its several upright forms—is an unquestionable asset to the landscape.

BEST CONDITIONS Willows need full sun and moist or even wet soils. They are traditionally grown at the edge of a body of water. They will grow in average soil if water can be supplied whenever the weather turns dry. The soil need not be of greater than average fertility.

PLANTING Transplant in fall or early spring.

ROUTINE CARE Willows are known for their greediness. Unless they are planted in wet soil, be prepared to water them in dry weather. An organic mulch helps keep average soil moist for willows.

PRUNING Pruning should enhance natural beauty of tree. Prune selectively back to larger branch. Remove branches that drag on the ground, but don't create a neat edge! Because willows "bleed" sap, they should be pruned only in winter or spring.

SALIX BABYLONICA (BABYLON WEEPING WILLOW) Deciduous. 10 years: 15 feet; 20 years: 30 feet; 50 years: 40 feet; maturity: to 40 feet. Wide head, best weeping shape, narrow silver-gray foliage. Full sun, moist or wet soil of average fertility. Zones 6-9.

SALIX CAPREA (GOAT WILLOW) Deciduous. 10 years: 13 feet; 20 years: 25 feet; 50 years: 30 feet; maturity: to 30 feet. Loose open shape, somewhat pendulous; foliage remains dark green all summer; small fuzzy catkins appear in early spring. Full sun, moist or wet soil of average fertility. Zones 4-8.

SASSAFRAS ALBIDUM (SASSAFRAS) Deciduous. 10 years: 13 feet; 20 years: 25 feet; 50 years: 40-45 feet; maturity: to 50 feet. Rounded clusters of yellow-green flowers, interesting lobed leaves, small blue-black fruit. Full sun or light shade, rich, moist soil; tolerates adverse conditons, somewhat invasive. Zones 4-8.

SCIADOPITYS VERTICILLATA (JAPANESE UMBRELLA PINE) Evergreen. 10 years: 5 feet; 20 years: 10 feet; 50 years: 25-30 feet; maturity: to 60 feet. Symmetrical conical habit, dense, lustrous dark green needles with yellow markings; mature trees produce 5-inch cones. Full sun, slightly acidic soil. Zones 6-8.

INVASIVE TREES

Some trees are avoided because they can be invasive, crowding out other plants and taking over the area. In some area, weed trees imported from other climates have overtaken native plants. It is important to remember that the level of weediness will depend on the climate in which a plant is grown. A tree that will grow slowly in one area may become invasive in another. Some gardeners consider a tree to be invasive only if it is not native. The following trees are problematic in the Midwest because of their tendency to send out seedlings (except for ailanthus, which sends out root suckers): *Acer negundo* (box elder); *Acer saccharum* (silver maple) *Ailanthus altissima* (tree of heaven), phellodendron, *Syringa reticulata* (tree lilac, particularly in shade), and *Ulmus americana*. For areas of the country which are milder, be cautious of koelreuteria and paulownia.

PROPAGATION It is easy to propagate willows from cuttings taken anytime.

PESTS, DISEASES, OTHER PROBLEMS Willows have weak wood that is easily damaged by ice and wind. They are also prone to insect damage, particularly from caterpillars. Avoid injury to the wood when pruning, as this increases the possibility of insect damage. Do not plant near septic tanks, drains, or in cultivated areas because they tend to seek water and become a nuisance.

USE Willows are striking specimen plants, especially at water's edge; they are most effective when viewed from across water. When adjacent to water, they also serve to shore up the edge of the bank.

SELECTIONS *S. alba* (white willow) has an excellent loose and open shape and delicate texture, growing to about 30 feet tall and is hardy in Zones 3-7. It has yellow wood and catkins. *S. a.* **'Tristis'** (golden weeping willow) is readily available, hardy to Zone 2 and also has good yellow bark. *S. a.* **'Argentea'** has stunning silver foliage. *S. babylonica* (Babylon weeping willow) is known for it shape; it is considered the best of the weepers. But it is hardy only in Zones 6-8 and is subject to canker, twig blight, and powdery mildew. *S. b.* **'Crispa'** has interesting curled leaves. *S. caprea* (French pussy willow, goat willow) produces winter flowers tipped with fuzzy gray. It grows 25 feet tall and is hardy in Zones 4-9. The cultivar **'Pendula'** is a weeping form. Several colored pussy willow species are also available.

SASSAFRAS ALBIDUM SASSAFRAS *Lauraceae (Laurel family)*

All parts of the sassafras tree contain an oil that was used in numerous folk remedies, patent medicines, and sassafras tea until research showed that oil of sassafras is carcinogenic and should not be ingested in any form; it has been banned by the FDA. Of easy culture, sassafras trees are among the first to invade abandoned fields. They range from 35-50 feet tall and are characterized by fragrant, yellow flowers in spring, blue-black fruits in summer, and oval, three-lobed, or unique mitten-shaped green leaves. Mature trees exhibit a candelabra branching effect, particularly when adorned with flowers; autumn brings a show of brilliant orange, scarlet, and yellow, sometimes in a single leaf.

BEST CONDITIONS Although wild colonies may be seen in shaded areas, sassafras is best sited in sunny locations. Moist well-drained soil is ideal but fertility and moisture beyond average are not necessary. This tree does not tolerate high pH soils and is hardy in Zones 5-9.

PLANTING Purchase healthy looking plants in containers or balled and burlapped; sassafras has a deep tap root and long lateral roots. Robert Bowden recommends planting from container-grown stock whenever possible. Transplant in spring; mulch and water generously. Think twice before planting in a cultivated area: sassafras trees send up numerous suckers which will form colonies if transplanted.

ROUTINE CARE Additional water is usually unnecessary after establishment. Addition of fertilizer is never needed.

PRUNING Sassafras trees have a natural candelabralike habit that can be enhanced with good pruning.

PROPAGATION Sassafras is propagated easily—sometimes too easily—by suckers.

PESTS, DISEASES, OTHER PROBLEMS It is usually free of diseases and pests, but the first Japanese beetle found in Galen Gates' garden was munching on sassafras leaves.

USE Though picturesque when planted as a specimen, one must accept that sas-

SEQUOIADENDRON GIGANTEUM (GIANT SEQUOIA) Evergreen. 10 years: 10-12 feet; 20 years: 20-25 feet; 50 years: 50-60 feet; maturity: to 110 feet. Massive trunks, very tall straight habit, densely covered with spirally arranged needles. Full sun, deep, fertile, well-drained soil. Zones 6-8.

SOPHORA JAPONICA (JAPANESE PAGODA TREE) Deciduous. 10 years: 12-15 feet; 20 years: 24-30 feet; 50 years: 50-60 feet; maturity: to 70 feet. Tall tree with large branches, feathery compound leaves (similar to locusts), showy pealike flowers in spikes. Full sun or very light shade, sandy or loamy soil, acidic to slightly alkaline. Zones 4-8.

SORBUS x LATIFOLIA Deciduous. 10 years: 8 feet; 20 years: 15-20 feet; 50 years: 35-45 feet; maturity: to 45 feet. Round to oval toothed lobed leaves, small white flowers. Full sun or partial shade, any soil, but acid is best. Zones 5-8.

SORBUS ALNIFOLIA (KOREAN MOUNTAIN ASH) Deciduous. 10 years: 10 feet; 20 years: 20 feet; 50 years: 35-40 feet; maturity: to 50 feet. Pyramidal and upright, becoming rounded at maturity; simple, oval, toothed foliage, lustrous green turning brown and orange in fall; 2- to 3-inch white flowers in corymbs. Full sun or partial shade, any soil, but acid is best. Zones 4-8.

THE TALLEST TREES

Calaveras County, California, enjoyed national fame even before Mark Twain's 1865 story about the jumping frog. In the spring of 1852 a hunter named A. T. Dowd, lost in the woods, found himself standing in the middle of a forest of giant sequoia trees. His reports were dismissed as "tall" tales until while hunting a grizzly bear he managed to lead others to the grove. News of the towering trees soon spread, and Calaveras became a tourist mecca, complete with hotel. One of the largest trees–called simply The Big Tree–was felled in 1853; it took five men 25 days to bring it down, and they reported that mud splashed 100 feet in the air when it crashed to earth. The trunk was 302 feet long. Its rings were counted, and it was found to be 1,300 years old; by way of giving people something to go by, the tree was said to have been standing for nearly two centuries when Charlemagne was born. For many years the stump of the tree, 30 feet across, was used as a dance floor, while its trunk served as a bowling alley.

Below: Sequoidendron giganteum.

safras is best suited to a natural landscape. Though it behaves itself in garden settings when planted in the heavier soils found in much of the Midwest, suckers may run rampant in the garden if the tree is moved. In lighter soils, it can be rapacious. In nature, this tree produces colonies, often along fence rows, and is responsible for some of the best fall color in the Midwest.

SCIADOPITYS VERTICILLATA UMBRELLA PINE *Taxodiaceae (Taxodium family)*

L. H. Bailey, an eminent botanist, called the umbrella pine (native to a small area of Japan) "one of the most handsome and distinctive of conifers." Its uniform conical habit, complex texture, and glossy dark green foliage combine to make it an elegant addition to any garden. It grows 20-30 feet tall (and up to 60 feet) and 15-20 feet wide.

BEST CONDITIONS Like most conifers, umbrella pine prefers slightly acid and alkaline, moist, well-drained soil; it grows best in sun with some afternoon shade, particularly in hot climates. It does not do well in windy sites. Zones 5-8.

PLANTING Transplant balled-and-burlapped or container-grown stock.

ROUTINE CARE An organic mulch is beneficial. Water deeply during drought.

PRUNING Prune out dead branches. Heavy pruning will only destroy its excellent natural shape.

PESTS, DISEASES, OTHER PROBLEMS None serious.

PROPAGATION Propagation is accomplished by seed or cuttings, but is not easy and is best left to professionals; purchase plants.

USE Umbrella pine is an excellent choice as a specimen tree or an accent tree in a shrub or perennial border. It is very slow-growing and will remain small for many years; it can also be used in a rock garden.

SEQUOIA REDWOOD *Cupressaceae (Cypress family)*

These massive trees reach extraordinary proportions in their native habitats–300 feet tall is not uncommon, and trunks are often 50 feet in diameter–but in cultivation typical speciments reach only 75-100 feet. The wood is useful for making furniture and exterior and interior housebuilding; unfortunately, this has caused the destruction of many of these noble trees, which are the largest and among the oldest of native North American trees.

BEST CONDITIONS Sequoias need full sun and deep, rich soil. They are hardy in Zones 7-9.

PLANTING Provide protection from wind and deep, regular watering for the first years after planting.

ROUTINE CARE Water deeply and frequently during dry spells. An annual application of fertilizer can be beneficial.

PRUNING Pruning of lower branches is sometimes done so that the attractive bark is visible.

PROPAGATION Propagate by seeds and cuttings.

PESTS, DISEASES, OTHER PROBLEMS None serious; the sequoia's bark is thick enough and of such a composition that it deters pests.

USE A redwood tree is an impressive specimen in any setting; a grove of redwoods is truly awesome.

SELECTIONS *S. sempervirens,* California or coast redwood, is a narrower but taller tree than the giant sequoia, growing up to 350 feet but rarely having a trunk diameter over 30 feet. Forests of California redwood on the West Coast are a national treasure.

S. giganteum [Sequoiodendron giganteum], giant sequoia, has the largest trunk width of any tree in the world; champion specimens are up to 80 feet across. In cultivation, specimens usually grow 30-100 feet tall. The largest specimen in the East is at Blithewold, and is about 90 feet tall.

SOPHORA JAPONICA JAPANESE PAGODA TREE *Fabaceae (Pea family)*

Japanese pagoda tree is native to China and Korea and was frequently planted near Buddhist temples in ancient times. It is a handsome, tall tree with wide-spreading branches. Its very showy panicles of white pealike flowers appear in mid to late summer, but it takes several years to reach flowering size. In some area, it flowers well only in alternate years.

BEST CONDITIONS It should be planted in full sun, where the soil is fertile and well-drained. Japanese pagoda tree adapts to average soils and to acid or alkaline pH.

PLANTING Plant balled-and-burlapped stock in spring, when the plants are still young. Typical of the pea family, Japanese pagoda tree has a strong tap root and is difficult to move when older. Water well and mulch. Young plants are somewhat tender but when the trunk diameter (caliper) exceeds 1½ inches they become hardier. Bear in mind the potential size of the tree.

ROUTINE CARE When established additional water is seldom required, but routine mulching is beneficial.

PRUNING Prune after flowering in fall, to shape the tree and remove crossing branches. When young, prune to develop a good leader.

PESTS, DISEASES, OTHER PROBLEMS Powdery mildew may need to be controlled, especially if the tree is under drought stress. Canker and twig blight should be cut out and affected wood destroyed. Be alert for leaf hoppers, especially the potato leaf hopper, which can kill young tissue causing witches brooms to develop.

PROPAGATION Easy to grow from seed, especially when it is fresh. Stored seed should be scarified to hasten germination. Best grown in a container to contain the taproot. The cultivars are budded.

USE This fine-leaved tree develops a dense crown and is an elegant specimen in the large landscape. Useful as a shade tree in lawns. It tolerates urban pollution well and if space allows is a good city tree.

SELECTIONS 'Pendula' is a weeping form that rarely flowers. It is often grafted on a standard to show off its weeping habit. It may reach 15-20 feet tall; a 100 year old specimen at Blithewold is about 15 feet in height.

'Fastigiata' ['Columnaris'] has a very upright habit.

'Regent' from Princeton Nurseries, was selected for its rapid growth, straight trunk, and uniform growth habit. It has shiny dark green leaves and a large oval crown. It blooms at an earlier age than the species.

SORBUS MOUNTAIN ASH *Rosaceae (Rose family)*

This deciduous tree provides shade, clusters of white flowers in spring, and bright orange berries and bright red foliage in fall. It is an excellent choice for gardens in cool regions, growing 40 feet tall and wide. Native species, such as *S. americana,*

Sophora japonica.

Sorbus alnifolia in autumn.

are common in northern woodlands and are part of the picture-postcard autumn in New England that never fails to take our breath away.

BEST CONDITIONS Mountain ash prefers a cool climate; it is hardy to Zone 2, but does poorly in climates warmer than Zone 7 (except in the Pacific Northwest, where they do well in Zone 8). Full sun or partial shade is acceptable. It adapts to many soil types, though acidic soil is best. The soil must be well drained. Mountain ash does best at high altitudes.

PLANTING Plant in fall or spring from container or balled-and-burlapped saplings. Protect young trees from wildlife, which enjoy the tender bark.

ROUTINE CARE Although it does not like wet feet, mountain ash does not do well in overly dry soil–water in dry spells.

PRUNING Mountain ash has a naturally attractive shape, stays a reasonable size, and usually does not need pruning. When necessary, prune dead wood in the spring.

PESTS, DISEASES, OTHER PROBLEMS A relative of many fruit trees, mountain ash needs the same disease and pest control programs as these do. In the Chicago area, fireblight can be fatal.

PROPAGATION Ripe seed can be planted in the early fall or in the spring if stratified over the winter.

USE An excellent shade or specimen tree in the North where fireblight is not a concern.

SELECTIONS S. *americana*, a native species, has dark brown, smooth bark and outstanding fall color.

S. *alnifolia*, Korean mountain ash, has gray bark and pink-orange fruit and is an excellent species for hot, humid areas.

S. *aucuparia*, European mountain ash, has redder fruit; the cultivar **'Cardinal Royal'** has been selected for larger, redder berries.

S. *hupehensis* is one of the best mountain ashes in the Pacific Northwest. Its sea-green leaves, white flowers, good fall color, and pink to white fruit make it interesting through most of the year.

STEWARTIA OVATA MOUNTAIN STEWARTIA *Theaceae (Tea family)*

Mountain stewartia is a native of the southeastern U.S., where it is an understory plant and grows as a large shrub or small tree. In summer its beautiful white camellialike flowers open 1-4 inches across with white stamens. In the fall the handsome dark green leaves put on a brilliant display, turning bright orange-red. The smooth bark is brown, but multicolored underneath flaking patches; not as colorful, however, as other species of this genus.

BEST CONDITIONS Plant in an open position, but provide some shade during the hottest part of the day. The soil should be acid (pH 4.5-5.5), moisture retentive and highly organic. Mountain stewartias do not care to dry out.

PLANTING Difficult to transplant; best results are with container grown plants. Look for strong, vigorous plants, no more than 5 feet tall, with a good branching structure.

ROUTINE CARE Keep soil moist at all times, especially in warm regions. Mulch.

PRUNING Pruning seldom necessary.

PESTS, DISEASES, OTHER PROBLEMS No major pest or disease problems.

PROPAGATION Stewartias are difficult to propagate from either cuttings or seeds. Sow seed in fall in pots plunged into the ground to overwinter.

USE Mountain stewartia is very useful as a specimen plant in a prominent position in the garden as it is attractive at all seasons. It also does well in woodland areas and near water gardens.

SELECTIONS *S. ovata* var. *grandiflora* has flowers that are larger and have purple stamens; the 4-inch flowers may have up to eight petals. Native only to Georgia.

S. pseudocamellia has a pyramidal habit and grows to about 40 feet. Its white 2- to 2½-inch flowers open in midsummer. In autumn the foliage turns yellow, orange, red, or purplish before dropping, then exposing the colorful exfoliating bark of gray, red, brown and orange.

S. koreana is difficult to distinguish from *S. pseudocamellia,* but is popular for its upright pyramidal habit and thick leathery leaves. More tolerant of full sun and dry soil.

STYRAX JAPONICUS JAPANESE SNOWBELL *Styracaceae (Storax family)*

One of the earliest plants of Japanese origin to be planted in the U.S., the first specimen was sent in 1862 by Thomas Hogg, the U.S. consul in Japan. This small delicate tree is native in most of eastern Asia and is a handsome but under-used addition to residential gardens in the U.S. Its beautiful, white bell-shaped flowers bloom in hanging clusters in late spring or early summer. Fall color is minimal.

BEST CONDITIONS Light shade is preferable, but full sun is also acceptable. Soil should be acid, porous but well-enriched with organic material to retain moisture. Does not tolerate alkaline conditions.

PLANTING Plant balled-and-burlapped stock in spring. Water well and mulch. Leave sufficient space for the tree to show its wide-spreading habit at maturity. Select a sheltered spot in cold areas.

ROUTINE CARE Water routinely in dry weather, and keep mulched.

When we plant a tree, we are doing what we can to make our planet a more wholesome and happier dwelling place for those who come after us, if not for ourselves. As you drop the seed, as you plant the sapling, your left hand hardly knows what your right hand is doing. But Nature knows, and in due time the power that sees and works in secret will reward you openly.

OLIVER WENDELL HOLMES

STEWARTIA PSEUDOCAMELLIA (JAPANESE STEWARTIA)
Deciduous. 10 years: 7-10 feet; 20 years: 14-20 feet; 50 years: 25-40 feet; maturity: to 40 feet. Pyramidal shape, interesting flaking bark, bright green oval leaves, large white flowers with yellow centers. Partial shade, moist, rich soil with good drainage. Zones 5-9.

STYRAX OBASSIA (FRAGRANT SNOWBELL) Deciduous. 10 years: 7-10 feet; 20 years: 14-18 feet; 50 years: 20-30 feet; maturity: to 30 feet. Large green leaves, tiny bell-shaped white flowers on long racemes. Full sun or partial shade, moist, rich soil. Zones 5-8.

SYRINGA RETICULATA (JAPANESE TREE LILAC) Deciduous. 10 years: 10 feet; 20 years: 15 feet; 50 years: 20-30 feet; maturity: to 30 feet. Open, pyramidal form; large leaves (larger than most lilac species), small creamy white flowers in cone-shaped clusters up to 6 inches long in early summer, reddish bark. Full sun, acid and alkaline soil. Zones 4-8.

TAXODIUM DISTICHUM (BALD CYPRESS) Deciduous. 10 years: 16 feet; 20 years: 30 feet; 50 years: 60-70 feet; maturity: to 90 feet. Tall straight trunk, open head of flat light green needles that turn orange in fall, small cones. Full sun or light shade; slightly acid or alkaline, moist or swampy soil; tolerates somewhat drier conditions. Zones 4-10.

PRUNING Prune to shape and to remove crossing branches in winter.

PESTS, DISEASES, OTHER PROBLEMS Mostly pest and disease free; in eastern U.S., ambrosia beetle has caused great damage to styrax.

PROPAGATION Softwood cuttings root readily treated with a rooting hormone and kept under mist. Seedlings often appear at the base of established plants but seeds exhibit double dormancy and are tricky to germinate.

USE This excellent small tree or shrub combines well with perennials in the mixed border and with other shrubs and trees. It is ideal for planting near the patio or terrace (and seen from below) and makes an attractive specimen plant in the lawn. Good effects can be had from massed plantings on banks or hillsides.

SELECTIONS *S. obassia,* fragrant snowbell, is not as dainty, but recent research has shown it to be hardier. Its leaves are larger and often hide the beautiful flowers. There are also pink and weeping forms.

A thousand-year-old bald cypress.

SYRINGA RETICULATA, SYRINGA PEKINENSIS TREE LILAC

Oleaceae (Olive family)

S. reticulata, Japanese tree lilac is one of the late-blooming lilacs, and is valuable to extend the lilac season. The pungent white flowers are carried in 6- to 12-inch panicles and open in early summer for about two weeks. Their odor is similar to that of privet, a close relative. The bark is brown and similar to cherry bark. *S. reticulata* and *S. pekinensis* are the only trees among a genus of shrubs, they have far fewer pest and disease problems than the rest but gardeners must still remain vigilant. Galen Gates rarely sees problems in Chicago.

BEST CONDITIONS Plant in full sun for best flowering. The soil must be well-drained and slightly acid. Regions where summers are cool are best for tree lilac.

PLANTING Transplanting is easy; select vigorous, well-balanced balled-and-burlapped stock and space 15-20 feet apart. Be sure to allow plenty of space for good air circulation around the plants. Water well.

ROUTINE CARE Water well until established, then only in times of drought. The best defense against pest and disease problems is to keep the plants healthy.

PRUNING Prune after flowering as needed to keep in shape.

PESTS, DISEASES, OTHER PROBLEMS There are plenty of possible problems for lilacs, but tree lilacs are among the least affected. However, be alert for bacterial, phytophtora and leaf blights, powdery mildew, leaf spots and wilt. Insect attackers include lilac borer and leaf miner, scale, caterpillars and leopard moth. In severe seasons, frost injury may occur.

PROPAGATION Take softwood cuttings after flowering and treat with a high level of hormone rooting powder.

USE A good specimen tree, but spectacular in bloom when massed.

SELECTIONS *S. reticulata* is described above. ***S. reticulata* 'Ivory Silk'** is a choice cultivar that flowers at a young age and has a compact habit. .

S. pekinensis, (Pekin lilac) is a multistemmed small tree, to 20-40 feet tall; loose, open habit; 3- to 6-inch-long white flowers appear before *S. reticulata*'s. ***S. p.* 'Morton' (China Snow™)** has beautiful exfoliating cinnamon bark..

TAXODIUM BALD CYPRESS *Cupressaceae (Cypress family)*

From Florida to Virginia, in Texas, and in southern Illinois, massive bald cypresses with buttressed trunks dot the landscape and line the swamps and riverbanks; its wood resists rotting even over centuries. This tree, native to northern

Taxus baccata.

Delaware and southern Illinois–is hardy to the Boston area. It needs a large space and commands respect for its tall, dignified bearing and interesting textures.

BEST CONDITIONS These trees can grow in swampy soil, but take less moist conditions fairly well. Like most conifers, they prefer slightly acid, well-drained moist soil, but they will thrive in moderately alkaline soils and all but the poorest of soils. Full sun is best for them, but light to medium shade will not harm them. They are hardy from Zones 4-10.

PLANTING Follow general planting procedures for conifers.

ROUTINE CARE Like most conifers, bald cypresses benefit from an organic mulch that improves fertility and keeps in moisture. They are native to areas that are very wet and swampy, but can withstand dry conditions.

PRUNING These trees do not need pruning.

PROPAGATION Propagate by seeds or cuttings.

PESTS, DISEASES, OTHER PROBLEMS Bald cypresses are sometimes attacked by twig blight, canker, wood decay, and spider mites.

USE Though too large for small or even medium-sized yards, bald cypresses are majestic in larger estates or parks; naturally suited to riverbanks and ponds and useful in stree tree situations, they are valuable for fine texure and orange fall color.

SELECTIONS *T. distichum,* common bald cypress, is hardy to Zone 4 (but only if grown from northern trees) and grows 50-70 feet tall. The cultivar **'Pendens'** has drooping branchlets; **'Shawnee Brave'** has a more narrow pyramidal habit; its parent tree is 75 feet tall and 18 feet wide.

T. ascendens, pond cypress, thrives in wet or dry sites and in windy areas; it is smaller than *T. distichum.*

TAXUS YEW *Taxaceae (Yew family)*

Yew trees have the distinction of being the darkest green of all the conifers; many consider them to be the most striking. In autumn they provide small dull red poisonous berries if male and female plants are grown; they keep their needles through the winter.

BEST CONDITIONS Yews are not fussy about soil. They prefer slightly acid, well-drained moist soil, but they will thrive in alkaline and all but the poorest of soils. They do not do well with wet feet, though. Full sun is best for them, but light to medium shade will not harm them. Various species are hardy from Zones 4-7.

PLANTING Follow general planting procedures for conifers.

ROUTINE CARE Like most conifers, yews benefit from an organic mulch that improves fertility and keeps in moisture.

PRUNING Prune out dead branches. Yews can be sheared to formal shapes if desired.

PROPAGATION Propagate by seeds or cuttings.

PESTS, DISEASES, OTHER PROBLEMS None serious; strawberry or black vine weevils may attack, but they are controlled fairly easily with traps and organic sprays. Yews are a favorite food for deers.

USE Yews have a multitude of uses in the gardens. They are eminently shearable, and are often used for formal hedges and even topiary. Their dark green color makes them very useful as backgrounds to flower borders, or as accent plants at the edges of beds.

SELECTIONS *T. baccata,* English yew, is the most common. Almost 100 cultivars

TAXUS BACCATA (ENGLISH YEW) Evergreen. 10 years: 5 feet; 20 years: 10 feet; 50 years: 15-20 feet; maturity: to 30 feet. Pyramidal form with dense branches covered with dark green needles; red berries in fall. Full sun, will tolerate some shade; slightly acidic, well-drained soil. Zones 6-8.

TAXUS CUSPIDATA (JAPANESE YEW) Evergreen. 10 years: 5 feet; 20 years: 10 feet; 50 years: 15-30 feet; maturity: to 40 feet. Irregular, multistemmed habit; can be trained as shrub or tree. Dark green leaves with yellow undersides. Full sun or partial shade; slightly acidic, well-drained soil. Zones 6-8.

THUJA OCCIDENTALIS 'PLUMOSA SUDWORTHII' (AMERICAN ARBORVITAE) Evergreen. 10 years: 3 feet; 20 years: 6 feet; 50 years: 15 feet; maturity: to 25 feet. Narrow, almost columnar habit, flat, scalelike leaves. Full sun or light shade, slightly acid to alkaline well-drained soil, cool climates. Zones 2-7.

THUJA OCCIDENTALIS 'LUTEA' (AMERICAN ARBORVITAE) Evergreen. 10 years: 7 feet; 20 years: 14 feet; 50 years: 30-35 feet; maturity: to 40 feet. Narrow, almost columnar habit, flat, scalelike leaves, greenish gold. Full sun or light shade, slightly acidic to alkaline well-drained soil, cooler climates. Zones 2-7.

THUJA PLICATA (WESTERN REDCEDAR, GIANT ARBORVITAE)
Evergreen. 10 years: 12-15 feet; 20 years: 25-30 feet; 50 years: 60-70 feet; maturity: to 90 feet. Narrow pyramidal form, lustrous scalelike needles. Full sun or light shade, slightly acidic to alkaline well-drained soil, cool climates. Zones 5-9.

THUJA OCCIDENTALIS 'TECHNY' (AMERICAN ARBORVITAE)
Evergreen. 10 years: 9 feet; 20 years: 18 feet; 50 years: 40 feet; maturity: to 50 feet. Narrow, almost columnar habit, flat, scalelike leaves; 'Techny' stays green all winter. Full sun or light shade, slightly acidic to alkaline well-drained soil, cooler climates. Zones 2-7.

TILIA PLATYPHYLLOS (BIGLEAF LINDEN) Deciduous. 10 years: 12-15 feet; 20 years: 25-30 feet; 50 years: 55-60 feet; maturity: to 90 feet. Broad pyramidal form; oval to roundish green leaves, 2 to 5 inches long. Full sun or light shade, deep, organic moist soil; does not tolerate heat, wetness, or cold. Zones 5-8.

TILIA TOMENTOSA (SILVER LINDEN) Deciduous. 10 years: 12-15 feet; 20 years: 25-30 feet; 50 years: 55-60 feet; maturity: to 90 feet. Broad pyramidal form; 3-inch-long shiny green leaves with white undersides. Full sun or light shade, deep, organic moist soil; does not tolerate heat, wetness, or cold. Zones 5-8.

exist, ranging in size from tiny shrubs to 60-foot trees. It has narrow very dark green needles, is unfussy in its requirements, and grows slowly. It is hardy to Zone 6.

T. cuspidata, Japanese yew, is just as attractive, and hardy to Zone 4.

T. x media, AngloJap yew, a cross between English and Japanese yews, is also hardy to Zone 4. Many selections are available; some are tree forms that grow to 40 feet and have strong central leaders and red fruit.

THUJA ARBORVITAE *Cupressaceae (Cypress family)*

Native to the forests of the Northwest and Northeast, and to Asia, arborvitaes have been used extensively in cities and courtyards across North America for their slender pyramidal form, dense glossy foliage, and easy care.

BEST CONDITIONS Like most conifers, arborvitaes prefer slightly acid and alkaline, moist, well-drained soil; they grow best in sun or light shade. Hot, dry areas are not good sites for arborvitaes.

PLANTING Conifers are easy to transplant in any season.

ROUTINE CARE Like most conifers, arborvitaes benefit from an organic mulch that improves fertility and keeps in moistures. Water deeply during drought.

PRUNING Prune out dead branches. Arborvitaes can be sheared to formal shapes if desired.

PROPAGATION Propagate by seeds or cuttings.

PESTS, DISEASES, OTHER PROBLEMS Though healthy plants will repel disease, a stressed plant will fall prey to any of several problems. Keeping the soil well-mulched will avoid problems.

USE Arborvitaes are valuable where their stiff, pencil-point shape is useful as an accent in the landscape.

SELECTIONS *T. occidentalis,* American arborvitae, can grow to 60 feet and has fan-shaped leaves. The foliage turns bronze in fall. It is hardy in Zones 3-7. Often browsed by deer.

T. orientalis, Oriental arborvitae (see *Platycladus*).

TILIA LINDEN, BASSWOOD *Tiliaceae (Linden family)*

Lindens are excellent ornamental trees, but their value does not stop there. They also provide valuable timber and a nectar that bees adore; a linden tree in your

Top: Roots of *Thuja plicata.*
Above: Fleshy cones of *Thuja orientalis.*
Below: Tilia cordata 'Greenspire'.

yard will ensure a large group of pollinating bees nearby. They are very undemanding about conditions, and will survive where other trees won't (though not in stressful parking lot or street tree situations).

BEST CONDITIONS Lindens will survive in nearly any situation except severe drought or heat, but their ideal conditions are full sun or light shade, and deep, organic, moist–but not wet–soil. They are hardy in Zones 3-8.

PLANTING Lindens transplant easily in winter or early spring.

ROUTINE CARE Lindens won't tolerate drought; water during very dry times. Organic mulch will help keep soil moist and fertile.

PRUNING Prune out overcrowded branches; bottom branches are sometimes removed.

PROPAGATION Sow seed in fall. Grafting can be done in winter.

PESTS, DISEASES, OTHER PROBLEMS Heat sometimes browns leaves; on city streets, this is often the result of winter salt damage. Aphids are a problem in the Pacific Northwest, Japanese beetles in New York. Healthy trees are disease resistant.

USE Linden are used as street trees, shade trees, and hedges. They do well in city conditions if they have adequate root space.

SELECTIONS *T. americana,* American linden or basswood, has light gray bark that turns reddish in winter. The culivar **'Redmond'** was selected in Nebraska for its hardiness.

T. cordata, little-leaf linden, has a conical shape and green leaves that turn yellow-green in fall. **'Glenleven'** has larger green leaves than the species, and **'Greenspire'** grows more rapidly, with a central leader and a uniform habit.

T. x euchlora, Crimean linden, grows 40-60 feet tall, 20-30 feet wide; its lower branches ring the base and its leaves turn shiny yellow green in autumn.

T. tomentosa, silver linden, also called *T. argentea,* has a conical crown, 3-inch-long shiny green leaves with white undersides that shimmer in the breeze. It is hardy in Zones 5-8. *T. petiolaris,* pendant silver linden, is similar to *T. tomentosa* but has an extraordinarily graceful weeping habit. Zones 5-8.

T. platyphyllos, bigleaf linden, has heart-shaped leaves, dark green leaves, 2-5 inches wide. Native to Europe, where it is a popular shade tree, it is used less here.

T. mongolica, Mongolian linden, is a good choice for the Midwest, with small lobed leaves that turn red in late fall. It grows to about 30 feet tall. Zones 4-8.

TSUGA HEMLOCK *Pinaceae (Pine family)*

Hemlocks are a major character in our forests, growing from coast to coast. They have massive trunks and wide branches with deep green or blue-green needles and grow up to 200 feet in the wild, 50-70 feet in cultivation. This tree is not related to the poisonous herb known as hemlock.

BEST CONDITIONS Avoid very warm, windswept or dry areas. Otherwise, hemlocks will thrive in either full or partial sun.

PLANTING Plant in spring or fall from balled-and-burlapped or containerized stock. Follow general planting procedures for conifers.

ROUTINE CARE An organic mulch will improve soil moisture and fertility; irrigate only in drought.

PRUNING Prune lightly to restrain growth. Heavy pruning can result in a smaller tree or a more formal one if that is desired; hemlocks shear well.

PROPAGATION Propagate by seeds or cuttings.

This is the forest primeval.
  The murmuring pines and
  the hemlocks,
Bearded with moss, and in
  garments green, indistinct in
  the twilight,
Stand like Druids of eld, with
  voices sad and prophetic,
Stand like harpers hoar, with
  beards that rest
  on their bosoms.
HENRY WADSORTH LONGFELLOW,
  HIAWATHA

Opposite: Tsuga canadensis.

plant selector

Full in the midst a spreading
elm displayed
His aged arms and cast a
mighty shade;
Each trembling leaf with some
light visions teems
And leaves impregnated with
airy dreams.
VIRGIL

PESTS, DISEASES, OTHER PROBLEMS Rust, botrytis, spruce mite, black vine weevil, and strawberry weevil sometimes attack, but more often the only problem is debris from heavy needlefall. Scale insects are sometimes severe in hot and dry conditions. A more serious problem is the wooly adelgid (an aphid with a white woolly appearance) that is slowly spreading from the Carolinas into the heart of hemlock country in the Northeast. Some horticulturists believe this pest can destroy the hemlock population, other think that though it mars their appearance, the trees survive. The only reliable control is well-timed spray with horticultural oils (which are non-toxic).

USE Hemlocks are useful in screens or background borders, or as part of a woodland garden.

SELECTIONS *T. canadensis,* Eastern or Canadian hemlock, though common, is one of the most admired and respected trees in North America, growing long, tall, and graceful; trees that were recorded at the time of William Penn are still alive in Pennsylvania. Hardy to Zone 3. There are hundreds of dwarf and weeping selections available, suitable for smaller landscapes and excellent for shade.

T. caroliniana, Carolina hemlock, can be grown as tall tree, up to 75 feet, or pruned to smaller size. It is hardy to Zone 4.

T. chinensis, is native to China and Taiwan and is not susceptible to the woolly adelgid. It grows 20-50 feet tall in cultivation.

T. heterophylla, western hemlock, is the tallest species. It needs humid air and moist soil. It grows well from the coast to the Cascade Mountains of the Pacific Northwest.

T. diversifolia, northern Japanese hemlock, has beautiful dark green foliage with contrasting nearly white undersides. Although it grows 40-60 feet tall in the wild, it remains small (20-30 feet) with multiple trunks in cultivation. It is susceptible to scale, but less so to the woolly adelgid.

T. mertensia, mountain hemlock is native to mountainous areas of the Northwest, where it grows to 90 feet tall; it stays much smaller in cultivation, usually under 30 feet. It has silvery blue-green foliage and is useful in rock gardens. Zone 4.

ULMUS ELM *Ulmaceae (Elm family)*

Elms are magnificent trees and were a major part of the American rural and urban landscape until the attack of Dutch elm disease. Several species resist this fatal illness, but many elms can be grown today only if aggressive, and often unacceptable, pest controls are used. The species listed tolerate Dutch elm disease.

BEST CONDITIONS Elms will grow under several types of unfavorable conditions, like those in cities or at the seashore. They do best in full run and moist, rich soil.

PLANTING Transplants and grows easily in winter or early spring.

ROUTINE CARE Additional water and fertilizer, and/or an organic mulch, will help elms stay healthy.

PRUNING Prune lightly to cut out dead wood and remove crossed branches.

PROPAGATION Propagate by seeds, cuttings, and grafts.

PESTS, DISEASES, OTHER PROBLEMS The Dutch elm disease is the only major problem; unfortunately, it is often insurmountable.

USE Elms are excellent shade and specimen trees. At one time, they lined the major avenues in many of our cities. The disease that killed these trees taught us not to plant a single type of tree in great quantities.

TILIA MONGOLICA (MONGOLIAN LINDEN) Deciduous. 10 years: 8 feet; 20 years: 16 feet; 50 years: 30 feet; maturity: to 40 feet. Compact pyramidal form; deeply serrated green leaves, 1-3 inches long, good winter color. Full sun or light shade, deep, organic moist soil. Zones 5-8.

TSUGA CANADENSIS 'PENDULA' (CANADIAN HEMLOCK) Evergreen. 10 years: 3 feet; 20 years: 6 feet; 50 years: 15 feet; maturity: to 20 feet. Squat form with pendulous branches covered densely with dark green needles; small oval cones. Full sun or partial shade, slightly acidic or alkaline soil, cool climates. Zones 3-8.

TSUGA CAROLINIANA (CAROLINA HEMLOCK) Evergreen. 10 years: 8 feet; 20 years: 20 feet; 50 years: 45 feet; maturity: to 60 feet. Tall narrow tree, branching on top. Full sun or partial shade, slightly acidic or alkaline soil, cool climates. Zones 4-7.

ULMUS AMERICANA (AMERICAN ELM) Deciduous. 10 years: 20 feet; 20 years: 40 feet; 50 years: 70-80 feet; maturity: to 90 feet. Vase-shaped tree with strongly arching branches ending in pendulous smaller branches; shiny dark green leaves turn yellow in fall. Full sun, adapts to many soil types, moist rich soil is preferable. Zones 5-8.

ULMUS PARVIFOLIA (CHINESE ELM) Deciduous. 10 years: 12 feet; 20 years: 25 feet; 50 years: 45-50 feet; maturity: to 60 feet. Oval head, sometimes widespreading branches; dense foliage, sometimes turns yellow, red, or purple in fall; attractive bark. Full sun, adapts to many soil types, moist rich soil is preferable. Zones 5-8.

UMBELLULARIA CALIFORNICA (CALIFORNIA BAY) Evergreen. 10 years: 10 feet; 20 years: 20 feet; 50 years: 40 feet; maturity: to 50 feet. Broad-leaved evergreen with spicy scent. Full sun or light shade; fairly moist, deep, rich soil is best, but tolerates dry, poor soil. Zones 7-10.

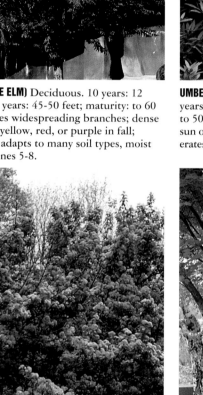

VIBURNUM SIEBOLDII (SIEBOLD VIBURNUM) Deciduous. 10 years: 9 feet; 20 years: 18 feet; 50 years: 35 feet; maturity: to 25 feet. Small tree or shrub can be trained to a single stem. Large, toothed coarse bright green leaves, turn purple or red in some areas; flat-topped clusters of creamy white flowers. red berries turn black. Full sun or up to half shade, moist, well-drained soil. Zones 5-8.

ZELKOVA SERRATA (JAPANESE ZELKOVA) Deciduous. 10 years: 15 feet; 20 years: 30 feet; 50 years: 60-65 feet; maturity: to 80 feet. Short trunk, round top, many upward-arching branches; medium-sized dark green leaves turn yellow in summer. Full sun, moist deep soil, tolerates drought once established. Zones 5-8.

PESTS, DISEASES, OTHER PROBLEMS Historically, elms have been plagued with problems but the new selections are highly resistant and viable landscape options. Dutch elm disease is the major problem, and it is unfortunately fatal; *Nectria* canker and verticillium wilt are also possible. However, people should not stereotype elms as disease prone, particularly with the new cultivars available.

USE American elm's strongest attribute is its upright arching habit. Additional characteristics of this urban tree include tolerance to soil compaction, drought, a wide range of soil types, and atmospheric pollutants; ease of maintenance; and, in some selections, fall color and ornamental bark.

SELECTIONS There are three excellent breeding programs in the United States, at the Morton Arboretum in Illinois (under George Ware), at the University of Wisconsin (under Guries and Smalley), and at the National Arboretum (under Alden Townsend). At this writing, Ware, Guries, and Smalley are on their way to China to look for new genetic material from lacebark elm, which holds tremendous potential for the next century.

U. americana American elm selections exist, but they differ in their resistance to DED and PN. **American Liberty** is a mixture of six clones with typical upright, vase-shaped crowns and high degree of resistance to DED. Susceptible to PN. Zone 3.

U. parvifolia, lacebark elm, is an Asian tree with excellent resistance to DED, PN, and elm leaf beetle. Like other elms, this tree has good stress tolerance. The species has ornamental bark. There are currently 38 selections. **'A. Ross Central Park'**, a clone of a tree planted in Central Park over 100 years ago and selected for cold hardiness and urban tolerance, has a spreading branching habit with strong wood that rarely is damaged in storms; dark green leaves turn yellow in fall. Zone 5. **'Drake'** is an evergreen of medium size, with weeping branch tips, a rounded habit, and handsome bark. Zones 7-9. **'Dynasty'** is vase-shaped, vigorous in growth and hardy in Zone 5. **'Emerald Vase'** has the attractive habit of the American elm, ornamental exfoliating bark, and a fluted trunk. The fine-textured branches carry lustrous green leaves that turn a subdued yellow in fall. **'Pathfinder'** has leaves that turn a brilliant red in fall. In was registered in 1990 by Alden Townsend. The parent tree, at the age of 27, was 35 feet tall and 28 feet wide.

Note: In this entry, Dutch elm disease is abbreviated as DED and phloem necrosis, a fatal vascular disease, is noted as PN.

Left: Ulmus americana was a favorite among American trees and its strongly upward branching habit is a part of the history of the American landscape. Unfortunately, the species is susceptible to Dutch elm disease and is therefore not recommended today. However, people should not assume that all elms are disease-prone. Although selections from *U. americana* are often susceptible to DED, and selections from European species tend to be susceptible to leaf miner, there are many available choices. Most of those listed below are, at least in part, of preferable Asian descent.

'Accolade' has a splendid vase-shaped habit, vigorous growth, and extremely shiny green leaves. Noted for excellent resistance to DED, elm leaf beetle, and leaf miner. Zones 4-5.

'Danada' is a rapid-growing, uniform tree which shapes up nicely, even when young. The new growth is an attractive red and the trunk sports exfoliating strips of bark as it matures. Name was selected to honor Dan and Ada Rice, founders of the Rice Foundation of Chicago. Highly resistant to DED, elm leaf beetle, and leaf miner. Zone 4-5.

'Homestead' is a fast-growing selection with excellent resistance to DED and PN. It has a pyramidal to globe-shaped habit rather than the arching habit of the American elm. It has shown some susceptibility to elm leaf beetle. Zones 4-5.

'Pioneer' is another vigorous elm with tolerance to urban stress. It has a globe-shaped habit and medium texture. It has a high degree of resistance to DED but suffers some damage from elm leaf beetle. It can exhibit yellow fall color. Zone 5.

'Regal' is a narrower and more upright tree, which makes it a valuable choice for storefront or street tree use, where its narrow habit and stress tolerance are ideal attributes. It has good resistance to DED. Zones 4-5.

Above: Ulmus rubra, the slippery or red elm, is brittle, weedy, and disease prone in most regions; in the Pacific Northwest, however, it is recommended for its hardiness and fast growth.

UMBELLULARIA CALIFORNICA CALIFORNIA BAY *Lauraceae (Laurel family)*

This California-to-Oregon native, also called Oregon myrtlewood, California laurel, pepperwood and spice tree, is a fine broadleaved evergreen for Pacific Coast gardens; its leaves emit a spicy scent when bruised. It grows slowly, but will eventually reach 75 feet tall.

BEST CONDITIONS California bay will thrive in full sun, or in shade if it is not too dense. It prefers fairly moist and rich soil, but will grow, though slowly, in dry, poor soil. The tree has a complex root system and requires deep soil. It is hardy in Zones 7-10.

PLANTING Plant in spring or fall; transplants easily.

ROUTINE CARE California bay will grow more quickly if the soil is kept evenly moist and fertile.

PRUNING California bay can be pruned and trained to grow with a single stem or several.

PROPAGATION Propagate by seeds or cuttings.

PESTS, DISEASES, OTHER PROBLEMS None serious.

USE California bay is often used as a hedge or screen; it also provides excellent shade.

VIBURNUM SIEBOLDII SIEBOLD VIBURNUM *Caprifoliaceae (Honeysuckle family)*

Viburnums are some of the most useful shrubs for the Northeast and Midwest; some species, such as *V. sieboldii* serve as small trees with single or multistemmed trunks. Growing 15-20 feet tall, this species has fine, clean-looking foliage that stays attractive until fall and produces abundant 3- to 6-inch clusters of creamy white flowers in mid to late spring. From late summer through much of the fall, the branches are covered with beautiful red and black berries that attract birds. After the fruit is gone, red fruitstalks persist, imparting a red cast to the tree.

BEST CONDITIONS Siebold viburnum thrives in full sun or partial shade. It prefers moist, well-drained soil, but is tolerant of other types and of a wide pH range. It is hardy in Zones 5-8.

PLANTING Look for strong, vigorous, well-branched plants. Viburnums transplant easily in spring or fall. Space 10-15 feet apart.

ROUTINE CARE For the first two years after planting, supply 1 inch of water per week. Thereafter, water during dry spells, if soil has dried out; plants that are stressed by dryness can develop leaf scorch. If soil is poor, fertilize in early spring.

PRUNING Prune out dead wood or other problems.

PROPAGATION Softwood cuttings root easily.

PESTS, DISEASES, OTHER PROBLEMS None serious.

USE This viburnum works as a single specimen or in a group; it is also attractive displayed against large buildings.

SELECTIONS *V. s.* 'Seneca' is an excellent upright fruiting form.

V. prunifolium (black haw) grows 15-20 feet tall and is hardy in Zones 4-10. Its stiff branching pattern is similar to that of the hawthorn; because it is generally pest free, it can substitute for hawthorns, providing good fall color and edible fruit. It thrives in dry soil, sun or shade, and many types of soil. It can be invasive; plant far from woodlands.

ZELKOVA SERRATA JAPANESE ZELKOVA *Ulmaceae (Elm family)*

This handsome elmlike deciduous tree is native to Japan, Korea and China. At maturity it develops a vase-shaped habit to 50-80 feet tall and as wide. The leaves are fine textured and deep green in summer turning to rusty brown or orange-yellow in fall. The spring blooming flowers are inconspicuous. In well-drained soil zelkovas may live over 100 years and with age they become tolerant of both wind and drought. Fairly resistant to pollution. Because it is resistant to Dutch elm disease, it is being used to replace the American elm in some cities.

BEST CONDITIONS Grow in sun or partial shade, in deep, moist soil. They do poorly in heavy, clay or badly drained soils. Fairly adaptable to a range of pH.

PLANTING Transplant balled-and-burlapped material. Water well and mulch. Site with the ultimate size in mind.

ROUTINE CARE Water young trees routinely during dry weather and mulch until established.

PRUNING Prune in the fall.

PESTS, DISEASES, OTHER PROBLEMS None serious. Susceptible to frost damage when young (in the North only). Notable resistance to Dutch elm disease, that has decimated populations of other members of the elm family. Good resistance to elm leaf beetle and Japanese beetle. Some susceptibility to mites.

PROPAGATION Seeds germinate without pretreatment but do so more readily if stratified for two months at 41° F. Take cuttings from seedlings and treat with rooting hormone. Cultivars are nursery-budded onto seedling stock.

USE For the larger landscape or as street trees. Too large for average residential properties, but beautiful as a lawn specimen and viewed from a distance, where there is space. It is often considered as a substitute for elms, though it grows more slowly.

SELECTIONS 'Green Vase' is a vigorous grower to 60-70 feet by 45 feet with a strong upright vase shape. Fall color is orange-red-bronze. **'Halka'** also grows rapidly but only to 50 feet by 30 feet. Its fall color is yellowish. Long graceful branches. **'Village Green'** is an upright grower that becomes more rounded with age, with rusty red fall foliage. Considered to be somewhat hardier than 'Green Vase'. Highly resistant to Dutch elm disease.

Z. carpinifolia, Caucasian or elm zelkova, has an oblong rather than vase shape. Its smooth beechlike bark flakes at maturity. Zones (6)7-9.

Z. schneideriana, Schneider zelkova, from eastern China, is rare in the U.S. It is quite similar to *Z. serrata,* but with a sandpaper-rough upper surface to the foliage; wine red fall color. Zones 6-8.

Z. sinica, Chinese zelkova, native in central to eastern China, is a promising new landscape species with strongly ascending branches and slightly spreading to weeping branch tips. Its foliage is narrower and grayer than other zelkova species, and it has an attractive exfoliating bark that flakes off to reveal gray, white, green and tan. It may be multistemmed and grows 30-40 feet in cultivation. The Arnold Arboretum has a specimen over 60 feet tall. Zones 6-8.

During a man's life, only saplings can be grown, in the place of the old trees–tens of centuries old–that have been destroyed. It took more than three thousand years to make some of the trees in these Western woods–trees that are still standing in perfect strength and beauty, waving and singing in the mighty forests of the Sierra. Through all the wonderful, eventful centuries since Christ's time–and long before that–God has cared for these trees, saved them from drought, disease, avalanches, and a thousand straining, leveling tempests and floods; but He cannot save them from fools.

JOHN MUIR

Acmena smithii, the lili-pili tree.

OTHER TREES

Although all trees have their uses and virtues, there was not enough room in this volume to include full entries on every one. The following trees were omitted because they are useful in only a small part of the country (see Chapter 5, Special Conditions), because they are weedy or disease-prone, because they are considered shrubs by most people, or because they are very rare.

Acmena smithii, lili-pili tree, evergreen, to 25 feet tall, clusters of small white flowers, useful as hedge or windbreak. Tolerates shade and salt. Zones 9-10.

Ailanthus altissima, tree of heaven, deciduous, to 50 feet. Compound green leaves, very invasive. Zones 5-10.

Bauhinia blakeana, Hong Kong orchid tree, evergreen. Shrub forms to 20 feet, taller forms to 60 feet. Grown for its large, orchidlike blossoms that bloom over a long period. Zones 9-10

Brachychiton, bottle tree, most species evergreen, 40-60 feet. Showy red, pink, or white flowers. Zones 9-10.

Broussonetia papyrifera, paper mulberry, deciduous, 40-50 feet with wide-spreading broad crown. Interesting catkins and round orange or red fruit; in China, paper is made from the bark. Zones 6-9.

Buxus sempervirens 'Arborescens', tree box, evergreen; tree form of the popular shrub grows to 20 feet; small glossy dark green leaves, grows to tree size in Zones 6-9.

Calocedrus decurrens, California incense cedar, evergreen to 70 feet. Narrow, columnar habit, flattened scalelike leaves; best on West Coast. Zones 5-9.

Castanea, chestnut, deciduous. Most species are very susceptible to chestnut bark disease and are rarely used. The following two species are resistant. ***C. mollissima,*** Chinese chestnut, to 60 feet tall with dense glossy leaves that turn yellow or bronze in summer; Zones 4-9. ***C. crenata,*** Japanese chestnut, to 30 feet tall, Zones 6-9.

Cercidium floridum, palo verde, to 30 feet, used in the Southwest. Attractive structure of blue-green-barked branches, hence the common name of palo verde, meaning green stick in Spanish. ***C. microphyllum*** and ***C. praecox*** are also useful. Zones 8-10.

Chilopsis linearis, desert willow, evergreen, to 20 feet or more. Flowers even in extreme heat, producing blooms of pink, lilac, or purple; foliage has a light, feathery texture. Zones 8-10.

Chorisia, floss-silk tree, deciduous, to 50 feet. Swollen trunk, thorny, light green bark, magnificent delicate pink and white flowers. Zones 8-10; very drought tolerant.

Cinnamomum camphora, camphor tree, evergreen, to 40 feet. Attractive, dense glossy leaves, often effected by camphor scale. Zones 9-10.

Clethra barbinervis, Japanese clethra, deciduous; tree form on the common shrub, with racemes of white flowers, brown shedding bark, widespreading, often multitrunked habit. To 15-25 feet. Zones 5-9.

Delonix regia, royal ponciana, evergreen, to 40 feet tall. Flamboyant orange blossoms for a long period, attractive flat-topped habit when not in flower. Zones 9-10.

Eriobotrya japonica, loquat, evergreen, to 20 feet. Long leathery leaves, edible, pear-shaped orange or yellow fruit. Zones 7-10.

Eucalyptus, gum trees, mostly evergreen. Many species of trees, most useful in California; many are very tall with open gray-green foliage and interesting bark. Zones 8-10.

Hemiptela davidii, deciduous, to 20 feet tall. Compact thorny tree with small dense leaves, can be used as a barrier. Zones 5-9.

Idesia polycarpa, deciduous, to 45 feet tall. Large clusters of orange berries persist until heavy frost; long leaves. Somewhat invasive. Zones 6-8.

Keteleeria fortunei, evergreen, to 90 feet tall. Pyramidal habit when young, turning flat-topped when mature. Withstands drier conditions than firs, to which it is similar. Zones 7-9.

Lagerstroemia indica, crape-myrtle, deciduous. This plant usually remains shrub-size in temperate regions; in warm climates, it grows to 20-25 feet. Many cultivars available with red, pink, or white flowers. Zones 7-10.

Laurus nobilis, sweet bay, laurel, evergreen, to 30 feet. Small, lustrous, aromatic leaves; usually kept small. Zones 6-9.

Lithocarpus, tanbark oak, evergreen, to 75 feet. Long leathery leaves, needs rich moist soil and is usually successful only in its native habitat of northern California and southern Oregon. Zones 7-8.

Melia azedarach, chinaberry, evergreen, to 45 feet. Clusters of fragrant, lilac flowers in spring, dense shade, ornamental yellow berries in fall. Tolerates heat and dry soil; tends to produce litter. Zones 7-10.

Myrica, bayberry, evergreen, to 30 feet tall. Very aromatic foliage, ornamental berries. Zones 7-10.

Olea, olive, evergreen, to 25 feet. Gray-green leaves, often twisted irregular habit in rich soil, though rounded and dense in dry soil. Olives are rarely produced, and tend to be a nuisance when they are. Zones 9-10.

Photinia, evergreen, to 36 feet tall. Usually multistemmed and shrubby, can be trained to tree form. Small white flower in large flat heads, bright red berries in fall and early winter. Zones 7-10.

Rhamnus davurica, Dahurian buckthorn, to 30 feet. Shiny red or black berries, glossy deciduous leaves. Very hardy and vigorous. Zones 2-10.

Sabal palmetto, palmetto, evergreen, to 90 feet tall. The hardiest of the palms, with fan-shaped leaves 5-6 feet across. Common from North Carolina to Florida. Zones 8-10.

Torreya nucifera, Japanese torreya, evergreen, to 75 feet. Similar to yew trees, with a very attractive pyramidal habit and dense foliage. Rare, but worth looking for. Zones 6-8.

Vaccinium arboreum, farkleberry, evergreen, to 25 feet tall. Small white flowers in summer, blue berries in fall.

Ziziphus jujube, common jujube, to 30 feet tall. Oblong dark red to black edible fruit in fall, spiny open habit, tolerant of heat, drought, and alkaline soils. Zones 7-10.

Torreya californica, California nutmeg.

Above: This ginkgo, planted outside a window can be enjoyed from indoors as well as out. *Below right:* This is just one example of how small scale, ornamental trees can be incorporated into the understory of an existing landscape.

Previous pages: This residence on Lake Michigan shows how a garden can be enhanced by using trees with a variety of habits, foliage color, bark, and flowering times. *Acer platanoides* 'Schwedleri' is behind the house and a large *A. p.* 'Crimson Sentry' is beside it. Amelanchiers flank the entrance. In the foreground are white-barked *Betula papyrifera* and spreading *Acer platanoides* 'Undulatum'.

Encountering trees in nature–a grove of river birch near a stream, a stand of lodgepole pines on a Rocky Mountain pass, a collection of brilliantly colored maples in autumn in a New England woodland–can make one's efforts to design with trees seem somewhat presumptuous. Trees are not to be trifled with: they are often more permanent than the houses they are meant to decorate and, once established, cannot be easily moved at the whim of the gardeners. Designing with trees means taking their needs into consideration as well as your own. But if properly chosen and sited, a tree will need little care and will provide pleasure and beauty for generations.

Designing with trees often involves working with existing trees as much as planting new ones. Removing an established tree should never be done lightly (in fact, there are laws against it in some areas). Rarely will you find a healthy tree that does not have its virtues. If you move into a new home in autumn, you may not see the magnificent display provided by a horse chestnut in spring or the dense shade it offers in summer; your row of Canadian hemlocks may seem ordinary until you see them covered with snow. Unless the tree is damaging the house or is unhealthy because it should never have been planted there in the first place, think about leaving it and designing around it.

On the other hand, there's something to be said for the blank palette. Sometimes an established tree makes it impossible for you to achieve your dream garden, or is causing serious problems–limbs are threatening the house, sun is blocked out, debris is scattered over the lawn, or the tree is taking up all available gardening space. In some cases, new cultivars that weren't around when your mature tree was chosen will work better in your site. Don't let an existing tree intimidate you; if it's wrong, a licensed arborist can usually remove it easily.

The first act of design, then, should be to view the site for at least four seasons. Study the conditions–does the site get sun throughout the year or does

the foliage of tall trees, once they are in full leaf, shade most of the site? A visit from a competent arborist is well worth the cost. A tree that looks scraggly or unhealthy may need only a competent pruning; often removing one or two trees that have been carelessly planted too near the house or too close together will allow you to rejuvenate and keep the rest of them. At the same time, learn the conditions in your garden so that if you decide to plant new trees you can choose those best suited to your site. Take a soil test, using soil from different areas in your site. Study the sun/shade, wind, and rainfall patterns. Visit botanic gardens and local nurseries to find out which trees thrive in your area; when you see a healthy tree on the street or in another yard, stop and find out what it is–if it works for someone near you, it will probably work for you.

Next, consider your own needs for shade, barriers against noise and poor views, borders between properties. Do you enjoy sun streaming into upper story window? Is there an eyesore you'd like to block, noise you'd like to muffle? Are there children or pets in the home who might be endangered by plants with thorny branches or toxins? Then, decide which aesthetic elements are most important to you–flowers? fall interest? architecture? bark? Are you looking for a formal tree to complement your home and garden, or a natural or even woodland style? Good garden design takes into account a multitude of factors: the overall type of garden, its color scheme, the mix of plants, their size and shape, the look of the landscape year-round, new or existing architectural elements, and the special uses required of individual plants. The best way to consider all the elements–and to avoid costly (or backbreaking) mistakes–is to plan first on paper: *Measure twice, dig once* might well be the garden designer's credo and caveat.

Planning on Paper Before drawing up your plan, choose a scale that fits the site. For small gardens, a scale in which ¼ inch equals one foot is suitable; for landscapes that exceed a ⅓ acre, an inch to the foot. (Highly detailed plans, even in smaller areas, require larger scales.) Next, take an inventory of the site,

Trees can be used as single specimen, like the purple beech (top) or combined to show contrast in their shape, color, and texture. *Top left: Acer palmatum* shrub, *Cedrus deodora* 'Aurea', *Cedrus atlantica. Above: Quercus alba, Cornus florida, Malus* cv.

Elements to consider when choosing trees include architecture (as shown in *Acer palmatum* 'Dissectum', above) shape (strong verticals like the *Juniperus communis* 'Suecica' or conical shapes like the *Chamaecyparis obtusa* 'Golden Spangle' in the top picture).

including buildings, property lines, walkways, walls, fences, and existing vegetation; learn and write down soil pH, soil type, hours of sun, prevailing winds, and drainage conditions. Armed with this information, you're ready to make a site analysis, which will consist of your opinion, both positive and negative, of existing elements. These could include problem views as well as panoramas, off-site noise, drainage problems, sunny exposed banks or highly shaded areas, and any other landscape blessings and blemishes. Keep in mind the general categories of plants that might solve your problems: a dense evergreen hedge to muffle noise, a group of moisture-loving trees to incorporate into a poorly drained area, a tree to shade a seating area—or flowering shrubs and perennials to brighten a stately elm or healthy but unexciting conifers. Consider, too, your intent: finding a spot for a pool, a backdrop for a flower garden, camouflaging a drab foundation. Then begin your sketch, which can usually be done on a single sheet of paper (though more ambitious plans may necessitate the use of overlays). Once the site has been successfully mapped out, pace it off in the landscape to make sure it will translate from paper to topsoil; strategically placed stakes or gardening hoses outlining beds will help you visualize the intended effect.

CHOOSING A SITE Unless your property is unusually large, possible sites for new trees will be readily apparent by the time your plan is ready. Planting a tree in a spot visible from a window will allow you to enjoy it from inside as well as outside the house. If your property slopes, consider a tree (like davidia, halesia, pterostyrax, or styrax) that is particularly attractive when viewed from beneath. If your space is limited, consider dwarf conifers or other small trees; understory trees like redbud, dogwood, and amelanchier will accept some

shade and can be planted under existing taller trees. Choosing trees for the understory of the garden as well as the overstory provides a more layered look that is attractive in all seasons. Many smaller trees, like Japanese maples, redbuds, dogwoods, crabapples, and witch-hazels are more ornamental than huge trees like oaks and beeches and their small stature allows several to grouped for a more interesting texture.

USES FOR TREES Trees used in home landscaping can be broken into some very general categories. Specimens are sited so that they can be seen from all angles, with nothing around them; these are usually particularly dramatic trees that can make a statement without any help from other plants; weeping willows, large crabapples or cherry trees, umbrella pines, and purple beeches are often used as specimens. Borders and hedges can be used to divide properties or screen unattractive views; typically conifers such as firs and pines are used for this purpose, which they fulfill handsomely, but other choices like poplars, hawthorns, and maples can do the job as well. Backdrops to flower gardens are usually neutral and dark in color; some designers believe that yews are far and away the best for this purpose because they are dense, do not create litter, and provide evergreen foliage in winter; other gardeners use hollies, hemlock, and umbrella pine. Within a flower garden, trees are used as accents or focus plants, creating a skeleton that is filled in by herbaceous plants and small shrubs; Japanese maples and fringe trees are small enough to be integrated comfortably into even a small garden and create a focal point without taking over. Until recently, trees have been used to surround doorways; all too often arborvitae or junipers stood as sentries in these "foundation plantings"; this practice is out of favor today as more varied and interesting

Top left: Cornus florida contrasts in size and color with a purple beech.
Top: A lightly pruned amelanchier is in perfect scale for a small house.
Above: The texture and color of the foliage of Japanese maples like *Acer japonicum* 'Aconitifolium' are invaluable additions to the garden.

Plantings under trees should not disturb the roots systems and should not require more sun than the tree will provide. *Top right:* Daylilies under green ash, red maple, and honey locust—a simple way to add interest. *Center left:* Impatiens under a spruce tree; a poor choice in this case because the area did not drain well and, after a few years, the tree's root systems became waterlogged from the moisture demands of the impatiens. *Center right:* Daffodils combine well with daylilies for later season color. *Below:* Color, texture, and shape are contrasted in a stiff blue spruce, two beeches—one dark purple and one with hot pink-edged leaves.

groups of plants are used in their place. By using plants as specimens, borders, hedges, backdrops, and accents, the home landscape is defined by large and important plants that make filling in the rest of the garden easier and provide interest through the winter. In fact, a successful garden can usually be judged when its "bones" are visible in winter, that is, when the trees stand alone.

SPACING No matter the need your tree will fill, it must have enough room to grow properly. Be sure you know the height and width that all parts of your tree—trunk, branches, and roots—will achieve in five, ten, twenty, and even thirty years down the road. Probably the greatest mistake made in planting trees is not allowing them room to grow or planting them too close to the house or other structures. The problems this causes include trees that overshade a house, grow too closely together to be healthy, don't have room to look attractive, get tangled in electrical wires, and spread their roots to where they damage foundations or take over the garden.

CHOOSING A TREE Just about everyone has a favorite tree that they've seen and admired, and taste is probably the most important criterion in this important choice. Some other factors to take into account:

Style A tree can harmonize with the style of the garden and house or fight with it. Some trees that complement a formal setting are sheared yews, spruce, and linden; birches, hemlocks, and hornbeam fit better into an informal or woodland garden. Live oaks and Southern magnolias evoke a Southern flavor, Mesquites, palo verdes, and acacias fit desert gardens well. Palms are probably the quintessential trees for tropical gardens, but purple orchid trees and mangos work as well. Native trees, by definition, can be counted on to fit into the landscape.

Scale and size Do you prefer a small tree—an amelanchier or star magnolia—nestled against your house, or a massive elm or oak towering above it? Landscape architects try to balance the largest components of the landscape—usually the house and the biggest tree—against each other. Consider, too the possibility of two trees of different sizes complementing each other—a large beech set off by a compact flowering tree like dogwood.

Shape The term "habit" is used to denote the shape of a tree, and trees come in a myriad of shapes, from stiff triangles like pine and fir to spreading masses like oak and corktree, from open forms like ginkgo to those with dense, closely packed crowns like flowering pear. A tree with an open habit, like a honey locust, gives a much airier feeling—though less shade—than one with a dense crown. Trees with architectural shapes, like strongly vertical junipers or Lombardy poplars provide strong definition; those that are softer contrast beautifully with them.

Texture Smooth, shiny holly berries, fuzzy sycamore fruit, lacy false cypress foliage, coarse horsechestnut leaves, incomparably fine threadleaf maple leaves, peeling bark of a paperbark maple, soft flowers of a flowering cherry, intricate pine cones, ferny willow branches—these are only a few of the textures that can be combined and contrasted in your garden.

Color Anyone who assumes that trees only have green leaves and brown bark isn't aware of how much color trees can provide. Besides every shade of green—from the chartreuse of *Sophora japonica* to the deep, almost black glossy green of magnolias—tree foliage comes in steely blue (spruces, firs, and pines), golden yellow (false cypress, Frisia black locust, larch) purple (beeches, maples), red (maples, crabapples) and silver-gray (firs, lindens, autumn olive). Tree bark can be glistening cherry red, as in *Prunus sargentii;* blue-gray (*Pinus bungeana*); pure white (*Betula papyrifera*); and salmon (*Acer griseum*). Flowers lend a whole new rainbow of color. Then, as seasons change, fruit and fall foliage change the palette entirely.

TIME PASSAGES A final and most important factor to consider in the planting of trees is their lifespan. There are trees that will grow relatively quickly, and become impressive within ten, five or even three years; if you can't wait, consider poplars or elms; liriodendrons, willows, and metasequoias are also relatively fast-growing. Many other trees—like Kentucky coffeetrees, beeches, and oaks— require a decade or two before they are truly beautiful; they sometimes require extra care or staking and look awkward or leave gaps in the interim. But a mature tree is a living symbol of the patience, effort, and foresight of its planter; like so many other of the best things in life, it only comes to those who are willing to sacrifice for it.

VIEWPOINT
PLANTING UNDER TREES

Any shade-tolerant plants–epimediums, hostas, bergenias, etc.–can be planted under trees; those with variegated foliage are especially appropriate. What is not appropriate is grass; it needs too much water and sun.
ETHAN JOHNSON, THE HOLDEN ARBORETUM,

We've used microbiota and liriope under deciduous trees with semi-dense shade and greedy roots. Native polystichum ferns also withstand the dry area under trees. Plants requiring evenly moist deep soil would not survive.
SUSAN THOMAS, HOYT ARBORETUM, PORTLAND, OREGON

Groundcovers such as *Pachysandra terminalis, Liriope muscari, Symphutum grandiflorum*, and *Vinca minor* do well. Avoid *Aegopodium podagraria* (goutweed) which is extremely aggressive and large forms of *Hedera helix* (English ivy) that don't remain as groundcovers, but prefer to climb the tree.
GERALD STRALEY, U. OF BRITISH COLUMBIA BOTANICAL GARDEN

It would be easier to list what not to plant under trees. So many wonderful, exciting bulbs, annuals, perennials, small shrubs and trees perform very well and provide a diverse palette of color in the home landscape. The secret is to choose plants that require the same cultural conditions–wet plants with wet trees, dry plants with dry trees.
ROBERT BOWDEN, HARRY P. LEU GARDENS, ORLANDO

Under trees that are shallow-rooted and heavy-canopied. I would plant hostas, astilbes, or ferns along with periwinkle or the old standby, pachysandra. Under trees that don't like their roots disturbed, I would much rather mulch than plant and disturb roots.
MIKE RUGGIERO, THE NEW YORK BOTANICAL GARDEN

Some good performers: Shrubs such as *Acanthopanax* 'Variegata', aronia, *Clethra alnifolia* for summer fragrance, *Viburnum carlesii* for spring fragrance, *Cotoneaster lucidus* for great fall color, daphne, fothergilla, hydrangea, lindera, physocarpus, ribes, rubus, sambucus; Perennials: ajuga, aquilegia, brunnera, corydalis, dicentra, geraniums, iberis, pulmonaria, trillium, and many other native spring wildflowers.
GALEN GATES, CHICAGO BOTANIC GARDEN

Key
A=*Magnolia virginiana*
B=*Thuja plicata*
C=*Ulmus americana*
D=*Acer saccharum*
E=*Cornus florida,*
Hamamelis virginiana,
Viburnum
F=*Quercus rubra*
G=*Betula populifolia*

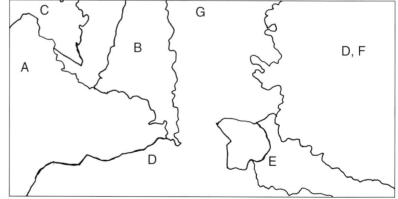

The Director's residence at The Holden Arboretum includes trees for all seasons; in spring, dogwood, witch hazel, magnolia and viburnum flower; in summer the landscape is cool, lush, green; in fall oak, maple, and birch provide brilliant flowers; and in winter the evergreen redcedar and the bare, spreading branches of the American elm contrast with snow.

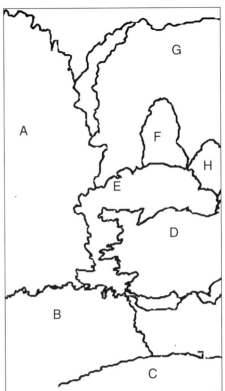

This scene at the Gottelli Collection of conifers at The National Arboretum in Washington, D.C. is an excellent example of contrasts in size, color, and texture. The gold and blue foliage of the chamaecyparis and *Picea pungens* 'Compacta' will provide weight, structure, and interest to this garden through winter. Note the shades of yellow and green during the growing season, and the vivid red of the maple foliage.

Key
A=*Picea abies*
B=*Spiraea bumalda*'Lime Mound'
C=*Pinus flexilis* 'Pendula'
D=*Acer palmatum* 'Sherwood Flame'
E=*Picea pungens* 'Compacta'
F=*Pinus sylvestris*
G=*Quercus alba*
H=*Chamaecyparis pisifera* 'Gold Spangle'

CHOOSING A TREE TO FIT YOUR SITE

The most important skill connected to growing trees is choosing the right ones in the first place. Unless your goal is experimentation to see if a tree will grow in an inhospitable site, you are safest choosing one that local sources–botanic gardens, county extension agents, reputable nurseries–recommend. Finding a recommended species is not enough; you also have to ascertain that the cultivar you are buying is right for your garden. Study your site to determine the conditions your tree will encounter.

SUN/SHADE Observe all possible areas over a period of time. Note how much sun each site receives and whether it is direct sunlight, sunlight that is filtered through trees and fences, or if the sunlight is totally blocked by buildings or dense tree foliage; note whether conditions change at different times of the day and year. The plant portraits in Chapter 2 discuss the type and amount of sunlight needed by particular trees. In most cases, plants will not grow if not provided with the sunlight suggested.

SOIL There are three basic types of soil: clay, sand, and loam. Clay soil has very little space between its particles; clay soil is often very rich in nutrients, but water and nutrients have trouble traveling through clay soil to the roots of the plant. Sandy soil transports material easily, but it can't hold nutrients and water for very long. Clay and sand together, along with fibrous organic matter, or humus, comprise the ideal mix: loam, which is light but rich; this type of soil is often called "friable," which means it is easily pulverized. If you are buying soil, take care to avoid pulverized material; the pulverization process destroys soil structure that has taken thousands of years to develop; it is much better to buy "rough black" top soil.

Below: When looking for a consistent trait in a plant, it is best to select a cultivar. The two trees below (both *Acer saccharum*) vary because they are seedling grown, not clones or special selections.

Right: Hawthorns were planted on both sides of this Manhattan street; on the north side, which receives light and sun from the south, the trees bloom profusely. On the south side, where the sun is blocked by tall buildings, the flowering is sparse. Most trees will color and flower better in sun.

To identify exactly what the soil in your garden needs requires a soil test. A small–but representative–amount of garden soil is analyzed for nutrient deficiencies and excesses. The acidity or alkalinity–pH–of the soil can be measured with a simple home kit. A full analysis can be done by a county extension service, an agricultural university, or perhaps even a local garden center. The analysis will generally be accompanied by recommendations for needed nutrients and their application rates.

There are many ways to maintain good soil; simply adding a lot of chemical fertilizer is not one of them. It takes experience to understand what your soil needs and to provide it. It is important to match the proper plant to the soil; the wrong plant will usually fail, and it may also damage the soil. Use organic matter generously for plants that need it, particularly when they are young. Adding compost and other forms of organic matter will keep your soil rich. Use fertilizers that add missing ingredients, including trace elements, only when you have reason to suspect that they are necessary. If you manage your soil properly, it will increase in fertility after several years of cultivation and provide the best possible home for your plants. However, in the case of trees, you should try to match the plant to the natural level of fertility–although adding fertilizer while the trees are being established is helpful, once the trees have spread their roots deeply, surface applications of fertilizer are usually sufficient. Contrary to popular belief, tree roots, with only rare exceptions, are no more than 2 feet deep.

SOIL PH Acidity and alkalinity of soil is measured on the pH scale; a measurement of under 7.0 indicates an acid soil, above 7.0 indicates alkaline soil, 7.0 is neutral. Many trees, including oxydendron and rhododendron, require acid soil. You can correct overly acid soil by adding limestone; this should be done several months before planting, and should be worked into the soil well. Overly alkaline soil can be corrected by adding organic matter and elemental sulfur. However, these improvements will not last over time and must be done over a large area because the tree's roots will spread. In most cases, amending the soil around a large tree actually does it more harm than good, because it prevents the tree from sending its roots past the immediate area of the "good" soil. Unless you are prepared to amend the soil heavily each year, it is advisable to choose a plant that can grow well in the existing soil.

CLIMATE Wind, heavy rain, humidity, heat, and cold are damaging to many trees. If your area experiences extreme climate factors, take them into account when choosing trees.

DRAINAGE Drainage is the ability of soil to move water so that the roots don't get too waterlogged and nutrients can percolate through the soil to the roots, where they are used. Most trees require well-drained soil.

MICROCLIMATES No matter how small your site is, it probably encompasses several sets of conditions. The area near the protection of a wall or building is probably warmer than the open space in front. The strip that faces the street may receive more pollution than the yard behind the house. The spot right in front of the house may be affected by limestone in the foundation.

SITE IMPROVEMENT

Your plants will grow better if you take the time to improve the ground in which you put them. The first step in preparing a garden site is a general

Trees are more often harmed by drowned roots caused by poorly drained soil than by drying out. *Above:* To determine whether your drainage is adequate, dig a hole large enough to hold a gallon pot. Fill the hole with water, and see how long it takes to drain. If water stands more than a few hours, drainage is probably a problem. There are several ways to correct poor drainage:

1. Use raised beds, which always provide better drainage and also allow you to mix better soil from elsewhere into your site.

2. Insert a drainage pipe. These pipes, usually plastic, can be purchased at most garden supply or hardware stores and move water to a place where it will do less harm.

3. Add sand and organic matter to the soil. Sand plus clay results in cement; but sand, clay, and organic matter will give you friable soil. To significantly improve the soil, you need to add about 90% sand.

4. Grade the area with terraces or retaining walls.

5. If your problem is serious, or if you think it is worth the investment, talk to a professional landscaper who can install tile, gravel beds, or drainage ditches.

Above: The containerized tree above is potbound and has less chance of successful transplanting; the one on top is a better choice. *Below:* A bare-root tree with dead roots.

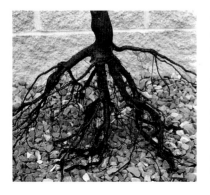

cleanup, the removal of rocks, sticks, stumps, or other debris. Once the area is relatively clean, lay out the boundaries of your site using string, garden hose, or spray paint.

PREPARING THE SOIL Loosen the soil to a depth of 4-6 inches. If there is tender vegetation growing on the site, turn it into the top part of the soil. If there are serious weeds like bindweed or dandelions, spray them first with an herbicide like RoundUp (glyophosate). Pull out any woody stems. Wait at least two weeks after tilling to allow the tilled plants to decompose and again turn the soil under to a depth of 4-6 inches to ensure the breaking up of dead plants and to further loosen the soil.

After the second tilling, apply soil amendments such as fertilizer, lime, compost, or sand. Till once again, this time to a depth of 8-10 inches with a tiller, or 12-18 inches by hand with a spading fork.

BUYING TREES

When buying trees, you can usually choose between bare-root, containerized, and balled-and-burlapped specimens. Bare-root trees should be planted only during their dormant seasons. Containerized and balled-and-burlapped specimens can be planted at any time when conditions are not harsh–the newly planted tree should not have to deal with midwinter cold or midsummer sun, especially in extreme climates. Buy plants from reputable nurseries, and make sure that they have healthy root systems before you put them in the ground. If you cannot plant your new trees immediately, store them in a cool place and water them regularly. If possible, dig a trench, lay each tree into it, and cover it with soil up to the lowest branches.

PLANTING

Planting is a gardener's most rewarding task and also one of the most crucial. Without the right start, even the most carefully tended trees will languish. Whether the tree is bought bare-root, containerized, or balled-and-burlapped, the roots need to be kept moist before planting. The maxim is simple, but apt: if they dry, they die. When digging the planting hole, make sure it's large enough to fit the roots without crowding. Prune any crushed or damaged roots back to sound wood. Finally, be sure to plant at the proper depth; too deep is just as wrong as too shallow. The hole should be at least as wide as it is deep, and the sides should be roughed up so that the soil around the roots does not become solid. Rule-of-thumb is that the hole should be two to three times as wide as the rootball; Mary Irish of the Desert Botanical Garden in Phoenix recommends that the hole be five times wider than deep, and only as deep as the container. Do not dig deeper than the bottom of the ball or the container or the tree will sink. Never dig when soil is very wet or very dry, as this will damage the soil structure.

To plant a bare-root tree: Because very little soil is packed with bare-root trees, they must be kept moist. Remove packing material, clods of earth, and broken or dead roots. Prune off dead or broken branches, and soak the plant for at least one, and not more than four hours. Mound soil in the bottom of the hole so that the center of the plant can be placed on the mound with the roots resting around it. Fill in half the soil; pack the soil firmly enough to avoid large air pockets, but not so firmly as to compact it. Water thoroughly; fill with soil; water again.

1. Dig a shallow hole, wider than deep; see page 195 for current research on the planting hole.

2. Scatter necessary amendments; at Holden, a handful of phosphorus (which is not mobile and therefore can't be used on the surface) is the main amendment. See page 194 for information on soil amendments–usually not recommended–at planting time.

3. Place the tree. Find the root flare, the place where the trunk of the tree hits the roots. Nurseries sometimes cover this up and you may have to remove burlap or soil. Place root flare at a point ⅓ of rootball higher than existing grade in heavy soils, level in light soils.

4. Fill in the hole.

5. Firm up the soil before you water. If you water first, you will compact the soil.

6. Create a 3- to 6-inch mound, called a berm, around the outer edge of the roots to hold water that can soak in deeply.

techniques

SOIL AMENDMENTS

Research has shown that it is best to plant directly into the soil that the tree will live in. Amendments can create a "potted plant" effect when roots move readily through the improved soil and stop at the unimproved earth; at that point, they stop growing or begin to encircle the "pot." This is not a serious problem with houseplants, which can be repotted in larger containers. But trees become rootbound as the roots fill the improved soil and they will will suffer and potentially, in time, perish. In extreme cases, the soil can be improved, but it should not be altered by more than 50%. The soil should also be well tilled or roughed up with a spade on the outside of the planting hole to encourage root penetration into the existing soil.
GALEN GATES,
CHICAGO BOTANIC GARDEN

I'm more concerned with good drainage than anything else. However, since the soil at Blithewold is heavy and claylike, we add our own compost to the hole when planting and dig the hole wider than usual rather than deep. After planting, we do little to amend the soil other than mulching, which keeps mowers from injuring the bark.
JULIE MORRIS, BLITHEWOLD GARDENS, RHODE ISLAND

We add some compost or mulch to the backfill; nothing beyond that.
MARY IRISH,
DESERT BOTANICAL GARDEN

We generally try to avoid amending so that we will not create a "pot" effect. However, we do try to thoroughly loosen the soil in a larger area beyond the plant to allow for better root penetration by young plants. Sometimes we add a small amount of organic matter to soils (20% by volume) to create aeration and porosity for new roots exploring soil, with a secondary benefit of a small amount of nutrition.
RICK LEWANDOWSKI, MORRIS ARBORETUM OF UNIV. OF PENN.

Rather than a one-shot soil improvement, we plant large logs in the soil near new trees, providing avenues for roots to move around through dense clay. Logs can also be left on the surface, as often occurs naturally in the woods. As they decompose, the logs are the best source or nutrients, and become sponges for moisture that is ready when needed.
ETHAN JOHNSON,
THE HOLDEN ARBORETUM

To plant a containerized tree: Containerized trees are started above ground in special plastic pots; they do not need to be dug up, and their roots are not damaged by transplanting. Remove the container (even if the manufacturer suggests leaving it on). It is important to break the rootball only if it has become potbound. Using a sharp knife or pruning shears, make cuts into the roots on all four sides of the rootball. Fluff out the roots with your fingers. Place the plant into the hole, and fill in soil.

To plant a balled-and-burlapped tree: The burlap needs to be removed halfway down the ball (entirely if it is synthetic), and all string, twine, and other packing material should be taken off. Place the plant in the hole and make sure it is at its proper depth by placing a rod across the hole; if the top of the rootball is not level with the rod, put in more soil, or dig deeper. Dorthe Hviid of Berkshire Garden urges gardeners to make sure the hole is not dug too deep in the first place; if soil has been dug below the rootball it is likely to settle. Fill in remaining soil, and firm.

At some nurseries, a metal cage is placed around the rootball; in that case, make sure to cut the metal cage in many places so that the rootball is not restricted. Bend back the top of the wire cage but don't attempt to lift the tree out of the cage or to cut the cage before the tree is in the hole, as the rootball is likely to fall apart.

It is a good idea to create a 3- to 6-inch mound, called a berm, around the outer edge of the roots to hold water that can soak in deeply. When the plant is in place, water well. During the first few months (and up to two years) after establishment, check frequently to make sure that the plant is kept moist. Inserting your finger into the root zone 1-2 inches will let you know if you need to water.

At the Desert Botanical Garden in Phoenix, weekly watering is recommended for the first summer, every 10 days or so for 2-3 years after that, then every 3-4 weeks until the tree is in the ground for 5-7 years. By that time, most desert trees are well enough established to be on their own with only a monthly soaking in very hot or dry seasons.

Most trees do not need staking; staking can prevent the tree from developing properly. However, in areas with high winds, new trees may need staking.

Sometimes, you will decide to move a tree that is already growing. This is

After planting, water and mulch.

not always easily accomplished and requires quite a bit of preparation; if the tree is more than a few years old, only an experienced arborist or landscape contractor should attempt it. On a small tree, you can root-prune the tree one year before moving it; some nurseries follow this practice. To root prune, dig a trench around the tree, about 2 feet deep and 6 inches wide; the trench should be out 10-12 inches for each inch of the trunk diameter at the base. Backfill with soil. If this procedure is properly accomplished, the plant will form a compact root system and will be better able to withstand the move, though you will still sever many roots when you move a tree of any size. It is best to move a tree during its dormant season, in early spring or in fall; early to mid summer is the most difficult time to move a tree successfully.

When you are ready to move the tree, dig a trench in a circle around the tree, 12 inches from it for each inch of trunk diameter. Dig down at least 2 feet, segregating a ball of earth that includes the tree's roots. Cinch the soil and roots as tightly as possible with burlap and nails. Rock it gently until it can be removed; you will have to cut some of the roots. Place the removed tree, with the ball of soil around its roots, on burlap, and remove to a protected spot. Even small trees are heavy, and you may need help with this procedure. For a large tree, place a board under the tree to move it. Replant immediately or keep the tree in a protected area, watering it gently and frequently.

Success and failure in transplanting. How many times have you purchased a beautiful, healthy, tree from the local nursery, planted it in a hospitable site, and had it die in just a few weeks? You are certainly not alone; this problem has occurred at botanic gardens and arboreta around the country and much research has been done to find and eliminate causes.

Ethan Johnson at Holden Arboretum believes that a major cause of transplant failure is planting trees that are too small or have underdeveloped roots. Industry standards exist for the caliper of trees suitable for transplanting; caliper refers to the size of the trunk measured a specific distance from the roots. These standards vary from state to state and are not easy for the homeowner to find or check, so one must rely on the nursery to uphold them. Unfortunately, even at excellent nurseries, trees are usually dug up by transient laborers who get paid by the unit—and undersized trees are easier to dig up than large ones. Some nurseries will guarantee their trees; their prices reflect this. Whenever you buy a tree, have the people at the nursery check its size and roots before you take it home.

Recent research at The Morton Arboretum in Lisle, Illinois concerns the planting hole; they have published their results in an excellent booklet, entitled "Selecting and Planting Trees."* They find that the planting hole should always be considerably wider than the roots or rootball; three times wider is best. The sides should slope gradually, making the hole saucer or bowl-shaped. They recommend against digging any deeper than necessary to cover the roots so that the tree will have the firm support it needs to support and stabilize it; it also saves work. Planting a tree too deep will kill it. Roots of bare root plants should be spread out in the wide, shallow hole. Never allows the roots to circle or kink in the hole.

Another issue discovered to cause transplant failure at the Morton Arboretum is poor drainage; trees can die from root drowning. They find that

*It can be ordered from The Morton Arboretum, Route 53, Lisle, Illinois 60532, Phone 708-968-0074

Bamboo stakes are used to hold young whips straight. The tree may be "guyed" to another stake to avoid blowdown in windy sites. It is a good idea to label the tree with full name, date planted, and nursery where the tree was obtained.

1. Cuttings are usually 4-6 inches long and have several sets of leaves.

2. To prevent the spread of disease, clean and disinfect all surfaces before you start.

3. Propagation supplies: rooting hormone, soil mix, cuttings.

4. After stripping off leaves, dip cutting in rooting hormone.

5. Insert the cutting into rooting medium to a depth of one-third to one-half of its length.

6. After misting, place the entire cutting-filled container into a plastic bag and seal.

near a slope, small drains may be able to run water to some lower point. On level ground, planting the tree on a slight mound may be necessary to get the root system out of the saturated soil.

Robert Bowden of Harry P. Leu Botanical Gardens reports on another area of importance: water; his notes are based on recent research from the University of Florida. Rapid root growth following tree installation in landscape soil is crucial to success; the root system must expand into new surrounding soil before shoot grows resumes. Soil factors including texture of growing medium versus landscape soil, compaction, drainage, and depth of the water table, plus irrigation before, during, and after planting, influence root growth. When planting container-grown trees, remember that until the root system extends into the new surrounding soil, the transplant depends on the one- or two-day water supply retained in the soil around it. The newly planted tree must be watered often, as it was in the nursery. The plant loses water by transpiration and when water is "wicked" from the coarse-textured container soilless mix into the finer textured landscape soil; studies show that 85% of available water is lost within hours after planting. Water will not move into the pot's media; only water applied directly on the rootball enters the rootball. Field-grown plants will not lose as much water because the soil around them is not so different from landscape soil. However, unlike container-grown plants, whose roots remain intact, only about 10% of the roots of hand-dug or spade-dug plants remain with the plant. For that reason, recently transplanted trees and shrubs require daily watering to lessen the dramatic shock to the root system. Although roots begin to grow within a week or two after transplanting, water demands require that the roots stay moist at all times. Trees will show signs of stress until root system is restored to the original pre-transplant size, which can take from one to as many as ten years. Traditionally, branches were removed to compensate for root loss, but this has proved to do more harm than good. To summarize the results of the University of Florida studies, water is the best soil amendment to help a newly planted tree survive; water often, making sure the original rootball as well as the surrounding area is kept moist for the first several weeks; supply water until the tree is firmly established; soil amendments such as fertilizer do little good and can actually cause harm; don't plant too deeply; and don't trim branches before planting.

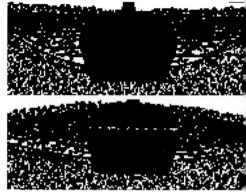

These illustrations, from the Morton Arboretum's booklet 'Selecting and Planting Trees' indicate current research. The planting hole should be considerable wider than the roots or root ball; three times wider is best. The sides should slope gradually, making the hole saucer- or bowl-shaped. Do not dig any deeper than necessary to cover the roots because the tree needs firm support below to stabilize it (and to save work). Planting a tree too deep can kill it. Roots of bare-root plants should be spread out in the wide, shallow hole. Never allow the roots to circle or kink in the hole. The lower picture shows how the hole should be dug in an area with poor drainage, elevating the root ball above the grade and gradually sloping soil around it.

PROPAGATION

To the avid gardener, nothing is as exciting as receiving a cutting of a long-sought plant; and nothing is more frustrating than watching it fail, often in a glass of water on the kitchen windowsill. With understanding and a little planning, this kind of disappointment can be avoided with relative ease, but you must keep in mind that no single method works for every plant all of the time.

Plant propagation is the art and science of reproducing plants. Plants can be propagated in several ways, including seeding, grafting, cutting, and tissue culture. The method selected is determined in large part by the plant's genetic characteristics and growth habit, the available facilities, the number of plants desired, and the skill and knowledge of the propagator. For home gardeners looking to produce a few favorite trees without great expense, cutting, layering, and division are generally the most appropriate techniques.

SOFTWOOD CUTTINGS Many popular trees can be propagated by softwood cuttings;

Top: A cutting of willow.
Above: Seeds sown in a pot.

it is a good idea to try this method while you are gaining experience in propagation. The optimum time to take cuttings can vary somewhat among species, and for certain plants, such as tree lilac, the period available may be limited. However, most trees will root well from cuttings taken in late spring and early summer. At this time, the new growth is soft enough to root rapidly but is sufficiently ripe to prevent premature wilting and deterioration. Ideally, the cuttings should be collected in the cool early morning hours from vigorous, healthy, insect- and disease-free plants. Using secateurs (pruning shears) or a sharp knife, take cuttings from terminal or lateral shoots of the current-season's growth. To prevent the possibility of spreading disease, spray cutting tools with a solution of one part household bleach to six parts water before moving to the next plant (you'll risk contaminating the solution if you dip the pruners in it). Cuttings are usually 4-6 inches long and have several sets of leaves. Moisten the cuttings immediately, place them in a plastic bag, and store them in a cool place out of direct sunlight. Refrigerated cuttings can last several days.

To prepare the cuttings, first remove flowers, buds, and seed heads; strip all leaves and buds from the lower half of the cutting. Next, make a fresh cut one-eighth to one-quarter inch below a node (where the leaf joins the stem—the site at which most rooting activity takes place). Usually two or more sets of leaves will remain on the upper portion; if they are very large, reduce them by up to half to lessen water loss from the cutting and conserve space in the rooting container. The bottom inch of the cutting should then be dipped in a rooting-hormone/fungicide mixture. Several liquid and powdered formulations of varying strengths are available, each with its own merits; experience will suggest which is most effective for specific plants (or check a manual on plant propagation).

Almost anything can be used as a rooting container, provided it is well drained, clean, and appropriately used. For most tree cuttings, a clay or plastic 6-inch bulb pan works well and will accommodate six to ten cuttings. Recycled pots must be washed and rinsed with a bleach solution to ensure sterility.

Rooting media should be light and well drained. They may contain peat moss, vermiculite, perlite, coarse sands, or even polystyrene beads, alone or in combination. Experienced propagators alter the composition of the medium to suit the growing conditions and needs of specific plants, but a 50-50 mixture by volume of peat moss and perlite is a good general-purpose starting point. Before filling containers with the selected rooting medium, moisten the mixture to the consistency of a wrung-out sponge.

Insert the prepared cuttings to a depth of one-half to one-third their length and space about 2 inches apart: spacing will vary depending on the size of the cutting, but avoid the temptation to overcrowd. Mist the cuttings lightly and place the entire cutting-filled pot inside a clear plastic bag. Seal the bag and move to a shady location in the garden. Particularly softwood cuttings may wilt initially but should soon recover. Check the cuttings once a week and remove any leaves that have dropped or cuttings that have begun to rot. If the initial moisture content of the rooting medium was correct and the bag is properly sealed, no additional watering will be required throughout the rooting process. Depending on the type of plant being propagated, rooting can take 2-10 weeks.

When the cuttings are well rooted, remove the bag. At the first required watering, use a water-soluble transplanter (or "starter") fertilizer. Continue to grow the cuttings in the rooting container for two to three weeks, then transplant to a protected nursery site in the garden or cold frame where the plants can grow until they are large enough to be moved to a permanent location. Early autumn plantings will benefit from a protective mulch; late-fall plantings, especially in colder regions, should be avoided since the cuttings will not become established before winter. Alternatively, allow the cuttings to go dormant and store them in a cold frame or unheated but frost-free garage or cellar until spring.

HARDWOOD CUTTINGS Propagating deciduous trees and evergreen genera such as *Taxus, Chamaecyparis, Juniperus,* and *Ilex* from hardwood cuttings is a useful method for home gardeners since the cuttings are relatively nonperishable, easy to prepare, and require no special equipment or facilities for rooting. Unlike leafy softwood cuttings, which are prepared in spring or early summer when plants are actively growing, hardwood cuttings are made in late autumn, after defoliation but before severe winter weather has arrived.

Cutting wood is collected in the form of long, healthy, vigorous stems of the past-season's growth. These will vary in length depending on the species, and diameters will range from ¼-1 inch. In most cases, each stem will be sufficiently long to yield more than one cutting. To prepare the cuttings first remove and discard the thin terminal portion of the stem. The balance of the stem is then cut into 4- to 12-inch uniform lengths so that each cutting has at least two sets of buds. Where possible, make top cuts just above a bud and ½ inch below a bud at the base. Dust the lower inch of the cuttings with a rooting-hormone/fungicide mixture formulated for hardwood cuttings and secure with elastic bands in conveniently sized bundles. If you are making a lot of cuttings, make the bottom cut on a slant so you can easily tell top from bottom.

Pack the base of the cuttings with damp sphagnum moss and place them in a plastic bag. Seal the bag with a twist-tie and attach a label that indicates the date, name of plant, and required treatment. Store the bag at temperatures of 55-65° F for 14-21 days to promote callusing, and then place it in cold storage (the refrigerator will do) at 35-40° F until spring.

Spring planting should be done as soon as the ground is workable. Select a particularly well drained area of the garden and plant the cuttings deeply so that only one or two buds are above the soil. The location and spacing of the cuttings must be adequate to allow the plants to grow undisturbed for a year.

In mild areas, the period of cold storage may be dispensed with and the cuttings planted out directly in the autumn. For colder regions, however, this is not advisable as repeated freeze and thaw cycles during the winter and early spring will heave the cuttings from the ground.

Not all deciduous trees will root from hardwood cuttings, but for those that will–including willow and dogwood–the method provides a simple, low-cost form of propagation.

PRUNING

There are three basic reasons to prune a tree: to keep the plant healthy, to promote flowering and fruiting, and to shape and maintain the tree's size. Pruning for health entails the removal of dead, diseased, and weak wood; pruning for flowering and fruiting encompasses thinning, deadheading, and the removal of old wood; pruning for shape and size is essentially the selective removal of both old and new growth.

Extensive pruning of mature trees is serious business. Trees can be severely

When pruning limbs, make an undercut to prevent bark tear, and leave the branch collar intact.

damaged by incompetent pruning, and, unfortunately it happens often. Aside from damage to the tree, pruning–particularly if done with a chainsaw, high in the tree, or anywhere near power lines–endangers the pruner's limbs and even life. We strongly recommend that arborists certified by the International Society of Arboriculture be hired for all except the most simple pruning tasks such as removing a low limb, removing dead wood, shaping young trees, and cutting off the tips of low, damaged branches. Make sure the person pruning your tree (and not just the contractor/owner) is licensed and check references.

To prune effectively and safely, you will need a few basic pieces of equipment: scissor-type (not anvil-type) hand shears (which perform a clean cut that doesn't promote a way for disease to enter plant), hedge shears (electric or manual), lopping shears (wooden-handled or steel with ratchet), a hand saw (sheathed or folding), gloves, and eye protection. Store all tools out of the reach of children, and maintain them regularly, keeping them sharp and free of dirt and moisture.

Whatever your reason for pruning, a few general caveats apply. When removing branches, cut as close to the branch collar of the main stem as possible, but do not cut into the branch collar. Leave only $\frac{1}{8}$-$\frac{1}{4}$ inch on smaller plants. Do not paint over the pruning wounds; this once-popular practice only promotes rot by providing a moist, sheltered environment for fungal organisms. Blooming trees should be pruned within two to four weeks after flowering, since next-season's flower buds will be formed on the new wood. Desert trees such as acacia, palo verde, and mesquite should be pruned in late spring and summer. Structural pruning can be done in winter, when the branching habit is clearly evident.

To maintain a tree's optimum health, prune regularly to remove dead, diseased, and weak wood and crossing branches. An experienced pruner will also remove branches that are growing toward the inside of the tree or the ground and weak crotches.

Two techniques encourage heavy bloom. Deadheading, the removal of spent flowers shortly after the blossoms fade, conserves the energy that would normally be spent on fruit production; it is commonly practiced on trees with profuse floral displays and nonornamental fruit, including rhododendrons, magnolias, and lilacs. Selective removal of old stems coupled with shortening and thinning of the remaining growth in early spring not only helps to maintain flowering trees, but is the key to better yield in fruiting trees.

Pruning to shape need not be daunting, especially if it is practiced regularly. To prune an ornamental tree, begin directly after planting by cutting out all dead, diseased, and weak wood. Then evaluate the branching structure and consider removing branches that overlap and rub, and those that form V-crotches that are likely to split apart; branches that have a crotch angle of less than 45° should usually be removed. Retain branch collars and keep branch stubs short (no more than ½-inch on younger trees); there should never be a stub.

Shape formal hedges twice a year, informal hedges just once; in the North, July 4 is generally considered the cut-off date for shearing. Remove one-third to two-thirds of the new growth at each pruning until the hedge nears mature size, then prune more severely. Hedges should be narrower at the top than at the base, so that adequate sunlight can reach the lower leaves. Though personal aesthetics and garden style will dictate the shape of a hedge, avoid flat-topped trees to minimize snow- and ice-load damage.

To reduce a tree's size without shearing, reach into the canopy and selectively prune branches back to a major limb, standing back from time to time to assess your progress. This method not only hides the cuts behind the remaining foliage, but gives the tree a more open and natural appearance.

ROUTINE CARE

WEEDING Rare is the gardener with an affection for weeds. Not only are they unsightly, but they compete with desired plants for available water and nutrients. By their very nature, weeds are prolific and tenacious; few gardens can be weed-free, but with a bit of knowledge and some assiduous elbow-bending, gardeners can maintain the upper hand. There are two approaches to weed control: chemical and manual. In home gardens, chemical controls are usually unnecessary, and can be hazardous if misused—to the environment and to the health of plants themselves. Fortunately, most weeds can be controlled with a good hoe, a cultivator, and a little exertion. The trick is to cultivate regularly and eliminate the weeds when small. Large, established weeds require a great deal of effort to remove, and if allowed to go to seed provide an endless source of future aggravation. Mulching helps reduce the weeds.

Though rare, there are times when chemical controls are the only alternative. Perennial grasses with rampant root systems, for instance, can be particularly difficult to dislodge. Often the only practical method for ridding the garden of such stubborn interlopers is the application of a systemic, nonselective herbicide containing glyphosate; these will kill anything that is green. Fortunately, these products are quickly degraded and have no residual effects. Always follow label directions.

WATERING Water is becoming an increasingly precious resource, and restrictions on its use are already in force in many areas. It is therefore sensible when designing a

Creating intricate forms from plants is known as topiary; it involves pruning and the use of armatures. Yews and boxwoods are often used in topiary.

Espaliering is the practice of encouraging horizontal growth by anchoring a tree to a wall or other structure and pruning selectively. It is often done with fruit trees or vines. Above: *Cedrus atlantica* 'Glauca'.

Often, a branch of a cultivar will revert to the species habit; in this case, the desirable compact growth of *Chamaecyparis obtusa* 'Gracilis' has reverted to the more open habit of the species. If the branch is not removed, the tree will lose its unique form.

VIEWPOINT

MULCHING

I mulch conifers when they are first planted, with an organic mulch, 2 inches deep that extends out just past the tips of the branches. As conifers become established, their annual dropping of older needles will act as a mulch and is usually sufficient. Mulch is important for all plants because it works to preserve moisture, inhibit weed growth that can compete for nutrients, and insulate roots from temperature extremes. An organic mulch also breaks down over time, improving the soil.
GALEN GATES
CHICAGO BOTANIC GARDEN

Mulches of any kind are not often used in the Pacific Northwest. In fact, they can be detrimental, holding in too much moisture, especially from September to May, our rainy season.
GERALD STRALEY,
UNIVERSITY OF BRITISH COLUMBIA
BOTANIC GARDEN

To maintain roots in a cool, protected zone for optimum growth, 2-3 inches of mulch is recommended at least from the drip zone to the trunk. I encourage homeowners to use a mulch that does not deplete a region's natural resources–pine bark rather than cypress, for example.
ROBERT BOWDEN,
HARRY P. LEU GARDENS, ORLANDO

We use pine bark mulch or our own wood chips, 2-3 inches deep. We keep mulch away from base of the tree trunk. The mulch keeps in moisture and keeps weedwackers and mowers from injuring the bark.
JULIE MORRIS, BLITHEWOLD MANSION AND GARDENS, RHODE ISLAND

Below: **Protecting trees along a roadway in winter.**

garden to select plants that are adapted to grow with the moisture that nature provides. Nevertheless, some watering to help establish new plants or compensate for unexpected droughts is inevitable. The key is to water only when necessary, but then to do so very thoroughly. Frequent light sprinkling, especially in the late evening, is a waste of water and often does more harm than good by encouraging the growth of shallow root systems and creating ideal conditions for the spread of disease. The frequency and quantity of irrigation will be determined by a number of factors, including soil characteristics, exposure, and the type of plants being grown. However, most well-established trees growing in a good garden loam can easily tolerate a week or two without water.

Water may be applied in a variety of ways, from a simple watering can to a fully automated time-controlled system. Most home gardeners opt for driplines, soakers, or an ordinary garden hose fitted with an overhead sprinkler. Each method has its relative advantages and disadvantages with respect to convenience, maintenance, and cost. Whatever your method, however, you can conserve water by 1) selecting plants that will thrive with the moisture nature provides, 2) watering only when necessary, 3) watering in the early morning if possible, and avoiding midday, when evaporation is greatest, 4) using mulches over the soil, and 5) collecting rain water for future use.

MULCH The practice of mulching–covering the soil with protective and sometimes decorative materials–is as old as horticulture itself. Indeed, the first mulcher was Mother Nature, who wisely devised a way to spread leaves and other plant litter across the forest floor, thus creating an insulating, nutrient-rich, biologically active "duff" layer between bare soil and the elements.

Gardeners can also choose among several weed-barrier landscape fabrics; these are suitable as underlays for mulches to supress weeds.

Just before applying the mulch, cultivate the surface of the soil to eliminate existing weeds and break up any hardpan that has built up. Two to 4 inches of mulch are usually adequate, but be careful not to pile the mulch too high around trunks or plant stems, which can lead to basal rotting. Mulches should remain light and porous; too heavy or compact a mulch can prevent water and air from reaching the plant's root system. Because organic mulches use nitrogen as they decompose, they can produce a temporary nitrogen deficiency in plants. You can avoid this problem by applying a light dressing of a 1-2-1 all-purpose garden fertilizer each spring.

FERTILIZER Like all living things, plants require a variety of nutrients, primarily nitrogen, phosphorus, and potassium, for healthy growth. These and other trace nutrients occur naturally in the soil, where they are absorbed by the plant's root system and metabolized for growth. Alas, not all soils are perfectly nutrient-rich; overworked soils, in particular, may be deficient in one or more elements, and this deficit will manifest itself in stunted growth, poor flowering, or yellow leaves.

The only true way to determine which elements are lacking is to have the soil tested by a laboratory, which can also test for soil acidity. If you suspect serious deficiencies, have the soil tested once or twice a year.

Once you've determined the problem, you can amend the soil with the proper fertilizer. Fertilizers fall into one of two basic groups: organic and manufactured. Organic fertilizers include such naturally occurring materials as compost and well-rotted manure; they have the advantage of providing organic matter and microorganisms as well as nutrients, and because they tend to have low nutrient values, they can generally be applied without fear of damaging plants. Unprocessed organic fertilizers, however, may contain weed seeds, can harbor disease, and have unknown nutrient value. To avoid these problems, choose pasteurized and tested manures and composts, available bagged at many nurseries and garden centers.

Manufactured fertilizers can be granular or water-soluble. Their nutrient values are clearly stated on the label, with the percentages for nitrogen, phosphorus, and potassium listed in that order. A product marked 5-10-15, for example, contains 5% nitrogen, 10% phosphorus, and 15% potassium, with the remaining 70% nonnutrient filler which allows distribution of the nutrients without burning. If trace elements like iron and sulfur are present, they will also be listed as percentages. Most manufactured fertilizers contain no organic matter and must therefore be used at recommended rates to avoid burning the plants.

Nearly all new plantings will benefit from a generous application of organic fertilizer mixed directly into the planting hole, and subsequent applications of a high-phosphorus transplanter-type fertilizer during the first growing season. Compost is a good organic fertilizer, as is leaf mold up to 20% by volume. If too much organic matter is added, it can create a wet, "mucky" soil that is perfect for celery but not beneficial for most trees. Once established, however, most trees are neither fussy nor heavy feeders, and a yearly spring application of a general-purpose fertilizer with a 1-3-2 or similar ratio is generally adequate. Some plants may benefit from an additional light application in midsummer, but late summer or early autumn feedings should be avoided, since they encourage late-season growth that can easily be damaged by frost.

Because each plant responds individually to fertilization, only experience will show the gardener what modifications may be necessary in the regimens outlined above.

WINTER PROTECTION Most trees that are hardy in your area do not need winter protection. However, for trees that are only marginally hardy, be sure additional fertilizer is not added since this will extend growth into winter, and this growth can be damaged. Siting a marginally hardy plant in a microclimate (courtyard, alcove, under a larger tree, or within an evergreen planting) will increase your chances of success.

PEST MANAGEMENT

The best time to begin a program of pest management is *before* you plant. Carefully sited, well-tended plants require a minimum of intervention; weak or stressed plants, however, will be predisposed to the ravages of opportunistic insects and diseases. In fact, a whole host of horticultural disorders are caused not by living organisms but by poor cultural practices or environmental problems. Known as physiogenic diseases, these disorders commonly result from winter injury, poor drainage, air pollution, road salt, nutritional deficiencies, mechanical injuries, improper application of herbicides–even lightning and strong winds. Their symptoms–including stunted growth, yellowing or spotted leaves, and twisted stems–often resemble those of organically afflicted plants. The good news for gardeners is that, once identified, these physiogenic diseases can usually be corrected, or at least accommodated.

To keep organic pests and diseases at a minimum, begin by practicing proper hygiene; a clean garden is usually a healthy garden. Fallen leaves, weeds, and other litter are more than just unsightly; they can also provide the perfect breeding ground for disease. Of course, given the daunting list of potential pests (which includes insects, mites, nematodes, fungi, bacteria, viruses, and, of course, mammals), even the most carefully tended plant can succumb. To detect problems at an early, manageable stage, you'll need to monitor the garden on a regular basis. Make it a habit to stroll through the yard at least every two weeks, carefully examining plants for signs of trouble; don't forget to check the undersides of leaves, where pests and diseases often hide. Many insects, including aphids, beetles, scales, and caterpillars, are easy to spot, but you'll need a magnifying glass to detect smaller pests like mites and thrips. Borers and leafminers, which spend most of their life cycle inside stems and leaves, are difficult to see, but the damage they cause is obvious. Keep a record of the trouble you encounter: With experience, it's possible to anticipate problems on specific host plants.

For many gardeners, the words *pest* and *insect* are synonymous; rare is the rose that never serves as supper for a Japanese beetle, or the late-spring landscape untrammeled by aphids. Some insects can do serious, life-threatening damage; others are simply unsightly. Every gardener has to determine for him- or herself an appropriate and tolerable level of infestation. When control is deemed necessary, there are a number of choices, including soaps, oils, and synthetic chemicals. Whatever the product selected, it's essential to follow label instructions carefully, both to ensure the method's efficacy and to protect the health of the plant and the environment. One of the most promising new areas of insect management is biological control, which enlists the services of natural predators like parasites, diseases, and other insects. (Ladybugs, for example, prove to be voracious afficionados of the aphid.) In controlled environments like greenhouses, these natural methods have proven highly successful; their efficacy in the backyard is still haphazard, though, since they tend to have date-limited applications. Another common pest is the mite, a tiny spiderlike creature that sucks the juice from tender leaves and stems and causes stunted or abnormal growth in affected plants. There are several types, and most thrive under hot, dry conditions. While small, they can often be detected by the fine, gray webs they create. Chemical controls are available, and simply syringing with cold water will help check their spread.

Nematodes, on the other hand, are virtually impossible to control. These microscopic worms attack roots, causing them to appear stubby, knotted, or covered with lesions (leaves are sometimes a target as well). The roots soon lose their ability to function effectively, which results in wilted or stunted growth in leaves and stems. Alas, nematodes are very difficult to detect, and infected plants must be removed and burned or discarded. Since many nematodes are soil borne, it's unwise to place susceptible plants in the same location.

Fungal diseases are among the most common in the garden, affecting leaves, stems, flowers, and roots. Spread by spores borne on air currents, water, or gardening tools, they can cause wilting, cankers, lesions, galls, blights, and leaf spots. Fungal infection is highly plant-specific and weather-dependent,

spread generally during warm, wet, humid conditions. The most effective way
to control fungi in the garden is to plant new resistant cultivars. If this isn't
possible—or if your garden is established—you can prevent many fungal infections by keeping both garden and gardening tools as clean as possible. Prune
plants regularly to maintain effective air circulation, and never water in the
late afternoon or evening. If a plant does become infected, the application of
fungicides may be your only recourse. Preventative in nature rather than cura-
tive, fungicides will protect uninfected tissue but do nothing to restore areas
already penetrated by the fungi. Gardeners must therefore be vigilant and
apply fungicide at the first hint of infection. Repeat applications are usually
necessary during the growing season to protect new growth and replenish
whatever fungicide has been depleted by rain.

Above: An oak tree displays chlorotic
growth, often the result of extremes in
soil pH—soils that are either too acid
or too alkaline make it difficult for the
plant to take up iron and other minerals and nutrients.

Often spread by insects or gardening tools, bacteria are microscopic organisms that can cause foul-smelling rots, wilted or scorched leaves, and galls.
Given the right conditions, they multiply and spread at a prodigious rate.
Because no chemical controls exist, gardeners can fight bacterial infections
only indirectly, controlling possible insect vectors, removing and destroying
infected plants, and replanting resistant cultivars.

As in humans, the ultra-microscopic organisms known as viruses can wreak
serious damage in the garden. Affecting a wide variety of plants, they cause a
host of symptoms, among them stunted growth, leaf spots, and mosaics. Like
bacteria, viruses are spread by a variety of mechanical means, and chemical
controls are nonexistent. Once again, proper hygiene and resistant cultivars are
the most practical means of prevention for home gardeners.

Anyone who lives in rabbit or deer country knows how deleterious mammals can be to the garden. Some animals, like moles, wreak their destruction
in a search for grubs and pupae of insects; you can minimize this kind of damage by eradicating the insects. Other animals are strictly vegetarian and often
have selective appetites. You can try cultivating only those plants that don't
appeal to your marauders, but in the case of deer, for instance, this could leave
you with a fairly barren landscape. Among the general controls for mammalian
pests are exclusion from the garden by fencing or live trapping, the application
of taste or odor repellents to selected plants, and the use of cages and other
mechanical barriers to prevent browsing. Normally, some trial and error is
required to determine which combination of methods is effective and appropriate for your particular area.

This young cherry tree was easily trained when small by pruning the branches back to buds that were pointing in the desired direction for the next year's growth. Basically, there are three major scaffolding branches here. The larger, most central branch in the foreground will straighten back up, creating a modified-central-leader branching structure.

GROWING TREES FOR FRUIT

Special considerations must be taken when you plant a landscape tree for fruit as well as beauty. You will want to provide any edible, ornamental tree with the best possible growing conditions. Producing fruit—especially high-quality fruit—demands an extra measure of energy from a tree, so give the plant sun and soil to its liking. Pay special attention to the soil's acidity and water drainage.

Pests can present a special problem with landscape trees grown for their fruits, because those luscious fruits can be as attractive to pests as to us humans. Yet trying to spray one fruit tree nestled among other plants, or growing near a terrace can introduce a new set of concerns. You do not want spray to fall on nearby, nontarget plants, or in areas where people—especially children—play or lounge outdoors. And besides, most of us are not willing to douse a landscape tree with the regular sprays demanded by orchard trees.

Choosing a good site provides some measure of pest resistance to a tree, but this benefit can be supplemented with pruning when needed. By letting light and air in among the branches, pruning promotes quick drying of leaves and fruit, thus limiting disease problems. Cutting away any diseased stems also helps prevent the spread of disease.

The most significant way to eliminate or drastically reduce the need for spraying is something you can do even before you plant: Choose an appropriate tree. This may mean thinking beyond such common fruits as apples and peaches. Although both can be beautiful plants, over much of the country they are beset with too many pest problems to integrate into a landscape. There are plenty of beautiful landscape plants that yield edible fruits with little need for spraying; diospyrus (persimmon), asimina (pawpaw), and juglans (walnut) are only three examples. In Arizona, citrus, barberry, and elderberry fig have the same qualities.

The following entries cover popular fruit trees, detailing how their care differs when you are growing them for fruit instead of ornament.

MALUS APPLE

BEST CONDITIONS Full sun; moderately fertile, moderately well-drained soil; regular water throughout season; Zones 2-9.
PRUNING Train young trees to open center, central leader, or modified central leader. Prune mature plant when dormant and only moderately. Thin wood especially high in plant. Thin fruit-bearing spurs when they crowd or get old. Remove dead and misdirected stems.
PESTS, DISEASES, OTHER PROBLEMS Apple scab: plant resistant varieties, clean up or cover fallen leaves at end of season, spray very early in season to control primary infections from leaves on ground, prune for good air circulation.
Cedar-apple rust: plant resistant varieties, prune for good circulation, spray if necessary.
Powdery mildew: plant resistant varieties, prune for good air circulation, spray, prune off infected buds in winter.

Apple maggot: hang out traps (red spheres coated with Tangletrap) six weeks after bloom.

Plum curculio: spray, ignore superficial damage.

Codling moth: thin fruits adequately, spray, pheromone traps.

SELECTIONS 'Liberty' productive, precocious, tasty, and resistant to major diseases.

'Cortland' all-purpose apple excellent for fresh eating and for cooking; makes pinkish applesauce; fresh fruit does not brown when cut.

'Winter Banana' good for warm-winter regions; beautiful fruit with hint of banana flavor.

'Gala' one of the best early apples, but also stores well, until Christmas.

PYRUS PEAR

BEST CONDITIONS Full sun, moderately fertile, moderately well-drained soil; regular watering throughout season; Zones 2-9.

PRUNING Train young tree to open center, central leader, or modified central leader; keep pruning of young trees to a minimum; bend branches that are upright almost to horizontal. This will improve form and speed up fruit production at an earlier age. Prune mature plant when dormant and only moderately. Thin wood especially high in plant. Thin fruit-bearing spurs when they crowd or get old. Remove dead and misplaced stems.

PESTS, DISEASES, OTHER PROBLEMS Fire blight: prune out infected stems (sterilizing pruning tool between cuts made while plant is in active growth); avoid succulent growth caused by excessive fertilization or pruning; use resistant varieties.

Pseudomonas blight: prune out infections.

There are three basic types of pruning done to fruit trees to allow maximum air circulation and sun penetration: to a central leader (top); to a modified central leader (bottom); and to an open center (opposite page).

Left: A young girl walks through an apple arch on Chicago Botanic Garden's Fruit and Vegetable Island. Even at an early age, children can learn first-hand the benefits and effects of plants, seeing "apples like we buy on the store on trees," the dramatic difference in light and temperature as related to sun and shade, and the great variety of color, form, and fragrance found in all types of plants.

Sooty mold: spray for pear psylla, which drips honeydew that leads to mold.
Codling moth: thin fruits adequately. Use pheromone traps. Spray.
SELECTION 'Magness' excellent flavor; some resistance to fire blight; slow to bear and cannot pollinate other cultivars.
'Seckel' small pear with excellent spicy flavor; harvest fully ripe; cannot pollinate 'Bartlett'.
'Ya Li' Oriental pear with sweet, aromatic flavor; good for warm regions.
'Hosui' Oriental pear with sweet rich flavor and crisp texture; also stores well. Fruit is round.

PRUNUS CHERRY

BEST CONDITIONS Full sun, well-drained soil; water important early in the season, but no rain as fruit is ripening; Zones 4-8 for tart cherries, Zones 5-9 for sweet cherries.
PRUNING Prune sweet cherries to central leader or modified central leader when young; minimal pruning is needed when mature. With tart cherries, train young trees to open centers; minimal pruning is needed when mature.
PESTS, DISEASES, OTHER PROBLEMS Birds: netting; drape black cotton thread all over tree.
Plum curculio: spray.
Brown rot: clean up mummified fruit from tree and ground; spray.
Cherry fruit fly: trap on red spheres coated with Tangletrap after bloom.
Cherry leaf spot: rake up fallen leaves; use resistant varieties ('Northstar' and 'Lambert', for example).
Aphids: band trunks with masked tape coated with Tangletrap.
SELECTIONS 'Compact Stella' self-fruitful, compact sweet cherry.
'Sweet Ann' yellow sweet cherry that resists cracking and winter cold; excellent flavor.
'Northstar' naturally small tree bearing tart cherries; somewhat disease resistant, very cold resistant.

PRUNUS PEACH

BEST CONDITIONS Full sun, very well-drained soil, regular water, especially when fruit is swelling; Zones 5-9.
PRUNING Prune about time tree is in bloom. Train young trees to open center. Prune mature tree heavily, using both thinning and heading cuts to stimulate new growth (for next year's fruit) and let sun and air into canopy.
PESTS, DISEASES, OTHER PROBLEMS Plum curculio: spray.
Brown rot: clean up mummified fruit from tree and ground; spray.
Oriental fruit moth: spray; pheromone traps; *Macrocentrus* parasite.
Bacterial spot: spray; use resistant cultivars ('Redhaven' and 'Harrow Beauty' for example).
Peach leaf curl: use resistant varieties ('Redhaven' and 'Candor'); spray.
Borers: avoid injuries to trunk; keep plants vigorous; in late summer, put ring of mothballs at base of trunk, then mound up soil over it and against the trunk for one month. Spray.
SELECTIONS 'Redhaven' some disease resistance, good flavor, freestone (no pit).

'Babcock' excellent flavor, white flesh, good for West.
'Scarlet Pearl' excellent flavor, white flesh, good for East.

PRUNUS PLUM
BEST CONDITIONS Full sun, very well-drained soil, regular water, especially when fruit is swelling; Zones 5-10.
PRUNING Train young plants to open center form, except for upright-growing cultivars, which can be grown as central leaders; only moderate pruning is needed for mature plants.
PESTS, DISEASES, OTHER PROBLEMS Plum curculio: spray.
Brown rot: clean up mummified fruit from tree and ground; spray.
Bacterial leaf spot: spray; use resistant cultivars ('AU Roadside', 'AU Amber', 'Green Gage' for example).
Black knot: prune away diseased portions; use resistant varieties ('AU-Roadside', 'AU-Amber', 'Santa Rosa').
SELECTIONS 'AU-Roadside' soft, red, excellent flavor, disease resistant.
'Superior' very coldhardy; fruits are large and early.
'Mount Royal' a prune plum that is very coldhardy.

CITRUS ORANGE, LEMON, GRAPEFRUIT
BEST CONDITIONS Well-drained soil with pH 5.5-8.0; full sun, except in desert climates where some midday shade is tolerated; Zones 9-10.
PRUNING Prune anytime in perennially warm climates, just before the spring flush where winters are cool. Little pruning is needed for either the young or mature tree. Prune mature tree to keep it from growing too large and shading the interior excessively. Prune low-hanging branches to ease access to the fruits. Drastic pruning for rejuvenation is tolerated in mild areas, but causes too much stress in the desert. Mary Irish of Desert Botanical Garden recommends selective pruning.
PESTS, DISEASES, OTHER PROBLEMS Scale insects: spray with oil, introduce parasites.
Citrus scab: prune so foliage and fruits dry soon after rain and dew.
Brown rot: prune so no fruits hang near ground; mulch.
Greasy spot: spray; rake up fallen leaves; prune so foliage dries quickly.
SELECTIONS Ruby Blood Orange' adapted to deserts and interior California; few seeds; juicy berry-flavored flesh.
Honey Tangerine' widely adapted; honey-sweet fruits; holds well on tree.
Chandler Pommelo sweet aromatic flavor in the grapefruitlike fruit; widely adapted, but needs hot summers.
Washington Navel Orange large, flavorful, seedless. Holds well on tree; best for California conditions, but not hot, dry areas.
For the desert, Mary Irish of Desert Botanical Garden recommends **Arizona Sweet** and **Valencia,** oranges as well as limes (with some protection); lemons and grapefruits are outstanding.

<small>THIS SECTION PROVIDED BY LEE REICH, PHD.</small>

Calamondin orange, below, bears small, tart fruit in warm climates.

TREES FOR DRY CLIMATES

Common shade trees

Mesquite (*Prosopis juliflora, P. glandulosa, P. chilensis, P. nigra*)

Palo verde (*Cercidium floridum, C. microphyllum*)

Palo brea (*Cercidium praecox*)

Ironwood (*Olneya tesota*)

Sweet acacia (*A. smallii,* often sold as *A. farnesiana*)

Retama or Jerusalem thorn (*Parkinsonia aculeata*)

Acacia saligna

Acacia salicina

Smaller tree (to 20 feet)

Fern of the desert (*Lysiloma watsonii*)

Desert willow (*Chilopsis linearis*)

Texas ebony (*Pithecellobium mexicanum*)

Cascalote (*Caesalpinia cacalaco*)

Hackberry (*Celtis reticulata*)

Twisted acacia (*Acacia schaffneri*)

Screw-bean mesquite (*Prosopis pubescens*)

Little known but excellent

Mexican bird of paradise (*Caesalpinia mexicana*)

Kidneywood (*Eysenhardtia texanum*)

Arizona rosewood (*Vaquelina californica*)

Chisos rosewood (*Vaquelina coymbosa*)

Desert hackberry (*Celtis pallida*)

Palo blanco (*Acacia willardiana*)

Elderberry (*Sambucus mexicanus*)

Plants well adapted to desert, widely used, but not strictly desert plants (some need a lot of extra water)

Aleppo pine (*Pinus halapensis*)

Eucalyptus species

Australian willow (*Geijera robusta*)

Silk oak (*Grevillea robusta*)

Floss silk tree (*Chorisia speciosa*)

Olive (*Olea europea*)

High elevation/dry climate plants

Arizona cypress (*Cupressus arizonicus*)

Junipers (*Juniperus monosperma, J. socpularum,*

Alligator pine (*J. deppeana*)

Pinyon pine (*Pinus edulis, P. cembroides*)

Ponderosa pine (*P. ponderosa*)

Picea pungens 'Hoopsii'–a drought-tolerant cultivar.

GROWING TREES IN DRY CLIMATES

Trees in very arid climates–the desert Southwest and southern California–are not only beautiful structural features in the garden, but vital partners in making a garden a pleasant place to grow and enjoy plants. By choosing well-adapted trees and providing them with regular, adequate irrigation, any dry area garden can become an oasis of comfort and beauty.

As in any area, the most important part of planting a tree is selecting the right type for your needs. Most trees in dry climates are planted for shade, so choose species that have spreading crowns, such as palo verde, mesquite, palo vera, or desert willow.

Trees in dry climates need a very good start to set a strong root system, grow steadily and eventually be able to grow on their own. Plant a tree as young as you can find it; a tree from a five-gallon container will catch up with and overtake a tree planted from a 24-inch box container in five years or less. For the first 2-3 years, water regularly and deeply every 7-10 days in summer, every 2-3 weeks otherwise. Gradually extend the time between waterings to every 3-4 weeks in cooler seasons, ever 2-3 weeks in summer until the tree has been in the ground 5-7 years or is quite large. By that time, a well-adapted tree can live without supplemental irrigation except for the hottest months of the summer, and than a deep soak every 3-4 weeks is sufficient.

Desert-adapted trees have few pests and problems in the region, but keeping them healthy, pruning out crossing and dead limbs, and providing adequate water when needed will assure a sturdy, long-lived tree. Trees which are watered too shallowly, or frequently but not deeply (as happens when grass is planted under a tree) often develop root systems that are unable to support the top growth of the tree. Sweet acacia is particularly susceptible to this problem. It can be solved in the short term by pruning to open the dense crown and to cut back long hanging stem growth. In the end, the best prevention is to water deeply and thoroughly the encourage a strong root system.

Many desert-adapted trees are long lived and if treated well will remain healthy throughout your lifetime. More than just plants, they are investments in the shape and form of the garden. Choose carefully, plant wisely, and enjoy them for a very long time.

GROWING TREES IN WARM CLIMATES

Warm climates–in the South and Southwest of the United States and the Pacific Northwest of the United States and Canada–provides hospitable conditions for a wide variety of plants, encouraging gardeners to experiment with specimens from many different regions. However, since trees are planted as near-permanent contributors to the landscape, a few special factors need to be considered.

Trees that are accustomed to cooler climates may need to be protected from the more intense sun. Especially when young, plant them in a shadier spot then they would need further north. Shade will help them deal with the heat. Sunscald is also a common problem, so the trunks of young trees should be wrapped to protect their bark. Since many trees in this region are grown for the purpose of shade, don't overlook the fact that the longer growing season will cause trees to mature faster and possibly grow larger than they do in cooler habitats. Give them enough room, especially away from structures they are meant to protect.

The greatest danger for all trees, even the hardiest natives, is summer drought. Aside from watering when possible during these periods, the best preparation is giving young trees a good start and keeping them healthy.

The South tends to have soils rather thin in organic matter. A summer mulch is not only essential for keeping the ground cooler, but for adding essential nutrients to the soil (it also helps to keep down the weeds). When planting, make sure the hole is wide enough for the roots to spread, and enrich with a healthy proportion of loam or compost.

Pruning young trees in warm climates, especially when planting, should emphasize the production of roots. Keep branches to a minimum for the first season or two at least, so that growth is directed to below the surface. Long-term pruning should have a two-part strategy because of the mild winters, which can include several triggers to spring growth. Prune in early winter to remove dead or diseased wood, then again in late winter to shape and control growth of the new buds.

Some northern trees, such as needle conifers, are not meant to be grown in the South. There are many compensations for this. The South is the perfect place for extending the zones of many plants, especially if you attempt to grow plants that are borderline for the zone at both ends of the spectrum. Many tropical plants can be grown in the middle of the South if winter protection is provided, and many northern plants can be coaxed to thrive in spots where summer afternoon heat can be reduced. Camellias are a wonderful example of trees growing outside their normal range; *Camellia japonica* varieties will grow in many areas often believed to be too cold. The trick is to grow early and late varieties. The early varieties bloom before the onset of cold weather, and the flowerbuds of the late bloomers remain tightly closed and protected until warmer weather arrives. Other trees that can be grown in the warm climates include acacia, araucarias, arbutus, brachychiton, cedrus, cinnamomum, citrus, eriobotrya, ficus, gordonia, lagerstroemia, maytenus, and olea; the magnificent live oak (*Quercus virginiana*) and southern magnolia (*Magnolia grandiflora*) are treasures for warm-climate gardens.

Warm-climate trees–for Zones 8-10, and for protected areas in Zone 7– include those with magnificent flowers (like *Bauhinia purpurea,* top). Most member of the large and varied family of palms (including *Phoenix canarienis,* above), are reliably hardy only in Zone 10, though some, such as the palmetto, are hardy in Zone 8.

GROWING TREES IN COLD CLIMATES

Since trees are expected to last for a long time, it is crucial to ascertain their hardiness—which is defined as their ability to tolerate the coldest temperatures of a region's winter, as well as early winter freezes and spring thaws—before planting them. Plants adapt to cold weather by entering a dormant stage during which they reduce all activity. Plants that are able to enter this dormant period early are more effective in cold climates; those that begin the process later are less hardy.

Locating the tree in a sheltered area will help some marginally hardy plants survive. Try to find an area that is protected by a wall or large trees, creating a microclimate that is warmer and less exposed than the rest of the garden. If your property is large, you will note that there are several microclimates within it—hilltops, valleys, and open areas will usually be the coldest, areas protected by trees and walls will be the warmest. But don't allow your protective device to block out sunlight. Exposure to southern currents is advantageous.

A plant will have less trouble adapting to cold if it is well-nourished in other respects; northern gardeners should pay particular attention to soil maintenance, supply sufficient water, and monitor diseases and pests. A plant that is already weak because of moisture or nutrient deficiencies will be the first to die in the event of a cold spell.

It is important to purchase only plants grown in colder regions, or to exchange with neighbors. Plants grown from seeds or seedlings that originate in warm regions are often less adapted to cold weather—even if they are the exact same species.

In addition to cold temperatures, most plants in northern climates must contend with desiccating winds that speed up evaporation of moisture from plant tissue; strong sun can also dry out a plant. Many broad-leaved evergreens are not able to survive these winds; narrow-leaved evergreens (conifers) have adapted to this problem by reducing their leaf structure to a small size.

A deep layer of snow actually benefits many trees, providing an insulating layer under which the roots can survive. A continuous layer of snow if actually the best protection that a plant can be given. Young trees can be protected by wrapping their trunks during severe weather, but most gardeners find this to impractical on a large scale for mature trees.

TREES FOR SMALL SPACES

Trees need space; one mistake often made by gardeners is planting a tree in a space just large enough to accommodate a sapling–sometimes surrounded by concrete or paving–so that the growing tree quickly becomes trapped. This is not good for the tree or for the surrounding area since roots can upheave the pavement. However, there are trees that will fit in small spaces nicely, adding a note of stability and grace to the landscape. Understory trees like cercis, amelanchier, and hamamelis fit nicely in small areas, and can easily be pruned in keep them within bounds.

When choosing a tree for a small area, look for a dwarf cultivars of larger trees; many slow-growing dwarf conifers are available. Some weeping varieties, particularly small cherry and birch trees, remain small even over time and provide a lush look in a small space. Japanese maples remain confined and add brilliant foliage colors, especially in fall.

Pruning should be done annually when necessary to keep tree in bounds; some trees, such as yews, accept heavy pruning and even shearing. If the tree becomes straggly or starts to grow past its space, a rejuvenation pruning may be in order, cutting back severely–to within a few inches of the ground; the tree will usually grow back within a few seasons and will be more manageable in the meantime.

One area that many gardeners ignore is the understory of the garden, the area shaded by larger trees. By using small trees in that space, a new layer of texture, color, and shape can be added to the garden. Many understory trees–cornus, cercis, amelanchier, hamamelis, chionanthus, acer–are particularly ornamental, providing colorful flowers and fall foliage; they can be planted in space that is often ignored.

A small weeping birch lends a graceful note to a pocket-sized garden.

ORGANIC GARDENING

Few gardeners today are unaware of the devastating effect pesticides and other chemicals used in the past have had on our environment. Rachel Carson's searing exploration of the subject, *Silent Spring* (1962), exposed the "needless havoc" wrought by products designed to promote healthy plants. Not only were the chemicals poisoning our environment, they were also killing the natural predators of the pests we were seeking to destroy, making it impossible for nature to come to its own defense.

In the past few decades a vast and successful effort has been made to find new ways to garden without using harmful chemicals. The approach is directed at the soil and at the measures taken to control pests.

The soil is built up through the addition of organic materials, especially compost. The addition of compost, homemade or store-bought, and other organic material such as peat moss, green cover crops, and bone meal makes the soil so fertile and productive that petrochemicals are not needed.

Pest problems are handled through a practice called Integrated Pest Management (IPM), developed by the Council on Environmental Quality. IPM is defined as "maximum use of naturally occurring pest controls, including weather, disease agents, predators, and parasitoids. In addition, IPM utilizes various biological, physical, chemical controls and habitat modification techniques. Artificial controls are imposed only as required to keep a pest from surpassing tolerable population as determined from accurate assessments of the pest damage potential and the ecological, sociological, and economic costs of the control measures." In other words, gardeners must make reasonable assessments of how much damage a particular pest will do. If the pest is just munching on foliage, let it be. If controls must be taken, nonharmful ones should be tried first. Only in extreme cases is chemical warfare waged—and then in the most nonharmful ways possible.

The weapons in the IPM arsenal include:

• Careful monitoring to identify problems before they become widespread.

• Beneficial insects, such as ladybugs, praying mantises, and some nematodes, which feed on garden pests. Some of these reside naturally in your garden; others can be bought and placed there.

• Bacteria such as Bt (*Bacillus thuringiensis*) that attack garden pests. These bacteria can be bought by the pound and dusted on the plants; strains have been discovered that breed and attack many common pests.

• Insecticides such as rotenone, pyrethrum, and sabadilla and insecticidal soaps.

• Pest-repellent plants such as marigolds, which is reputed to repel bean beetles and nematodes, and garlic, which repels whitefly.

• Hand-picking pests off foliage wherever they are seen in small numbers.

See pages 204-205 for more information about pest control.

Acid soil: Soil with a pH level below 7

Alkaline soil: Soil with a pH level above 7

Annual: A plant whose life cycle comprises a single growing season

Anther: The part of a flower that bears pollen

Axil: The angle formed by a stem and a leaf stalk

Balled-and-burlapped: Describing a plant that is ready for transplanting, with a burlap-wrapped soil ball around its roots

Bare-root: Describing a plant that is ready for transplanting, with no protective soil or burlap covering around its roots

Bipinnate: Having leaflets that are divided into second leaflets

Bract: A modified leaf below a flower, often showy, as in dogwood

Broad-leaved evergreen: A non-coniferous evergreen

Calcaceous: Containing calcium or calcium carbonate (lime), as soil

Candle: On a conifer, the new budlike shoot that sends out young needles

Cane: A long, often supple, woody stem

Capsule: A dry fruit having more than one cell

Catkin: A long flower cluster comprised of closely spaced, generally small flowers and prominent bracts, as in pussy willows

Chlorosis: A yellowing of the leaves, reflecting a deficiency of chlorophyll

Clay soil: A soil, usually heavy and poorly drained, containing a preponderance of fine particles

Clone: Vegetative produced plants from a single parent

plant; clones will not grow true from seed.

Columnar: Growing in the shape of column, not spreading.

Compost: Decomposed organic matter, usually used to enrich the soil

Conifer: Cone-bearing plant, usually evergreen

Container-grown: Grown as a seedling in the container it is to be sold in

Corymb: A flat-topped flower cluster in which flowers open successively from the outside in

Cross-pollination: The transfer of pollen from one plant to another

Cultivar: A variety of plant produced by selective hybridization

Cultivate: To work the soil in order to break it up and/or remove weeds

Cutting: A severed plant stem, usually used for the purposes of propagation

Deadhead: To remove spent blossoms

Deciduous: Losing its leaves at the end of the growing season; nonevergreen

Dieback: Death of part or all of the woody portion of a plant

Dioecious: Having both male and female flowers

Division: The removal of suckers from a parent plant, for the purposes of propagation

Double: In flowers, having an increased number of petals, produced at the expense of other organs

Drupe: A fruit with a fleshy covering over a hard-coated seed

Epiphyte: A plant that grows on another plant rather than in soil; "air plants"

Evergreen: Retaining foliage year-round

Exfoliate: To self-peel, as bark

Fertile: Having the capacity to generate seed

Filiferous: Threadlike

Foundation planting: A massed planting designed to mask, disguise, or enhance the foundation of a house or building

Friable: Ready for cultivation, easily cultivable, as soil

Genus: A group of related species

Germinate: To develop a young plant from seed; to produce a seedling

Glaucous: Blue-hued; covered with a bluish or grayish bloom

Graft: To insert a section of one plant, usually a shoot, into another so that they grow together into a single plant

Habit: A plant's characteristic form of growth

Harden off: To mature sufficiently to withstand winter temperatures

Hardpan: Soil sufficiently clogged with clay or other particles that draining is impossible

Hardwood cutting: Cutting taken from a mature woody stem for the purpose of propagation

Hardy: Able to withstand winter temperatures

Herbaceous: Without woody tissue

Humus: Soil composed of decaying organic matter

Hybrid: A plant produced by crossing two unlike parents

Insecticidal soap: Soap formulated to kill, repel, or inhibit the growth of insect pests

Integrated pest management (IPM): A philosphy of pest management based on the idea of using escalating methods of pest

control, beginning with the least damaging; incorporates the selection of resistant varieties, the use of biological and nontoxic controls, and the application of pesticides and herbicides only when absolutely necessary

Invasive: Tending to spread freely and wantonly; weedy

Leaf mold: A form of humus composed of decayed leaves, often used to enrich soil

Leaflets: the parts of a compound leaf

Lime: Calcium carbonate, often added to the soil to reduce acidity

Loam: A generally fertile and well-drained soil, usually containing a significant amount of decomposed organic matter

Lobed: Divided into segments

Pendulous: Hanging down, drooping (also pendant)

Microclimate: Climate specific to a small area; may vary significantly from that of surrounding areas

Mulch: An organic or inorganic soil covering, used to maintain soil temperature and moisture and to discourage the growth of weeds

Naturalize: To "escape" from a garden setting and become established in the wild

Neutral soil: Soil having a pH of 7—neither acid nor alkaline

Node: On a plant, the site at which the leaf joins the stem; the area where most rooting activity takes place.

Panicle: A branched raceme

Peat moss: Partially decomposed sphagnum moss, often added to soil to increase moisture retention

Pendulous: Hanging down, drooping (also pendant)

Perennial: A plant that lives for more than one growing season (usually at least three)

Perfect: Having stamens and pistils; bisexual, as a flower

Petal: Part of a flower's corolla, outside of the stamens and pistils, often vividly colored

pH: An expression of soil alkalinity or acidity; the hydrogen ion content of soil

Pioneer: A plant that flourishes in disturbed soil, as after a fire

Pistil: A flower's female reproductive organ

Pods: Dry fruits

Pollen: The spores of a seed-bearing plant

Pollination: The transfer of pollen from one plant to another

Pome: A fleshy fruit

Propagate: To grow new plants from old under controlled conditions

Prostrate: Lying or dragging on the ground.

Prune: To cut back, for the purposes of shaping a plant, encouraging new growth, or controlling size

Pyramidal: Broad on bottom, coming to a pointed top.

Raceme: An elongated flower cluster in which the flowers are held on small stalks radiating from a single, larger stalk

Rejuvenation pruning: The practice of cutting all the main stems of a tree back to within one-half inch of the ground during winter dormancy; renewal pruning

Remontant: Able to rebloom one or more times during a single growing season

Renewal pruning: See Rejuvenation pruning

Root cutting: A cutting taken from the root of a parent plant for the purpose of propagation

Root pruning: The act of removing a portion of a plant's roots to keep top growth in check

Rootstock: The root of a grafted plant

Runner: A prostrate branch that roots at its joint

Scarify: To sand, scratch, or otherwise disturb the coating of a seed in preparation for its germination

Self-pollination: A plant's ability to fertilize its pistils with its own pollen

Semidouble: Having more than the usual number of petals but with at least some pollen-producing stamens

Semievergreen: Retaining its leaves for most of the winter, or in warm climates

Semihardwood cutting: A cutting taken from a stem that has just begun to develop woody tissue, for the purpose of propagation.

Sepal: The part of a flower that is circularly arranged outside the petals

Serrated: Saw-toothed

Single: In flowers, having only one layer of petals

Softwood cutting: A cutting taken from a green, or immature, stem of a woody plant, for the purpose of propagation

Species: A subgroup of a genus, composed of reproductively similar plants or animals

Specimen: A plant deliberately set by itself to emphasize its ornamental properties

Spreading: Having a horizontally branching habit

Stamen: The male organ of a flower carrying the pollen-bearing anther

Staminoid: A pollenless stamen

Sterile: Unable to generate seed

Stolon: An underground shoot

Stratify: To help seeds overcome dormancy by cleaning and drying them, then maintaining them for a period of time under generally cool and moist conditions

Striations: Fine stripes

Sucker: A shoot growing from the root or base of a woody plant

Tap root: A strong, vertical-growing, central root

Topiary: The art of trimming or training plants into decorative three-dimensional shapes

Trifoliate: Having three leaflets

Truss: A flower cluster set at the top of a stem or branch

Understock: The stock or root plant onto which a shoot has been grafted to produce a new plant

Unisexual: Having either stamens or pistils

USDA hardiness zones: Planting zones established by the United States Department of Agriculture, defined by a number of factors, including minimum winter temperatures

Understory plant: A plant whose natural habitat is the forest floor; or one that can be used beneath a larger plant in the garden.

Undulated: Wavy

Variegated: Characterized by striping, mottling, or other coloration in addition to the plant's general overall color

Vascular system: The tissues that conduct water, nutrients, and other elements through plants.

Weeping: Having long, drooping branches

Winged: Having winglike appendages.

Winter kill: The dying back of a plant or part of a plant due to harsh winter conditions

Woody: Forming stems that mature to wood

Xeriscaping: Landscaping with the use of drought-tolerant plants, to eliminate the need for supplemental watering

NOTE: INCLUSION IN THIS LIST DOES NOT
IMPLY RECOMMENDATION AND THIS LIST
DOES NOT INCLUDE MANY FINE NURSERIES

MAIL-ORDER NURSERIES

Carrol Gardens
PO Box 310
Westminster, MD 21158
301-848-5422

Cascade Forestry Service
22033 Fillmore Rd.
Cascade, IA 52033
319-852-3042, fax: 319-852-5004

Eastern Plant Specialties
PO Box 226
Georgetown, ME 04548
207-371-2888

Forestfarm
990 Thethrow Road
Williams, OR 97544
503-846-7269,fax: 503-846-6963

Foxborough Nursery, Inc.
3611 Miller Road
Stree, MD 21154
410-836-7023

Girard Nurseries
Po Box 428
Geneva, OH 44041
216-466-2881, fax: 216-466-3999

Gossler Farms Nursery
1220 Weaver Road
Springfield, OR 97478-9663
503-746-3922

Greer Gardens
1280 Goodpasture Island Road
Eugene, OR 97401
503-686-8266,fax: 503-686-0910

Heronswoos Nursery
7530 Street Northeast 288th
Kingston, WA 98346
206-297-4172, fax:360-297-8321

Lamtree Farm
PO BOx 162, Route 1
Warrensville, NC 28693
910-385-6144

Melingers, Inc. *
2310 W. South Range Road
North Lima. OH 44452

Musser Forests, Inc.
PO Box 340, Route 119 North
Indiana, PA 15701
412-465-5685, fax:412-465-9893

Oikos Tree Crops
PO Box 19425
Kalamazoo, MI 49019
616-624-6233; fax: 616-342-2759

Owen Farms
2951 Curve, Nankipoo Rd.
Ripley TN 38063
901-635-1588

Pacific Tree Farms
4301 Lynwood Driva
Chula Vista, CA 91910
619-422-2400

Plants of the Southwest
Agua Fria, Route 6, Box 11A
Santa Fe, NM 87501
505-471-2212
800-788-7333 (orders only)

Roslyn Nursery
211 Burrs Lane
Dix Hills, NY 11746
516-643-9347, fax: 516-484-2155

Wavecrest Nursery
2509 Lakeshore Drive
Fennville, MI 49408
616-543-4174, fax: 616-543-4100

Weston Nurseries
30 Phipps Street, Route 135
PO Box 186
Hopkinton, MA 01748
508-435-3414, fax: 508-435-3274

White Flower Farms
Route 63
Litchfield, CT 06759-0050
303-567-0801,fax: 203-496-9600, mail
order: 1-800-503-9624

Whitney Gardens and Nursery
PO Box F
Brinnon, WA 98320
206-796-4411

Woodlanders, Inc
1128 Colleton Avenue
Aiken, SC 29801
803-648-7522, (phone and fax) take
orders only from Oct. 1st thru March

Yucca Do Nursery
PO Box 655
Waller, TX 77484
409-826-6363, (phone and fax)

OTHER SOURCES

International Society of Arboriculture
303 West University
PO Box 908
Urbana, IL 61801
217-328-2032

American Society of Consulting
Arborists
PO Box 6524
700 Canterbury Road
Clearwater, FL 33546
813-446-3356

National Arborist Association
PO Box 1094
Amherst, NH 03031
603-3311

The National Arbor Day Foundation
Tree City USA
100 Arbor Avenue
Nebraska City, NE 68410
(for information on community tree
programs)

Global ReLeaf
American Forestry Association
PO Box 2000
Washington, D.C. 20013

Holly Society of America
11118 West Murdock
Wichita, KS 67212
310-825-8133

The Magnolia Society,
Robert D. Hagen, Secretary
6616 81st Street
Cabin John, MD 20818

International Oak Society
PO Box 310
Pen Argyl, PA 18072
610-588-1037

Ontario Shade Tree Council
17-4 Carling Ave, Ste 301
Ottawa, ON CANADA K2A 1C7

CONTRIBUTORS

MAIN GARDENS
Ethan Johnson
The Holden Arboretum
9500 Sperry Road
Kirtland, OH 44060
With contributions by David Allen, Tabitha King, Heather Starr, Peter Bristol, and Charles Tubesing

Galen Gates
Chicago Botanic Garden
Lake Cook Road
Chicago, IL 60022

CONTRIBUTING GARDENS
Dorth Hviid
Berkshire Botanical Garden
PO Box 826
Stockbridge, MA 01262

Julie Morris
Blithewold Mansion and Gardens
Ferry Road
Bristol, RI 02809

Mary Irish
Desert Botanical Garden
1201 N. Galvin Parkway
Phoenix, AZ 85008

Susan Thomas
The Hoyt Arboretum
4000 S.W. Fairview Boulevard
Portland, OR 97221

Robert Bowden
Harry P. Leu Gardens
1730 N. Forest Avenue
Orlando, FL 32803

Rick Lewandowski
Morris Arboretum of the University of Pennsylvania
9414 Meadowbrook Avenue
Philadelphia, PA 19118

Michael Ruggiero
The New York Botanical Garden
Bronx, NY 10458

Gerald Straley
University of British Columbia Botanical Garden
6804 S.W. Marine Drive
Vancouver, BC V6T 1W5 CANADA

PHOTO CREDITS

All photographs ©Galen Gates with the following exceptions:

©Ian Adams: 7, 12R, 22-23, 49, 62, 74, 89BL, 90, 91BR, 92, 93, 109TR, 122BL, 152, 143BL, 168, 186, 188-89, 192-98, 200, 206-207

©Ethan Johnson: 31TR

©Dency Kane: 89TL, 176, 213

©Sylvia Martin: 113TR, 191

©Elvin McDonald: 211

©Sylvia and Steve Sharnoff: 18BL, 34BL, 36BR, 43BR, 52BR, 77BR, 79TR, 113TL, 113BR, 114, 117, 118, 121BL, 127, 143BL, 144BL, BR, 150BR, 156TL, 166TL, 172TR, BL, 177

©Albert Squillace: 1, 6, 28-29, 32, 43TL, 51, 52TL, TR, BL, 72TL, 79TL, 89BR, 98, 99BL, 108, 115, 126TL, TR, 129, 134, 135TR, BR, BL, 137, 138, 140, 142, 143TL, TR, 154BR, 159, 164, 165TL, TR, 171, 201, 215

©Lori Stein: 61, 63TR, 187

©John Trager: 31BR

©Chani Yammer: 12L, 33, 35, 36TL, 38, 40TR, BL, BR, 32BL, 47TR, 60, 63TR, 68TL, 70, 76, 78, 79BL, 81, 84TL, BL, 86BL, BR, 88, 116, 99TL, TR, 102, 109TR, BR, 111, 113BL, 120, 139, 150TL, BR, 151, 156BL, 158, 166BL, 174, 181, 182T, 184B, 187, 190B

llustrations on endpapers and on pages 16-17 by Delores Bego; illustration on p. 25 courtesy of U.S. Department of Agriculture. Illustration on p. 197 courtesy of The Morton Arboretum.

T=Top; B=Bottom; R=Right; L=Left